FEARLESS FREEDOM

Also by Arlan Simone

My Fabulous & Fearless Journey

Fearless Faith + Hustle: 21-Day Devotional Journey

The Fearless Money Mindset: Broke Doesn't Scare Me

FEARLESS FREEDOM

A Manifesto for Unlocking Wealth and Equality for All

ARIAN SIMONE

STOREHOUSE VOICES
New York

STOREHOUSE VOICES
An imprint of the Crown Publishing Group
A division of Penguin Random House LLC
1745 Broadway
New York, NY 10019
storehousevoices.com
penguinrandomhouse.com

Vintage paper backgrounds on pages 116 and 234: Shutterstock.com/Helga_creates

Detailed permissions acknowledgments on pages 263–64

Library of Congress Cataloging-in-Publication Data is on file with the publisher.

Hardcover ISBN 979-8-217-08761-7
Ebook ISBN 979-8-217-08762-4

Editor and associate publisher: Porscha Burke
Production editor: Natalie Blachere
Text designer: Andrea Lau
Production: Christopher Andrus and Heather Williamson
Copy editor: Aja Pollock
Proofreaders: Eldes Tran and Sarah Bean
Publicist: Jennifer Valentin
Marketer: Mason Eng
Publisher: Tamira Chapman
Editorial director: Jennifer Baker

Manufactured in the United States of America

1st Printing

First Edition

The authorized representative in the EU for product safety and compliance is Penguin Random House Ireland, Morrison Chambers, 32 Nassau Street, Dublin D02 YH68, Ireland, https://eu-contact.penguin.ie.

I dedicate this book to future changemakers and leaders.
We are counting on you all to finally get this thing right.

You must never be fearful about
what you are doing when it is right.
—Rosa Parks

Contents

by Ben Crump

Foreword

There are moments in history when a voice emerges so powerfully, so courageously, that it alters the course of the conversation, and with it, the trajectory of the world as we know it. Arian Simone is one of those voices and she demands to be heard. She is our Rosa Parks, our Ruth Bader Ginsburg, our Sojourner Truth, our Gloria Steinem, our Harriet Tubman—a trailblazer for justice and an advocate for opportunity. Through her life's work and experiences, she reminds us all that bravery is not the absence of fear but the strength to confront it head-on and prevail.

I've had the privilege of knowing Arian since her college days in Tallahassee, Florida. Even back then, her determination and brilliance were undeniable. Arian carried a vision for change that was as bold as it was inspiring, and through all life's journeys she transformed that vision into a movement. What sets Arian apart is her ability to see opportunity where others see obstacles.

Over the years, I've been fortunate to witness her growth and success, not just as a friend but as a champion of her cause. As a longtime supporter of her many accomplishments, I've been proud to stand alongside her as she pursues fair spaces for all.

Arian is not only giving people a seat at the table, she's leading the charge for economic freedom by educating and empowering others with the tools they need to build their own. Arian is the founding partner and CEO of the first venture capital fund built by women of color for women of color, the Fearless Fund. Women of color receive less than 1 percent of venture capital funding, and the Fearless Fund is changing that narrative by creating generational wealth and reducing the wealth gap, as they have raised millions of dollars to pave the way for countless entrepreneurs. This, for any fund, is no easy feat, and when it comes to someone as tenacious as Arian, I cannot help but admire the fruits of her labor. Unfortunately, there are individuals in this country who are driven by their desire to make sure those fruits are stripped away.

In a frivolous attempt to prevent progress, these enemies of equality leveraged a lawsuit against the Fearless Fund under the guise of discrimination. This case is just as important as George Floyd and Henrietta Lacks when highlighting the detrimental effects of those who will stop at nothing to make sure that we are marginalized for generations to come. I had the honor of representing the Fearless Fund in its lawsuit against Ed Blum—a fight that went beyond legalities. This battle was about affirming the rights of communities that have been historically excluded by people who don't want to see those with diverse backgrounds receive a chance at economic freedom. Despite the challenges they faced in court, the Fearless Fund emerged stronger, securing even more funds to continue their mission, and I am so proud to utter two simple yet monumental words: case dismissed.

Though we acknowledge the momentous occasion of the case being dismissed, we also acknowledge that this is only the beginning. This isn't just about one fund. It's about ensuring that we don't go backward, that we don't allow those who fear progress to erase the strides we've made. The intellectual justification of discrimination is running rampant in America, especially in light of the recent attacks on and recusal of DEI initiatives across the country. During the case, I often said, "The enemies of equality picked the wrong one." Arian's leadership and unwavering clarity in this season reemphasized what I have always known: she is cut from an impenetrable cloth that makes her a force to be reckoned with.

As a civil rights attorney, I've often spoken about the importance of standing firm against forces that seek to undermine equality. Arian does not simply stand in the gap; she builds bridges. She challenges systems, not with anger but with strategy and an unwavering belief in what is just. It's this level of understanding that defines true disruptors and lays the foundation for this groundbreaking piece of work. This book, *Fearless Freedom,* is more than a memoir; it is a collection of powerful moments, each yielding its own gravity. It is a manifesto for those who refuse to accept the status quo. As it's been said, "Nothing is more powerful than an idea whose time has come." This is an idea whose time has come.

Written histories like this one hold immeasurable value in moments like these. When society finds itself at a crossroads, we must uplift the voices of those who seek to provide guidance for future generations through sheer integrity. It is through accounts such as these that we preserve the truth and make sure that our children are more intelligent than those who seek to oppress them. In an era where books are being banned and erased, *Fearless Freedom* is a book to be kept, shared, and cherished, as Arian's decision to document her journey and lessons in this book ensures that her reach will outlast the challenges of the moment.

Books like *Fearless Freedom* become living, breathing narratives, and I would be remiss to categorize this book as anything less than the critical piece that it is: a playbook for how we achieve an equitable future in funding amid an evolving landscape. As barriers to access shift, the lessons and strategies laid out here serve as a guide for entrepreneurs, investors, and advocates striving to create meaningful change. Arian has provided a framework for how we build lasting opportunities and ensure that economic empowerment reaches those historically left behind. It will serve as a guide for those who dare to dream of a better world as her expertise and practical wisdom remind us that progress requires action and the persistence to not take no as an answer.

As I reflect on the countless battles I've fought for justice, I see in Arian the same determination and courage that fuel those efforts.

She is a leader who not only talks the talk but walks the walk. Her story is a testament to what happens when we refuse to let adversity define us. Instead, we use it to rise above fear, to push past limitations, and to embrace our roles as agents of change, because history is not something we passively observe. It is something we actively create.

To read this book is to be transformed. To embody its lessons is to be empowered. Arian is a living testament to the power of courage, vision, and action. Let her story remind you of what is possible when we dare to dream big and take bold action. Let *Fearless Freedom* inspire you to lead a life of impact and meaning.

—***Ben Crump***

FEARLESS FREEDOM

Introduction

We are all living in urgent times.

I write this book in 2025 as I travel between my longtime home of Atlanta, Georgia; my adopted home of Accra, Ghana, where I've been researching the work of W. E. B. Du Bois, Malcolm X, and other Black leaders who traveled here during the 1960s as they sought to improve Black people's worldwide financial freedom; and Côte d'Ivoire, where I founded a school for 180 kindergarten through sixth-grade students and have been officially enthroned as a queen who has moral, legal, and spiritual responsibilities to support the well-being of thousands of Ivorians.

As I fly over countless millions of human beings, I'm more conscious than ever that we all share one home: planet Earth. Our fates intertwine. Internet connections facilitate our witnessing and learning about locations far from our home locales, and if we learned anything from the Covid pandemic, it is that one person's well-being can affect others', all around the world.

In the United States, income inequality has reached extreme levels: The wealthiest members of society rig the economy to benefit themselves wildly, at middle- and lower-income people's expense. The richest 1 percent of earners in the United States control more than 30 percent of the wealth,[1] while the bottom 50 percent of earners hold only about 30 percent. Fifty-three percent of Americans couldn't cover a $1,000 emergency by tapping into their savings.[2] Among other things, this huge economic divide is creating and heightening racial and ethnic divisions, and people are losing trust in the willingness of political leaders to look out for their economic well-being. Particularly among many white people who believe in their supremacy (though not only among them), rising resentment of Black and brown people exists. There's also widespread fear that white people are losing the opportunity to live the good life the American Dream promises. Our society is becoming destabilized.

In 2025, more than four hundred thousand Black women were either pushed out of the workforce or left due to poor workplace conditions. And as income inequality rises, governments aren't the only ones fearing social unrest.

Knowing they can't outrun the extreme economic inequality they've set into motion, the world's wealthiest people are feeling afraid for their future.[3] Among them, Meta CEO Mark Zuckerberg is building an underground bunker in Hawaii, and PayPal co-founder Peter Thiel a luxury getaway in New Zealand.[4] Short of digging a hole in the ground or launching yourself off the planet in a spaceship as other members of the superrich are preparing to do, we cannot outrun the repercussions of widespread financial inequality.

Because we are human

This book is my effort to help the world understand why it's in everyone's best interest to reduce income inequality, rather than just accepting it as "the way things are." I will also explain why we must take an inclusive approach to financial freedom and economic justice, including and especially for people of African descent in the United States and around the world. Though many of us understand that race is not a biological reality, it is a sociological, cultural, and economic one. Of the roughly eight billion people on the planet, about two billion are Black.[5] If Black people continue to be denied economic freedom and justice, much of the rest of the world will have a difficult way to go. I will teach you in these pages that an overwhelming majority of Black people are experiencing economic injustice. When one of the largest racial groups in the world is struggling economically, it doesn't bode well for the rest of the planet. When you consider the entire world, people of African descent are the planet's fastest-growing demographic; Black people on the African continent have the largest youth population. As go Black people, so goes planet Earth.

When I use the terms *financial freedom* and *economic freedom,* I am talking about every human being's right to make their own financial decisions. This includes things like having the ability to work in the career they choose; start their own business and compete freely and without restrictions; own property and assets; and decide how they spend their own money. Research shows us that people with greater economic freedom have higher incomes and a better standard of living, engage in more innovation and business activity, and enjoy greater individual and political liberties.[6]

Economic justice includes allowing everyone the ability to live a dignified life no matter their identity, personal circumstances, or background. By *dignified life,* I mean every person should be able to access everyday necessities like food, housing, healthcare, education, and capital for their business if they have one.

I believe a person's ability to meet basic needs like these should not be determined merely by how much money they have or their standing within a society. To me this is their right because they are human. Unfortunately, because we haven't experienced it, none of us knows what economic justice looks like. I've spent some time imagining and thinking about it, so throughout this book I'll help you envision it. Because it can be difficult to imagine things that do not exist and that never have, I'll also help you understand what living in an economically unjust society is costing us.

We live in a world where the disparities between the uberwealthy and everyone else grow wider with each passing day. Don't get me wrong, I'm not against people having hard-earned wealth; I'm against obscene levels of inequality. Some of my Christian sisters and brothers are quick to remind us that Jesus said there will always be poor people (Matthew 26:11), but they forget the part where we are instructed to help them (Deuteronomy 15:11). Many people argue that extreme wealth disparities are just the way things are, or that helping those in need somehow detracts from the success of those who have already made it. Others claim social safety net programs give a handout to lazy people who haven't earned it. But I'm here to tell you that nothing could be further from the truth. I will reveal to you how the structure of venture capital increases both the extent and the pace of income inequality—particularly for Black, brown, and working people of all races.

I believe an inclusive society that allows all its members to fulfill their human potential financially benefits everyone, not just those who have been historically marginalized. When we uplift communities that have been excluded—by increasing access to nutritious food, clean water, education, healthcare, business opportunities, financial capital, and so on—we create a more robust economy, we expand the market for goods and services, we increase the size of the workforce, we lower unemployment, and we foster innovation and new ideas.

During the 2025 anti-DEI backlash, many people saw inclusion as merely an option or as just a moral "nice-to-have." The data are clear: inclusion is also a financial imperative. According to research undertaken by the consulting firm McKinsey & Company, the most diverse leadership teams are significantly more likely to financially outperform less diverse teams.[7]

However, economic justice doesn't happen all on its own. Bringing it about for everyone requires us to challenge systems and structures that create and perpetuate inequality, and advocate for policies that promote fairness and opportunity for each and every human being. No matter your race, ethnicity, gender, or nationality—or whether you're a CEO, a business owner, a DoorDasher, a politician, an educator, a nonprofit employee, a manual laborer, or a lawyer, or if you're someone simply navigating their own path in life—in this book I will help you understand why you have something to gain from creating a more inclusive world.

Truth be told, all of us know that change is needed, but far too often we talk about change without doing anything substantial to make it a reality. Meaningful change doesn't just happen on its own. It requires action. And in the context of financial justice for all, it means we all must be proactive in supporting systems that dismantle the barriers that hold others back.

My goal is to support people who desire change and are willing to take action to move us closer to a world where everyone experiences financial freedom.

Discomfort and growth

Though there are many dimensions of inclusivity, I will focus on racial inclusivity. I will also talk about how race and gender intersect.

In the United States and other locations around the world—especially those places where Black and/or brown people were enslaved, or live or lived under colonialism—economic freedom tends to be allocated by race, with people with more melanized skin tones often experiencing less economic freedom than the vast majority of their white counterparts.

I'm aware that I'm bringing up a difficult conversation. So many of us are hesitant, even afraid, to talk about race. I get it; the conversation can be very emotionally charged and uncomfortable. There are lots of long and ugly histories. But racism exists, and the racial economic disparities that result plague the world greatly.

In this book I invite you to consider issues related to racial justice while looking through the lens of resolving them. As someone who tends to turn toward hard things rather than running away from them, I have had the courage to engage in difficult conversations on diversity, equity, and inclusion (DEI) without creating hostility or being argumentative. This includes during my career as a venture capitalist, where a huge percentage of my peers in the field are white and male and Ivy League graduates; I am not.

Trust me, having conversations about financial equity, financial freedom, and fair funding is an art, not a science—one I've cultivated throughout a life in which I've been blessed to move back and forth across racial and geographic boundaries worldwide. I'm here to guide you through conversations that are often uncomfortable for the very people who need to engage in them most. But that's okay. I want to reassure you that this is a journey—one that may bring up feelings of discomfort, confusion, or even frustration. I will hold your hand through this. We will not shy away from the tough topics, the uneasy moments. But we will not stay in that space either.

The reality is that to get to a funding plan that truly works, we must be willing to engage in uncomfortable conversations. But here's the key: we will move through those challenging moments together, and I promise you, we will find common ground and come out the other side stronger and with solutions that make sense for everyone involved. I know that sounds like a tall order, but I've seen it happen. I've witnessed teams, corporations, and governments come together, setting aside their differences, to create funding plans that benefit not only their immediate stakeholders but entire communities and industries.

During the countless conversations I've had about race and racism, I've spoken to many white people who feel guilty or badly about what they've witnessed and experienced; for what they've done and not done; for what they know about their parents' and grandparents' views and behaviors, and what they suspect but don't even want to ask. Some white people have told me they fear their words coming out wrong, saying the wrong thing, being misunderstood by people of color, being ostracized by other white people, losing their job, getting kicked out of their family, being "canceled" in their community, revealing hidden racial bias to themselves and others, and so on. But the underlying and often unspoken fear many white people experience is that as America becomes more racially diverse, people of color will "take over" and white people will lose power. Even worse, many fear that people of color—Black people, in particular—will retaliate and do to white Americans what white Americans have done to Black people. What far too many white people fail to understand is that the world is very diverse. Globally, Black and brown people constitute a majority. To thrive, white people will need to work with people of color. I don't know why this isn't obvious.

As is the case with many white people, I've learned that many Black and brown people fear losing their jobs. They, too, fear being blacklisted at work, as well as being labeled "angry" or "militant," being "canceled" by their white peers and coworkers, being the subject of racist office whisper campaigns, and being pushed off their career track at their company and/or blackballed in their industry. Black people experience fear and shame for bowing to racism, for feeling afraid to stand up for themselves, for not speaking up out of fear they or their loved ones will experience negative consequences. Some of us also feel extremely uncomfortable thinking about what it would mean and who we could be if we could confront and overcome our racial fear and step more boldly into our lives and experience our destiny. Indeed, the price Black people pay for fear includes losing the possibility of their own liberation.

Fear is a natural human emotion. In fact, science tells us that to varying degrees every human body experiences the stress reaction commonly known as the "fight or flight" response. Our bodies are designed to move through our fear. Certain situations may honestly trigger our fear, but I'm here to remind you: we don't have to stay there.

As you read this book it's likely something I say will make you feel uncomfortable. Discomfort can be a part of growth. Human beings are often uncomfortable with unknown and unfamiliar things, but there's no need to stay stuck. For example, psychological research about the growth mindset teaches us that the key to growing and improving ourselves includes understanding that intelligence isn't a fixed trait but one that can be cultivated as we learn and try new things. It teaches us to embrace challenges, exhibit a sustained effort, be persistent, seek feedback even if it's critical, and become comfortable being uncomfortable as we practice, grow, and learn.[8]

In business, a growth mindset improves motivation, innovation, and productivity.[9]

In other words, when it comes to learning about tricky topics like race, you have to be willing to take a risk.

We will reach resolution and it will feel great for everyone.

Where I'm coming from

My ideas may strike you as ones you don't typically hear from either a Black woman, a business leader, or a serial entrepreneur—all of which I am. They're certainly not common to a venture capitalist, which I am as well. Let me be transparent about where I'm coming from:

- I practice Christianity unapologetically and bring a spiritual lens to life. I realize saying I'm Christian means different things to different people. Here are some of the ways my faith guides my thinking on these issues.
- I believe every human being is made in God's spiritual image and has the God-given ability to thrive when living in an environment where they can be their best self.
- I believe each person has unique gifts and talents to contribute to the world.
- I believe we are to love our neighbor, the stranger, the "outsider," and people we often see as the "other."
- I believe in justice and fairness. To me, extreme income inequality is a spiritual violation.
- I believe money is intended to flow in and out of our lives as a current—as "currency"—not to be hoarded in greed.

To paraphrase Mahatma Gandhi, there is enough for everyone's needs, though not for our greed.[10]

- I believe all human beings are equal in value and no one is superior to another.
- I believe the cultures, values, and beliefs of people of African descent are priceless in value.
- I believe that the greater the numbers of human beings who are thriving the greater the likelihood that everyone will prosper. I do not buy into "zero-sum" narratives, where for one person to win another has to lose, or if I get something it must take something from you.

I am also clear that almost all of us received an incomplete and even distorted education about Black history. If, for example, as an American you are under the impression that Dr. Martin Luther King's greatest dream was for his children to "live in a nation where they will not be judged by the color of their skin but by the content of their character"—language he used in his 1963 March on Washington speech—you are in good company. What you might not know as much about is Dr. King's fight for economic justice.

If you were taught European history in school but not African history, I'll expose you to some important history your education likely missed.

Over the years, many of us have also grown to understand that the media don't always portray Black and brown people accurately and in the fullness of their humanity. I'll share information to help fill in the picture.

Prosperity is possible

I welcome everyone into this conversation, no matter your race, ethnicity, or background. All of our lives depend upon our collective ability and willingness to address the existential issues we're facing, including reducing income inequality, increasing economic freedom, and closing wealth gaps within societies and around the world, including among Black people.

Remaining in fear is costing us our freedom and quality of life.

This manifesto is not just for one group, it's for everyone. I pray that people of all races, all backgrounds, from all walks of life can embrace it, receive it, and agree on it. Because though fear is universal, I believe freedom can be too. The freedom to speak. The freedom to create. The freedom to provide for ourselves and our loved ones. The freedom to build a world that endures.

We live in a time when divisiveness is easy. Fear thrives in uncertainty—it feeds on confusion, on isolation, on the idea that we are somehow separate from one another. But the truth is, we are all connected. And when we move beyond fear, when we step into courage together, we create a world where prosperity is possible for all of us.

If we can embrace fearless freedom, we can shape a future that is bold, just, and filled with opportunity.

This is the solution.

Chapter 1

Emergency

The purpose of the Fearless Strivers Grant Contest operated by Defendants Fearless Fund Management, LLC; Fearless Fund II, GP, LLC; Fearless Fund II, LP; and Fearless Foundation Inc. (collectively, "Fearless Fund") is to "bridg[e] the gap in venture capital funding for women of color founders building scalable, growth aggressive companies." . . . Fearless Fund's efforts on behalf of Black women entrepreneurs serve to remedy severe economic disparities that exist as a result of a long, sordid history of race and gender discrimination in this country, a legacy of inequity anchored in disenfranchisement and the exclusion of Black women from participation in the formal economy. These inequalities persist today, limiting the opportunities for Black women to start and grow their own businesses. By increasing access to capital for Black women entrepreneurs, Fearless Fund is not merely redressing centuries of marginalization—it is providing a much-needed foundation for growth and innovation that has been ignored for far too long.

—Black Economic Alliance Foundation, brief of amicus curiae in *American Alliance for Equal Rights v. Fearless Fund Management, LLC* in support of the Fearless Fund's opposition to the AAER's motion for preliminary injunction

AUGUST 2, 2023

I was working in my home office, soaking in the good energy streaming from the sun on a typical early-August Atlanta afternoon, when my cell phone began buzzing with text messages; I ignored them.

But then my phone rang.

"Arian, have you seen the news?" one of my staff members, whom I'll call Mary, asked, sounding distressed.

"What's wrong?" I responded calmly.

"The press is emailing me and other staff members, asking us to comment on our lawsuit."

"That's silly, we're not in a lawsuit," I said, feeling unbothered. "ChatGPT is probably mixing us up with somebody else. Whatever confusion is going on will work itself out."

I returned to the emails I'd been reading as CEO of the Fearless Fund, the women-of-color-founded venture capital (VC) firm I'd started in 2018 to help close the gap in funding available to businesses founded by Black and brown women.

Forty-five minutes later, Mary buzzed me again.

"Arian, major media outlets like Reuters and the *Wall Street Journal* are contacting us—some of the staff members are even getting phone calls."

"If there is a lawsuit, it's public record," I responded. "Just find me the filing and we can deal with it from there." I remained certain that this was an error. About forty-five minutes later, Mary called yet again.

"I just emailed the filing to you."

I opened the email and double-clicked on the attachment.

"IN THE UNITED STATES DISTRICT COURT FOR THE NORTHERN DISTRICT OF GEORGIA ATLANTA DIVISION," the top of the document read in all caps.

"Oh, sh—, this is a federal case!" I blurted out, my heart skipping a beat.

"AMERICAN ALLIANCE FOR EQUAL RIGHTS, Plaintiff, v. FEARLESS FUND MANAGEMENT, LLC; FEARLESS FUND II,

GP, LLC; FEARLESS FUND II, LP; and FEARLESS FOUNDATION, INC."

They are suing four of the Fearless Fund's six entities?

I scanned the document again to make certain I hadn't misread it; I hadn't. Then, mind racing, I called Mary back.

"Who is the American Alliance for Equal Rights?!"

"Do you remember Ed Blum?"

"I know that name. . . ."

"He's the person who filed the Supreme Court case that struck down affirmative action in colleges in June," she reminded me.

"Oh, yes!" I quickly recalled both the lawsuit and the conservative legal activist, Edward Blum, whose anti-affirmative-action group the American Alliance for Equal Rights, an organization dedicated to challenging "distinctions and preferences made on the basis of race and ethnicity," had filed it. When Blum's "reverse discrimination" lawsuit against Harvard and the University of North Carolina, Chapel Hill, first hit the news, I discussed it with several friends. We didn't believe he would be able to dismantle the laws requiring educators and employers to help rectify the nation's history of systemic racism in classrooms and workplaces by taking "affirmative action to ensure that applicants are treated equally without regard to race, color, religion or national origin."[1]

But on June 29, 2023, the Supreme Court struck down colleges' ability to use race as one factor among many in their admissions decisions. Still, what did this have to do with the Fearless Fund?

"Just go back to work; don't let this upset you," I told her. "I'll figure out what's going on."

How a leader shows up in times of crisis matters—and emotions are contagious. I wanted Mary to remain calm so she could work undistracted. I emailed a note telling the staff not to respond to the media but to stay focused on their work. I didn't want anyone becoming preoccupied with what might well be a social-media mistake gone viral.

I continued reading the lawsuit, noting the plaintiff had filed three critical motions against my companies all at once. The first was a temporary restraining order, demanding that we cease operations by August 17—just one day before our 2023 Fearless VC Summit, intended to provide education, networking, connections, and a marketplace for goods and services to two thousand women-of-color entrepreneurs. It was already August 2, and our conference planning was in full gear.

How could they be so blatant in their efforts to disrupt something so meaningful?

The second motion was a preliminary injunction order (PI) intended to stop the Fearless Strivers Grant program, an initiative run by the Fearless Foundation, our nonprofit providing grants and educational resources to Black women entrepreneurs and aspiring entrepreneurs. The Fearless Strivers Grant helped these enterprising women access resources, funding, and an ecosystem of support historically out of reach to people like them.

My gut became a bit unsettled.

The third motion consisted of the legal case itself, alleging that four of the Fearless Fund's six companies engaged in racial discrimination. As I attempted to digest what I was reading, I noticed Blum wasn't coming after Fund I, which had already invested almost $26 million in thirty-six companies founded by women of color. Nor was he pursuing the general partnership managing it. But he was coming after Fund II, which would soon invest in a new group of businesswomen; he was also suing Fund II's general partnership, the Fearless Fund's management company, and the Fearless Foundation.

That means he is after our future business, not past business—and the future of Black women's entrepreneurship!

I felt a bit shocked. This was a bit disconcerting, though I remained oddly peaceful as I tried to decipher the document.

This has to be some kind of mistake. Surely, someone will come forward to clear it up. The news media will retract it, and everything will return to normal.

Then something promising slowly dawned upon me.

Look at God—this is a setup for victory! I smiled as my deep faith welled up within me.

I reflected upon how the unexpected press the Fearless Fund received during the racial reckoning after the George Floyd protests in 2020 had positioned us to raise a lot more money than we normally would have through traditional efforts. The fund was currently raising capital for Fund II, which would increase the number of women of color we could support. We'd already secured $23 million and were in due diligence—when investors investigate us to ensure our business is legitimate—for more than another $100 million.

All this exposure will allow us to build a $200 million fund!

As I continued reading the filing, I noticed that the plaintiffs alleged not only that we were discriminating against white people but also that we were violating the 1866 Civil Rights Act.

Is that a typo or mistake? The Civil Rights Act passed in 1964. Or did it?

I reflected upon the history of the mid-1800s. The Emancipation Proclamation, which freed slaves in the Confederate states—Alabama, Arkansas, Florida, Georgia, Louisiana, Mississippi, North Carolina, South Carolina, Tennessee, Texas, and Virginia—was issued in 1863. However, slavery wasn't abolished until the end of 1865, when Congress passed the Thirteenth Amendment, which made slavery illegal. Reconstruction—the twelve-year-long era after the Civil War ended, when the US government attempted to reintegrate both four million newly freed Black people and the citizens of the defeated Southern Confederate states into the nation—took place after that.

But was there something else? I searched Google.

Oh, there is *an 1866 Civil Rights Act. . . .*

Congress passed it to help integrate formerly enslaved people into American society. The 1866 act declared that all people born in the United States are US citizens and that certain inalienable rights come with citizenship. The act also stated that it was illegal to deprive any citizen "on the basis of race, color, or prior condition of slavery or involuntary servitude."

Blum's lawsuit accused the Fearless Fund of violating Section 1981 of that 1866 act. Section 1981 grants all citizens the same rights as white people to make and enforce contracts, own property, sue in court, and enjoy the full protection of the law.[2] As they fought both to be paid for their efforts and to enjoy their lives for the first time, the ability of newly freed African Americans to enter a contract was critical to their ability to feed and provide for themselves and their families. Securing work often meant negotiating payment for their labor with the very same enslavers who previously owned, violently abused, and worked them from "can't see in the morning 'til can't see at night," paying nothing.

I became more alarmed.

I thought about the preliminary injunction focused on our foundation's Strivers Grant contest, a partnership with a major corporation that offered $20,000 grants and mentorship to businesses majority-owned by Black women, and Black women who aspired to be founders. The Strivers Grant offered many of our participants a lifeline, a financial opportunity they were unlikely to obtain elsewhere because the racial disparities in VC funding are so tremendous. Black women comprise 7 percent of the US population and start businesses at a faster rate than any other demographic group, yet they obtain only 0.0006 percent of the venture capital funding in the technology sector, where the overwhelming amount of venture capital funding is awarded. All women of color combined don't fare much better, comprising 20 percent of the US population but receiving only 0.39 percent of the VC funding across all business sectors. And though women comprise more than 50 percent of the US population, all totaled we obtain less than 2 percent of VC funding.

Hold up now, this makes no sense! How can we be violating a law that helped Black people get jobs? And how could helping Black and brown people be a civil rights violation when these acts were established to help us?!

I turned to the text messages and emails that had chimed on my phone.

This wasn't a glitch, a misunderstanding, or some temporary blip; it was real. The Fearless Fund was in the middle of a huge and serious situation. My heart pounded and thoughts raced chaotically as the weight of the situation, the gravity of what was unfolding, and the uncertainty of what would come next hit me at once.

This is an attempt to flip the law on its head! These people are trying to threaten Black people's ECONOMIC FREEDOM! Hell no!

I had to act quickly, and I knew who could help—renowned civil rights lawyer Ben Crump. My fingers flew across my phone keyboard texting him, "EMERGENCY."

Chapter 2

The Elephant in the Room

> Organizations like Fearless Fund play a critical role in closing the entrepreneurship gap and ensuring equity for Black women business owners. Fearless Fund and other organizations that promote minority businesses serve to remedy this historic and persistent inequality and, in so doing, create new avenues for economic growth and innovation. Indeed, the advantages of entrepreneurial opportunities for Black women extend not only to the recipients of funding—as one academic has noted, "[b]usiness ownership has allowed African American and other minority women to avoid discrimination on the job and to achieve occupational mobility" . . . —but also to the economy and society at large.
>
> —Black Economic Alliance Foundation, brief of amicus curiae in *American Alliance for Equal Rights v. Fearless Fund Management, LLC* in support of the Fearless Fund's opposition to the AAER's motion for preliminary injunction

I'm a straight shooter. I call a spade a spade and can be a very black-and-white person. I don't operate well in the gray.

We need to address the elephant in the room.

The reason the Fearless Fund was being sued was because white people who believe in white supremacy fear people in the numerical minority becoming the majority. When I refer to white supremacists, I am talking primarily about the type of overt Ku Klux Klan–style racists whom most Americans find repugnant. I'm also referring to people who don't engage in such odious action but who still fear a society where the number of Black and brown people combined comprises a majority.

In 2008, the US Census Bureau published its first projections that by 2043 those identifying as white will represent less than 50 percent of the population. After that, the country would become "majority minority," the mainstream media told us.[1] The total number of Indigenous Americans, Black Americans, Asian Americans, and Latinos combined will be greater than the total number of white Americans.

Those projections were solidified in 2012, when the census updated those data.

Suddenly, the media began reporting about "the changing face of America," "white decline," "anxious white people," and the "multicultural explosion" rattling them.

In reality, for decades many factors had been unsettling white America's well-being, including deindustrialization, job offshoring, manufacturing modernization, and the Great Recession. With the proliferation of smartphones, cell phone videos, and social media networks, suddenly everyday citizens could record and swiftly broadcast repeated incidents of violence unleashed upon unarmed Black citizens by law enforcement—violence African Americans had been complaining about and police had been denying for generations. A movement began to hold offending officers accountable. In 2013, Black Lives Matter sprang to life after a jury acquitted George Zimmerman of murdering an unarmed Black Florida teenager, Trayvon Martin. From Tamir Rice in Cleveland, Ohio, to

Freddie Gray in Baltimore, to Eric Garner in New York City, to Sandra Bland in Texas, seemingly countless defenseless Black people died at the hands of law enforcement. Racial justice activists demanded answers, reform, and greater racial and economic justice. This movement peaked in 2020, with widespread protests in the United States and all over the world after police officer Derek Chauvin choked George Floyd as he became the latest Black person to plead to police, crying, "I can't breathe."

Adding insult to what to certain white people felt like injury, in the aftermath of George Floyd's murder, increasing numbers of minority entrepreneurs and business leaders became visible; corporations made commitments to diversity, equity, and inclusion; people of color continued demonstrating tremendous impact in sports, entertainment, and other high-profile industries; and much of America began to witness many everyday Black Americans enjoying the American Dream, just as have generations of Americans of European descent.

Clearly the nation's economic and cultural narratives are no longer exclusively written by the historically powerful. Some see this as a threat, triggering their racial anxiety, and openly expressed displeasure with the progress of Black and brown people.

The backlash deepened: conversations about white people "losing jobs" to Black and brown people grew louder, though white unemployment generally had hovered between 3 and 4 percent since 2017, except for about eighteen months around the Covid-19 shutdown.[2] Mainstream media have continued to portray concerns about culture change and job loss as problems of white people living in rural and Middle America, as well as of the white working class and working poor. According to news narratives, these are the people who voted Donald Trump into office.

As a venture capitalist who travels the nation and the world, I can tell you firsthand these fears are not limited to low-income white people. In corporate conference centers, exclusive retreat spaces, and private boardrooms, I've encountered similar discomfort among some of this nation's wealthiest citizens. Compounding their unsettledness is a reality our nation has been too afraid to address for centuries but that many Black and brown activists now state publicly: a significant proportion of wealthy white people inherited social and economic privileges because their ancestors participated in the genocide, enslavement, and/or colonization of Black and brown people. The exposing of this unsavory past (or even present) makes some squirm, particularly when their own families are implicated. Still others object to terms like *privilege* and *structural racism*. It's clear a select few fear losing political control, the fading of their cultural dominance, and/or losing the economic power they and their ancestors have monopolized for centuries. To some who have profited from long-standing racial inequities, the idea that minorities, especially Black people, could demand and achieve economic independence and economic, political, and/or cultural influence threatens the very ideas upon which this nation was built.

The desire to oppress people of color is rooted in the fear of losing power and control. It's a fear that runs deep in the hearts and minds of those who believe in white supremacy, and it has shaped much of the history of this country. For many people who hold these beliefs, the increasing population of people of color is seen not as a sign of progress or a chance for greater diversity and growth, but as a direct threat to their power. I've observed that when you have been dominant for so long, the thought of that power slipping away can create deep, unsettling fear. That fear is not just about politics or social change; it's about the fundamental belief that a shift in the demographic balance could undermine the structure of society as they know it.

Little do they know that people of color are not trying to strip away power from anyone, but when you've been conditioned for generations to see yourself as superior, the idea of anyone else having a say, taking up space, or even thriving may feel like an existential threat. White supremacy, at its core, isn't about intellect or capability, it's about a deeply ingrained belief in white people's inherent right to maintain their dominance in every sphere, from politics to culture to economics.

When we think about the overwhelming support that President Donald Trump received during his 2024 campaign, it's easy to assume that his supporters were simply voting for someone who would improve the economy or bring back their jobs. Trump voters certainly were not voting for his intellectual ability or his understanding of complex issues. Many Americans voted for him because he represented power, a return to an era when white people were firmly in control. Many of his supporters had fears and anxieties about a changing America—one that was no longer going to prioritize white people's interests above all else but would instead cater to the diversity that is the fabric of America. In this way, it wasn't about who Trump was as a person or politician; it was about what he represented—a desperate attempt to restore what some felt had been lost.

For those who fear losing their grip on power, this shift feels like a betrayal. It challenges everything they've been taught about their place in the world, and that's not easy to accept. The fact that these fears are so deeply entrenched in the ideology of white supremacy makes it incredibly difficult to have honest conversations about race and power. When you've been taught your whole life that your race is inherently superior, the idea that other races are fighting for their own rights, recognition, and opportunities can feel like a rejection of everything you've known.

From voter-suppression tactics to the dismantling of affirmative action policies, the resistance to true equity is often set up as a defense of "traditional" values or a desire to protect economic and political stability. So many of these actions are based on the fear that if people of color have equal access to resources, power, and opportunities, society will fall apart, when in reality, our nation would be at its peak.

White supremacy isn't just about hatred; it's about fear. Fear of losing power. Fear of losing control. And when fear is allowed to guide policy, actions, and decisions, it leads to inequality and division. Just think about it: Can you name something good that came from the spirit of fear? No! But you can name many great things that came from the spirit of faith. If we can begin to lean boldly into unexplored possibilities, we can start to create the kind of change that we need in this country.

Though fear is a human emotion, there's no need to succumb to it. I named my business the Fearless Fund because I believe the biblical passage 2 Timothy 1:7: "God has not given us a spirit of fear but of love and power and a strong mind."

My faith teaches that fear does not come from God. That said, worry, anxiety, trepidation, distress, and even panic are part of the human condition. This reality is why many ministers teach that several hundred biblical passages speak to our unease. Phrases like "Fear not, for I am with you" (Isaiah 41:10), "Be strong and courageous" (Joshua 1:9), and "Let not your heart be troubled, neither let it be afraid" (John 14:27), and countless others support humanity in rising above its basic instincts. No fear comes from God, including the fear of Black and brown people taking over. Instead, the alarm we're seeing is the acronym FEAR in action: "false evidence appearing real."

As a serial entrepreneur—I have owned a retail clothing business, a marketing and PR firm, a magazine, and an online clothing company, in addition to being a venture capitalist—I deal in reality, not fiction. So let's get to the facts.

Leaders in corporate America and beyond know the results of the McKinsey & Company diversity report showing that companies with diverse employees outperform less diverse firms and that more-diverse workforces demonstrate better decision making and innovation. The May 19, 2020, McKinsey report "Diversity Wins: How Inclusion Matters" reads in part:

> The business case for diversity, equity, and inclusion (DE&I) is stronger than ever. Taking a closer look at diversity winners reveals what can drive real progress. . . . Our latest analysis reaffirms the strong business case for both gender

> diversity and ethnic and cultural diversity in corporate leadership—and shows that this business case continues to strengthen. The most diverse companies are now more likely than ever to outperform less diverse peers on profitability.

In fact, McKinsey's research showed that a company's commitment to diversity is so important to many job candidates that it helps them decide where they do and don't want to work.[3] In other words, DEI is good business.

In the venture capital space, the disparity between, on the one hand, Black women's percentage of the population and the rate at which they start businesses, and, on the other hand, the percentage of venture capital they receive is so immense, it ought not logically spark anyone's fear. Many women-of-color founders the Fearless Fund has invested in have white males, Black males, white females, and people of other races and ethnicities as cofounders and business partners.

We're paying a tremendous price for getting trapped in fear—the false evidence that appears to be so real.

In fact, I believe people's fear of losing economic control fuels the widespread resistance to policies that aim to redistribute resources more equitably—policies like universal healthcare, student loan forgiveness, and minimum-wage increases. These aren't just about ideology or political party lines. I believe opposition to these approaches reflects the fear of losing control over resources that have long been concentrated in the hands of a few. Though they're designed to help level the playing field so everyone can prosper, some see these policies as threats to their way of life—their economic status, their family legacy, and the immense power that comes with wealth.

Black people and other people of color pay a price for not showing up at work and other areas of life as their full selves. We fear speaking up would bring negative consequences—from the potential hostility of our peers all the way up to losing our paycheck. Fear is costing us our brilliance, our spiritual destiny.

But we aren't the only ones paying the price. Fear is costing non-Black people a world that's healed from all the division and strife because some white people want to oppress someone amazing. Our world experiences less innovation, less brilliance. And all of us live beneath the moral level and standard we were created to inhabit.

Beyond that, if people weren't being economically oppressed, we'd experience less crime. We wouldn't feel the need to live in gated communities, or reside in increasingly remote places, or feel so isolated from one another, or use security lights, or stockpile guns, or experience high rates of murder and death by suicide because weapons are so accessible. We wouldn't be cut off from members of our family who hold different political views. We wouldn't be polarized as a society because we fear people of color, immigrants, white supremacists, authoritarians, or fascists.

Our fear of the "other" is costing us all.

Even beyond the racial fears so prevalent these days, the shift in influence racial justice activists propose isn't about replacing one group with another or taking wealth from one group to give to another. It's about dismantling systems that have unjustly concentrated power in the hands of the few and instead distributing that power more equitably so that all human beings have the opportunity to thrive. Shifts toward greater equity have already taken place in other areas—politically, culturally, socially, and so on. Why should economics be any different?

We change agents don't desire to destroy anybody's lifestyle; we aspire to create ways to build our own opportunities. Despite very active societal narratives that accuse us of asking for handouts, we're not looking for favors; we're establishing fairness.

The Playbook

The Cure for Corporations

By enabling individuals to build their own wealth and businesses, corporations can support local entrepreneurship, help create jobs, stimulate innovation, and reduce poverty.

Corporate-backed entrepreneurship and innovation hubs can empower marginalized communities and nurture local entrepreneurs and innovators by:

- Providing seed funding
- Developing mentorship programs
- Partnering with educational institutions to create global learning networks, equipping youth—and particularly those in developing nations—with the knowledge and skills they need to thrive in the modern economy
- Focusing on sustainable and ethical business practices
- Backing renewable-energy projects
- Creating fair wage systems
- Investing in local communities
- Offering inclusive financial services: tailored products for marginalized groups (microloans, insurance, and savings accounts)
- Establishing financial literacy programs
- Establishing public-private partnerships, with governments and corporations working together to invest in transportation, healthcare, utilities, and technology infrastructure in underserved regions

- Advocating for global policy reform
- Using their influence to champion policies that promote economic justice, such as fair-trade agreements, tax reforms, and regulations to prevent exploitation
- Supporting local governments in crafting policies that foster inclusive growth
- Providing financial support for organizations working on racial and gender equality, access to healthcare, or education

When corporations lead by example and champion human rights, they set a powerful precedent for the private sector to become an active participant in solving global inequities. This not only drives systemic change but also empowers communities worldwide to achieve their economic potential. Every dollar invested in our markets, every initiative that supports education and entrepreneurship is a vote of confidence in a future where economic opportunity is not a privilege but a right for all.

Chapter 3

A Strategic Assault

Organizations like Fearless Fund continue the tradition of solidarity and investment pioneered by Booker T. Washington, Maggie L. Walker, and Madam C. J. Walker, bridging the opportunity gap for Black women and ensuring that new sources of economic growth and innovation are no longer ignored. While exploring the differing experiences of Black and white women business owners, one academic cited "access to minority loan programs and minority advocacy organizations" as advantages for the former. . . . But this access has not always been sufficient to meet the need. Writing a quarter-century ago, this same academic explained that, "[c]ompared to modern, voluntary immigrants, African Americans have fewer resources to pool in support of community-based businesses"—an historic detriment that "may be changing with inputs of wealth from successful new business started by blacks. . . ." Fearless Fund, the BEA Foundation, and other likeminded organizations are vindicating this promise, closing the historic gap between Black and white entrepreneurs and expanding opportunities for new Black businesses.

—Black Economic Alliance Foundation, brief of amicus curiae in *American Alliance for Equal Rights v. Fearless Fund Management, LLC* in support of the Fearless Fund's opposition to the AAER's motion for preliminary injunction

AUGUST 2, 2023

Civil rights attorney Benjamin Crump called within moments of receiving my "EMERGENCY" text.

"What's going on, Arian?" he asked in his trademark Southern accent.

I'd first met Ben in Florida when I was a student at Florida A&M University's School of Business and Industry, in Tallahassee, where he and Darryl Parks were running their law firm. A Florida State grad and a brilliant warrior for justice, Ben is known for taking on and winning difficult civil rights and wrongful-injury cases, including for the murders of innocent and unarmed Black people like Trayvon Martin, Michael Brown, Breonna Taylor, and George Floyd. The sound of his voice instantly comforted me.

"I think the Fearless Fund is being sued for reverse discrimination," I said, jumping right to the point. "Some organization called the American Alliance for Equal Rights is suing us for violating the Civil Rights Act of 1866. Have you ever heard of such a thing?"

"That's Edward Blum—the same guy who funded the *Students for Fair Admissions* Supreme Court decision, ending race-based affirmative action in higher education a few weeks ago, because it supposedly violates the Fourteenth Amendment's equal-protection clause," he said.

"Oh . . . ," I groaned, feeling the weight of his words.

"Arian, you're not alone in this fight."

It meant everything to have the support of such a capable and long-standing friend.

By nightfall, my team and I sat in a Zoom "war room" with Benjamin and some of the best and brightest minds in law and communications, including publicist and communications expert Rachel Noerdlinger, who has worked with attorney Johnnie Cochran, Reverend Al Sharpton, and the National Action Network, among other noteworthy clients. When Ed Blum succeeded in striking down affirmative action in higher education, I knew he wouldn't stop there. But I had no idea Blum would set his sights on private businesses—and

I darn sure never imagined the Fearless Fund's focus on women-of-color-cofounded companies would place us next on his hit list.

> When you disrupt a norm, some people and entities will try to push you back into what they see as your place.

Our legal team filled in the backstory for us. For decades, Blum has been pursuing a personal mission to build barriers to key pillars of the American Dream—particularly voting rights, education, and the economy. His deep-pocketed supporters have funded several anti-affirmative-action cases, including the 2013 *Shelby County v. Holder* Supreme Court decision, which struck down a key provision in the 1965 Voting Rights Act that determined which jurisdictions needed federal approval before changing their voting laws.[1] That victory paved the way for a decade-long assault. Many experts view the UNC/Harvard decision killing affirmative action as the death knell for DEI as well. It is just one facet of a multipronged assault by right-wing activists such as Blum, Christopher Rufo, and Robby Starbuck, who believe *Students for Fair Admissions* gives them the license to bully private companies committed to DEI.

Suddenly, the Fearless Fund found itself the inaugural defendant in that anti-DEI war.

What made our case stand out was it wasn't the usual attack on a government policy or even a public institution. The fact we weren't a traditional target sounded a wake-up call for many in the venture capital space. The Fearless Fund had been selected as the precedent case, where the plaintiffs clearly were trying to make an example of us. The attack on us signaled a forthcoming wave of attacks that could be waged against all types of organizations, including non-profits, from long-standing initiatives to businesses like ours just beginning to make a difference. It wasn't merely a broadside against DEI—it was an attempt to disrupt the funding and support systems that allow women-of-color entrepreneurs to thrive.

How dare they try to strip this away when we're actively having an impact!

Attorney Crump noted the case did not include Fund I. The fact the Fearless Fund had more than one legal entity but AAER wasn't coming after all of them made us curious. Was this an accident? Were they strategically avoiding Fund I since it was fully deployed? But how would they know that? Why were they so tuned in to our funding cycles? And what was so significant to them about our upcoming Summit that they wanted to shut it down one day before it took place? Clearly someone had been watching our every move.

The attorneys helped us understand the significance of the case, which was constructed not merely as a legal challenge but as a strategic assault intended to dismantle our entire operation. The plaintiffs had filed three critical motions, which are requests for a judge to issue a decision or a specific order.[2]

There was the temporary restraining order demanding that the Fearless Fund cease operations before our 2023 Fearless VC Summit. The lawyers explained that courts use temporary restraining orders—sometimes called injunctions—which are short-term directives that prohibit entities or actors from engaging in a particular activity. They often right a wrong in situations where financial compensation would be inadequate. Courts typically use them to prevent irreparable harm.

How could they be so blatant in their efforts to disrupt something this meaningful?

The second motion was the preliminary injunction order intended to stop the Fearless Strivers Grant program, which offered Black women entrepreneurs help with cash-flow management, product creation, and job creation. Funded by a reputable bank, the Strivers Grant was administered by the Fearless Foundation. The lawyers explained that courts issue a PI only after they've held a hearing and that a preliminary injunction usually lasts longer than a temporary restraining order.

Blum accused the Strivers Grant program of discriminating against non-Black founders; however, this didn't make sense. The Fearless Foundation offered several grant programs for women of color, including one specifically for Hispanic women. I was struck by the selective targeting of the program for Black women. More infuriating, over the three years it had been in existence, the Fearless Strivers program had awarded numerous grants of between $10,000 and $20,000. This year, we were awarding six grants; only one $20,000 grant remained. Yet this small amount of money had stirred up a ruckus. The plaintiffs were clearly attempting to roll back economic progress in the Black community post–George Floyd.

The third motion was a legal case alleging that four of the Fearless Fund's six companies engaged in racial discrimination: Fund II, its general partnership, our management company, and the Fearless Foundation. By that point I was raising money for Fund II and had already secured $10 million from General Mills, our first major investor, in addition to investments from Costco and other existing Fund I customers, such as Bank of America, which also reupped. We had closed on $23 million of these funds and were in diligence for an additional $100 million–plus across incremental closings.

Our attorneys noted that Blum wasn't coming after Fund I's general partnership or Fund I itself, which had already invested between $500,000 and $1.2 million in each of thirty-six companies run by women of color—a game-changing amount to the businesses in our portfolio, but a drop in the bucket in the $62 trillion venture capital industry. In 2022 alone, the various players in the industry deployed some $288 billion to US start-ups.[3] To provide a bit of context, if one million one-dollar bills were stacked with the front of one bill facing the back of another, just as you'd place them in your wallet, they'd reach about the length of a football field, according to FlowingData.com.[4] That means by comparison, $288 billion would be 288,000 US football fields long. I don't share that to diminish the impact of our work; it's only to give you a sense of the size of the Fearless Fund compared to the size of the industry. AAER was intentionally punching down at what they perceived as a very vulnerable organization they could easily defeat.

Clearly, this lawsuit wasn't just about the legality of what the Fearless Fund was doing—the plaintiffs were trying both to intimidate us and to stop Fund II from investing in future businesses. The attorneys noted that AAER filed the lawsuit in Georgia, a state known for its conservative legal climate. Clearly, Blum intended to halt our contest, disrupt our company, and undermine Black business formation. My livelihood and the livelihood of my team members were on the line. Broadly speaking, so were the livelihoods of all Black Americans.

But there's nothing I love more than helping people's dreams come true, so I continued doing that work with passion. After speaking with our attorneys, I also turned to the Black VC community for guidance. Our Fearless Fund team strategized and refused to back down. I did my best to shield our staff from the day-to-day associated with the legal case. I needed them focused on funding our women-of-color-cofounded companies. This lawsuit meant to break the Fearless Fund ignited a renewed commitment to our mission. The fact that Blum and the AAER were willing to go to great lengths to stop us meant one thing: we were doing something that mattered—and it was worth fighting for.

During this time a colleague generously offered me the opportunity to rest and restore myself from the demands of leading the Fearless Fund by spending time at their beach home in the Hamptons. When I arrived, their family was wrapping up a large reunion; they graciously welcomed me as though I were another member. They'd set up tables with games, one evening ended with a talent show, and delicious food was served in every corner of the house.

After the family departed, I stayed to think and decompress, blessed with not just a spectacular home but also maid service and chefs. I ate delicious food, and the cooks were even gracious enough to allow me to join them in the kitchen—one night sautéing onions, leeks, garlic, tomatoes, and other ingredients to make fresh fish soup together. This was heaven—a huge relief!

I viewed this time in the Hamptons as a sacred and quiet time to reconnect with God, journal my thoughts and ideas, and clarify my vision to continue building the Fearless Fund even in the face of this unexpected attack. I listened to sermons from my pastor, Bishop William Murphy III, lead pastor of the dReam Center Church of Atlanta, and other preachers I enjoy, including Bishop T. D. Jakes, and Touré and Sarah Jakes Roberts, to strengthen my spirit.

Evenings I sat on the back porch with a cup of green tea and reflected upon my childhood in Detroit, where I grew up with Rosa Parks, Coretta Scott King, Juanita Abernathy, Betty Shabazz, and other the iconic civil rights figures and Black luminaries in my family orbit.

They are your blueprints for resilience.

I meditated, watching the blue-green waves rise and then spray sea foam as they fell and crashed along the shoreline.

You were destined for this moment. You are well equipped for this divine disruption and whatever is coming on the other side of this lawsuit. You cannot remain silent about this vicious attack on the future of women-of-color entrepreneurs and their families.

I was built for this and I knew it.

Before the lawsuit even hit, I had been booked to speak with Gayle King on the *CBS Mornings* show to talk about the 2023 VC Summit. The appearance presented an incredible opportunity to sound the alarm on one of the highest-rated talk shows in the country—and to let Blum and America know that we weren't going to go down without a fight. I knew the moment presented the perfect chance to give CBS an exclusive news-breaking interview and to alert the world about what was going on.

Talk about divine timing! What are the odds?

I sat at the roundtable at CBS Studios in New York City wearing a black suit with gold buttons and a black button-up blouse. The producers positioned me between co-hosts Nate Burleson and Tony Dukoupil and directly across from Gayle.

"What's your response?" Gayle asked me about the lawsuit. "What are you all planning to do?"

"Our response is simple: we will continue to do the work that we do for women of color," I replied. "As you stated before, women of color are the most founded entrepreneur demographic; they are just the least funded."

Gayle described how shocked she was upon learning that less than 1 percent of VC money is awarded to women-of-color founders. We discussed the reasons, including the fact that 92 percent of the investors in venture capital are white males, who often lack proximity to women of color, so they don't benefit from knowing them or hearing their amazing ideas.

Then Nate jumped in.

"I never really understood how someone who had a head start in the race would look at those behind them and try to trip them up," he stated. "What is your message to those who are looking to trip you up?"

I shared that our corporate partners were standing by us as well as their DEI programs.

Tony inquired, "Arian, what do you say to people who say, 'However admirable your goal, however necessary the work you're doing, the law is just not on your side'? The law says racial discrimination is bad in all contexts—"

"And *that,* people argue, still is not fair," Gayle chimed in.

"Well, it's definitely unfortunate that things can be twisted," I responded. "I can't get into the details of the lawsuit, but what I can say is that certain laws were put in place to offer economic freedom for people of color, and somehow things keep getting misconstrued."

As the segment wound down, Gayle stated, "I don't care who you are, when you hear the word *lawsuit,* it does give you pause."

I talked about the widespread support we were receiving and invited *CBS Mornings* viewers to join in the fight.

"But am I scared?" I asked. "No, I am fearless."

The Fearless Fund soon benefited from our efforts. Blum and AAER withdrew the temporary restraining order they'd filed to keep the 2023 Venture Capital Summit from taking place. Even more inspiring, on the morning of the event, *Forbes* magazine ran an article titled "All for One: Over 70 Venture Funds Band Together, Sign Open Letter Denouncing Lawsuit Against Fearless Fund."

> Over 70 venture funds, many led by Black women GPs, including Arlan Hamilton of Backstage Capital, Melissa Bradley of 1863 Ventures, JoAnn Price of Fairview Capital and Monique Woodard of Cake Ventures, have signed an Open Letter denouncing the lawsuit against the Fearless Fund. These investors are part of a bold, class of diversity-focused capital allocators, committed to addressing the rampant racial, ethnic and gender disparities in venture capital.
>
> The Letter reads, "Black Women are grossly underrepresented as investors and underfunded as entrepreneurs. Over $288B of venture capital was deployed in 2022, with an estimated 0.41% share invested in Black Women founders. This approach to twist efforts to counter the impacts of racial and gender discrimination as harmful to women of color is not only transparent, unoriginal, and unconvincing, but it also unjustly targets Black Women while threatening the civil rights of all women. . . . We will fight and we will persist in

> doing this important work; anything to the contrary only perpetuates this attack and creates undue influence over our decision-making."
>
> The three women who organized the Open Letter: Shila Burney at Zane Ventures, Kimberley Nixon at Open Venture Capital and Tessa Flippin at Capitalize VC, also discussed the origins of the campaign.

The article included a statement of solidarity from Ed Zimmerman, a prominent white male start-up lawyer and angel investor who had invested in Fund I. The founding partner of First Close, a fund-of-funds backing underrepresented managers, Zimmerman posted this statement on LinkedIn.

> I stand with Fearless Fund (I didn't coordinate this statement with them & I speak here solely on my own personal behalf). The so-called "civil rights" lawsuit against Fearless Fund (& its program awarding grants to Black women who are small business owners) is a deeply problematic inversion of civil rights & social justice. I, personally, deeply & strongly denounce the suit & its plaintiffs. This lawsuit is a foreseeable outgrowth of the SCOTUS decision in the UNC/Harvard affirmative action cases, in which (I personally believe) the majority endeavors to protect structural racism. I'd encourage reading Justice Ketanji Brown Jackson's eloquent dissent in that (UNC/Harvard) case. Her dissent is brilliantly written & cites actual history—the very same history that some (like ron desantis) problematically seek to erase. Link to the audio of it by Alfre Woodard (below). Stay strong! Stay Fearless![5]

I really appreciated the support and encouragement of these powerful movers and shakers and peers, as the Fearless Fund's vision now lived and breathed, stretching far beyond what I'd ever imagined.

On August 17, our 2023 Venture Capital Summit for visionaries, trailblazers, and change-makers, held at Atlanta's Woodruff Arts Center, marked a triumph and a living testament to women of color who had been told no too many times. Day one focused on educating women of color and community members about venture capital and entrepreneurship. It included ten panels, keynote speeches by three industry leaders, and fireside chats featuring some of the heads of the companies in our Fund I portfolio. Some of the big names taking part included our attorney, Ben Crump; actor Jessica Alba; British entrepreneur and *Shark Tank* investor Emma Grede, who is CEO of Good American denim and a founding partner of the shapewear brand Skims; Rich Dennis, founder of the Sundial hair and skincare company; NFL quarterback Cam Newton; former *Teen Vogue* editor in chief Elaine Welteroth; entrepreneur and former Roc-A-Fella Records executive Kenny Burns; and attorney and former Atlanta mayor Keisha Lance Bottoms. Knowing that the Fearless Fund had been all over the news, Jessica Alba bravely stated, "When you threaten the status quo or the establishment, they're going to try and take you down, right? They will try to take you out." I felt proud of her for owning that moment instead of taking the safe route.

Day two was "demo day," where participants demonstrated their pitching skills in front of a panel of potential funders and the audience. Filled with hundreds of women of color, the room bustled with electricity, anticipation, and excitement. Our annual pitch competition featured some of the nation's top women-of-color founders. Each passionately presented her start-up business's promise and why she deserved a financial investment to take her dream to the next level. That day, the Fearless Fund selected three very different companies to invest in. One focused on creating more flexible meal plans for college students, another on the hair care and beauty sector, and the third on better hygiene products for women. Each founder walked out with a six-figure check that offered her the freedom to consider a future that would not have been possible before that moment and had the power to change her life.

I normally don't get emotional during our pitch competitions, but I was exhausted by the adrenaline rush and emotional high of keeping all the balls in the air. As my team members announced the winners, I silently wept. We'd created a fund that saw Black and brown women not as risks but as worthy investments. We put our money where our mouths were, stood firm under tremendous pressure, and made it clear we were here to stay. I believe when one of us rises, we all rise. Because having access to capital doesn't just build businesses, it builds legacies, shifts narratives, and creates the kind of generational wealth and opportunities that have been denied women of color for far too long. Our fight wasn't just about the Fearless Fund, it was about the thousands of women who deserve the right to build, to grow, to thrive. I refused to let them down.

I felt more committed than ever to continuing the Fearless Fund's work to create economic freedom for women-of-color founders. I had to continue the fight for economic justice that has been part of my family's mission and legacy for generations.

Pinky Cole, Founder, Slutty Vegan
(African American woman)

I am the founder of Slutty Vegan, a nationally recognized plant-based burger brand that has disrupted the fast-casual industry. What started as a food truck has grown into a multi-location empire, with celebrity fans, a loyal customer base, and millions in revenue. I have also expanded into franchising, consumer packaged goods, and multiple entrepreneurial ventures, all driven by my commitment to innovation, community, and Black business ownership. Fearless Fund has supported me along this journey, and I'm grateful for their commitment to empowering businesses like mine.

Fearless Fund has been an incredible champion for women-of-color entrepreneurs like myself. Their belief in my vision, their financial support, and their network of resources have played a key role in my entrepreneurial journey. Having their backing not only provided capital but also gave me confidence in expanding my business and pushing boundaries in the food industry.

Fearless Fund is leveling the playing field for women of color in entrepreneurship, a group that has historically been overlooked when it comes to funding and investment. Their mission isn't just about writing checks, it's about building legacies, closing the wealth gap, and empowering the next generation of successful business owners, and I am proud to be a part of that group.

Chapter 4

A Seat at the Table

The Alliance has not proved that any member is able and ready to apply for a grant in the imminent future. The Alliance fails to prove standing for another reason. The record does not show that Owners A, B, and C likely are "able and ready" to participate in the Foundation's grant program and will suffer an imminent injury if they cannot apply "on an equal basis." . . . The clearest way for a potential applicant to make this showing is to have applied and been rejected, as the Alliance's own cases illustrate.

—Gibson Dunn, amicus brief filed in *American Alliance for Equal Rights v. Fearless Fund Management, LLC* in support of the Fearless Fund

SEPTEMBER 7, 2023

AAER's argument seemed to center around several key points. First, they asserted that we excluded people from applying to the program based on their race. They also alleged that three members of AAER were ineligible to apply for the Strivers Grant solely based on their race. One, described as Owner A, supposedly lived in New York and would have used the grant to improve and expand her business. Owner B, in Virginia, ostensibly would have used the funds for website development; and the third, Owner C, also a Virginian, allegedly would have expanded her online presence. Next, AAER claimed the Fearless Fund violated section 1981 of the Civil Rights Act of 1866. They also wanted the Fearless Fund to pay nominal damages and to cover their costs and attorney's fees.[1]

The charges were ridiculous. First, the Fearless Fund wasn't excluding people, we were supporting Black women. Indeed, you name me a US immigrant or minority group, and I guarantee their community engaged in a tradition of self-help. There was the Charitable Irish Society. Check! Add another checkmark alongside the Sons of Italy. Jewish Americans had the Hebrew Free Burial Association. This is just the tip of the iceberg. As wave after wave of people immigrated to the United States, each leveraged organizations and traditions to support members of their ethnic or racial group.

African Americans also have a long tradition of self-help through various mutual-aid societies. There was Philadelphia's Free African Society during the late 1700s; the New York African Society for Mutual Relief, founded in 1808;[2] and the Grand United Order of Odd Fellows, founded during the 1840s and still existing today,[3] among many others.

Today, countless United Way charities also operate in this way, so this AAER argument really didn't make any sense.

Beyond that, who were Owner A, Owner B, and Owner C? Did they really exist? Did they run legitimate businesses? Did they actually meet the qualifications to be Fearless Strivers? Why were they hiding behind pseudonyms? Since there was no telling if these were real people, there was also no way to validate their claims or whether they even had the legal standing to file the complaint.

Our lawyers informed me that a preliminary injunction is an extraordinary and drastic legal measure. To request one based on just three anonymous people's declarations seemed like quite a stretch. With no information about them or their businesses, how could we investigate, much less refute, their allegations? How would we know if they'd suffered any injury at all, let alone irreparable harm? Maybe that was the point.

Then to claim we were violating Section 1981 of the 1866 Civil Rights Act put their complaint over the top. Did AAER really think they could undermine the rights of the very Black citizens the law was designed to protect?

The preliminary-injunction trial was scheduled for September 26, 2023. As part of the pretrial activities, several organizations filed what's called an amicus brief, which is intended to allow interested and informed parties to help the judge understand the issue being presented and reach a just decision. On September 1, the Black Economic Alliance Foundation—the nation's leading nonprofit harnessing Black business leaders' influence and expertise to build economic prosperity for African Americans—filed an amicus brief. Here's an excerpt:

> Black women have long been unrecognized and underappreciated pillars within the American economy, relegated first to the fields, kitchens, and nurseries of white homes and then to the least-favorable low-wage, labor-intensive positions in the broader economy.... Whether producing crops to be sold for profit or children to be sold as chattel, the considerable financial contributions of Black women historically did little to improve their financial or labor market position.... Even in times of purported equality, Black women—constrained by

both racism and sexism—have been excluded from better-paying positions that offered upward mobility and equity. . . . Their exclusion from these positions exacerbated the wage and wealth gap for Black women—and made assistance from within their community integral to their ability to overcome barriers to economic stability and independence.

Maggie L. Walker provides a compelling example of this phenomenon. In a 1901 speech, Walker, the daughter of a slave and the first American woman of any race to own a bank, asked, "Who is so helpless as the Negro woman? Who is so circumscribed and hemmed in, in the race of life, in the struggle for bread, meat, and clothing, as the Negro woman?" . . . As Black women were being systematically excluded from the workforce, Walker took action to address these inequities by helping them start their own businesses. In 1903, she opened St. Luke Penny Savings Bank and offered Black women entrepreneurs investment capital at significantly lower rates than the oppressive rates white-owned banks offered. . . . Access to the economic capital Walker provided created entrepreneurial opportunities for Black women that were long denied and allowed them to begin to confront institutional obstacles and gain their footing within the American economy.

The contributions of [Booker T.] Washington and Walker underscore the historic tradition of Black Americans—including Black women—starting their own businesses to circumvent the obstacles related to access, education, and experience needed to succeed in the formal economy. But notwithstanding the assistance provided by Black business leaders, entrepreneurship has imposed, and continues to impose, significant hurdles and inequities: "Black business owners usually lack key advantages that some white business owners enjoy," including education, startup funds, and familial connections. . . .

Black women seeking to own and operate businesses

> suffer not only from the disadvantages borne by Black entrepreneurs generally, but also obstacles unique to women. . . . These hurdles might include lack of managerial and business experience, limited access to startup capital, and family and household responsibilities. . . . Although all business owners, men and women alike, face challenges just to keep their ventures operating, the ability of women to own viable businesses has been further constrained by their marginalized status within the broader economy and a fundamentally segregated society. . . . For Black women looking to start their own businesses, these systemic and structural disadvantages—including wealth disparities, discrimination by lenders and financial institutions, credit history, and debt—conspire to deny them equal access to capital accumulation: Ultimately, Black women suffer the inequities experienced by both Black and women business owners.

My company may have been under attack—and the amicus brief laid out Black entrepreneurial women's challenges—but I'm sure Edward Blum and Co. didn't understand that I'm the descendant of people who have thrived in the face of adversity.

On my mother's side, my relatives come from in and around Macon, Georgia. Our family genealogist traces our ancestors back eight generations—unusually long for African Americans, since so many records documenting slavery have been scattered, have been destroyed, or are difficult if not impossible to find because census takers often listed our ancestors by race and/or age but without a name, and in the same records as their enslaver's animals.

For generations, the Calhoun family accumulated meaningful wealth. My great-great-grandmother Missouri McElmurray was born in 1864, shortly before the same Civil Rights Act of 1866 that Blum and AAER exploited to challenge the Fearless Fund. During slavery it was illegal for Black people to read or write, and it wasn't a whole lot easier during Reconstruction. Yet somehow Missouri earned a college degree from Morris Brown College in Atlanta. When she married my great-great-grandfather Joshua Calhoun, she already owned fifty acres of land. Together they transformed those fifty acres into five hundred, considerable landholdings for anyone of that era. As the area's only Black landowners, they experienced opposition from various white people; however, some form of protection allowed them to prosper. We suspect they possessed some economic leverage: their five hundred acres produced a considerable portion of the area's dairy products as well as corn, cotton, watermelon, lettuce, and other fruits and vegetables locals depended upon. Missouri's newspaper obituary reported she employed fifty-two sharecroppers, some white. In other words, Missouri was a Black woman entrepreneur. As I look back, she probably owned seven companies, including quite likely a perfume business. She ran some sort of import/export business involving flowers out of Jekyll Island, Georgia. All nine of their children were literate—rare for families of any race during the late 1800s and early 1900s. Missouri was a baaad girl! Many generations later, I benefit from having as ancestors some of the relatively few Black Americans who, 150 years ago, were able both to accumulate the insider knowledge required to build wealth and to actually build wealth itself.

Several Calhoun family members ran businesses in Macon. Family members owned a newspaper, which, among other news, reported racial-terror lynchings to document and end them, as so many Black newspapers of the time did.[4] Very common during that era, lynchings, cross burnings, and other forms of violence often targeted Black educators, preachers, and business owners. Many of my Calhoun ancestors were teachers, entrepreneurs, and doctors. One of my great-great-grandmother's children, Emory, called "Doc," was the first Black dentist in Macon. Reverend E. J. Calhoun was a well-known pastor whose impact was so widespread, five thousand people attended his funeral. My ancestors even owned a country club that bore the Calhoun name. My forebears stood up for what was right and proactively improved the welfare of Black people. They were activists back when activism required nerves of steel. I embody both their entrepreneurial legacy and their incredible bravery.

New experiences open your horizons and make new possibilities available to you.

After running AR PR Marketing, a very successful PR and marketing firm, for twelve years and serving both major corporations—think Sony Pictures, Walt Disney, Universal, and pretty much every major Hollywood studio—and celebrity clients like Chris Brown, Lil Wayne, and a whole host of others, I'd fought incredibly hard to create the Fearless Fund.

In 2016, two friends and I traveled to New York to pitch a business concept to Gary Vaynerchuk, a dynamic disruptor in entrepreneurship and venture capital. My friends—NFL defensive tackle Ndamukong Suh, a family friend who would eventually win a Super Bowl ring, and fellow entrepreneur (now publisher) Tamira Chapman—had been introduced to Gary by one of Ndamukong's business associates. Someone had run the numbers and we decided to pitch for $10 million. We stayed up late the night before the meeting to perfect our presentation. I brought to the conversation my panache from running AR PR Marketing. Pitching yourself for VC funds is very similar to what happens on the TV show *Shark Tank*. You present your business idea to one or more investors in hopes of securing cash to grow it. To acquire the cash, you exchange *equity*, an ownership stake in your company.

I strode into the conference room confident and dressed to the nines. Gary removed his jacket and shook my hand. Though this was my first time pitching to a venture capitalist and being exposed to the VC space, I wasn't exactly new to this game—in addition to coming from a family of entrepreneurs, I'd been speaking publicly and selling my ideas since I was a little girl. Not only did I know my numbers and business story, I also understood how to project my voice and my body into the room. My team and I felt confident until we discovered we had a problem—a big one.

We were pitching for a $10 million investment, but during the meeting we learned the fund was only $25 million in size—we wanted far too great a percentage. What's more, all $25 million was fully deployed. Surely, the well-meaning person who referred us hadn't possessed this information.

Afterward, we stood in the middle of the sidewalk as pedestrians scurried around us.

"I know what you are thinking," one of my friends said. "You don't want to be in here asking them for money—you want to be on the other side of the table."

"Exactly!"

At that point the Fearless Fund was born in my mind's eye, though I didn't arrive at the name until later. I knew in that moment I could make good on a promise I'd made to myself way back in college.

During the spring of 1999, my mother took some friends and me on a road trip to visit several HBCUs, including Florida Agricultural and Mechanical University (FAMU). Though my dad wanted me to attend Spelman College, followed by graduate studies at Harvard, as soon as my mom pulled onto FAMU's campus, I experienced love at first sight. Located atop one of the highest of Tallahassee, Florida's seven hills, I found FAMU's tree-lined campus of redbrick buildings and crisscrossing walkways beautiful. The staff members were warm and the students driven to be their best. Just two years earlier the Princeton Review and *Time* magazine had named FAMU "College of the Year." Even better, Sybil Mobley, the dean of FAMU's School of Business and Industry (SBI), was nationally recognized for creating a five-year program where graduates earned both a bachelor of science and an MBA degree. Several friends who accompanied us also chose FAMU. I matriculated to the five-year MBA program that August.

Day one, I started handing out my card for a beauty business. I was a graduate of Detroit's prestigious Cass Tech magnet school, where I'd taken the business track, so to me the university's eleven thousand students represented a target audience, a niche market, an opportunity. SBI students were required to wear corporate attire on campus. When I complained to my maternal grandfather about not wanting to be sweaty in class from wearing a suit in the eighty-five-degree heat and humidity, he used the corporate discount he'd earned working at Ford to buy me a $50,000 Mercury Mountaineer. Though I never abused it, from childhood I knew Granddaddy Roger would give me anything. Once when I was a young child, my mom took us to the beach. When we returned home, I told her I wanted sand. She told me I'd need to wait until we went back to the beach. But Granddaddy Roger built me a sandbox in our basement, where I could play in the sand all year.

From the time Granddaddy gifted me the car, I was on the move, scouting locations for various business ideas, eager to start something even though I didn't know what that "something" was yet. After hearing somewhere that it was an avenue to wealth, I tried my hand at real estate during my sophomore year, signing on with the realty company Keller Williams. I don't think I knew anyone in the business; otherwise, I would have called them to help me: "You've got to teach me, I don't know what I'm doing!" After a few months, when I wasn't experiencing the number of closings I wanted, I decided it wasn't for me.

I don't know if this is my calling.

I was used to rapid achievement—excelling in school, getting straight A's, success coming to me fast. Everything was a goal. If I didn't meet it, I moved on to the next thing. Perhaps I could have been good at real estate. I probably would have been amazing, but I'll never know because I was impatient.

I also threw myself headlong into campus life, excelling academically, serving as a student senator in the Student Government Association, and pledging the Beta Alpha Chapter of Delta Sigma Theta Sorority.

One day during my junior year, I was standing in line to pay a utility bill when I noticed a sign on the wall about obtaining a business license. It sparked my interest! I combined the experience I had from working in retail clothing stores during high school and skills I was learning at SBI to create a business plan. I got my plan for the Fabulous Clothing Store printed at Kinko's and scheduled an appointment with the manager of the Tallahassee mall. I went for my dream with little formal experience and not knowing what I wasn't supposed to be able to accomplish at such a young age.

> Sometimes there's power in being naïve, not knowing what's not possible, and not having been indoctrinated into what you are not supposed to be able to do.

I introduced myself as Dean Mobley's student and presented my business plan. Between Cass Tech and FAMU, I already knew how to pitch. Still, I wonder what made that mall exec take a chance on someone young and inexperienced who hadn't secured any financing. I didn't have much money of my own, so I asked family and friends. I managed to secure funds from my mom, several relatives, and a few friends. I also tapped my school "net checks"—whatever money remained after tuition, books, fees, and scholarships were paid for, which was returned to students. I still came up short, so I presented my business plan to loan officers at banks. The rejections piled up, and I discovered that raising capital is no easy feat.

Eventually the Fabulous Clothing Store opened its doors in part of a large space formerly occupied by Waldenbooks. I worked with whatever funds I had, throwing myself into hiring and training, managing inventory, making payroll, and balancing expenses and receipts. Juggling everything wasn't easy. I didn't know that nearly 50 percent of all new businesses in the United States fail within five years. Nor did I realize the risk of failure is even greater for minority-owned businesses, which experience tremendous difficulties securing fair funding. I didn't yet understand how hard it is to scale without the financial support required to cover inventory, payroll, marketing, and other essential expenses. That's not to mention what it takes to achieve long-term success. But I loved fashion, had heart, and was extremely resilient, determined to make it work. To differentiate Fabulous from other clothing stores, I attended industry events like the MAGIC trade show in Las Vegas, sourcing clothes, connecting with designers and creatives, and learning about upcoming trends. At this young age I met countless influential people in retail and fashion: Kimora Lee and Russell Simmons, the rapper/businessman Nelly, and many urban fashion execs. The MAGIC show also threw lots of celebrity parties. Rappers, singers, athletes, entertainers—everyone who was anyone—attended.

As my store grew, it took over all of the two-thousand-plus-square-foot space. But some days our business bank account showed $50,000; on others we were in the red. Meeting payroll felt especially stressful because people I cared about were relying upon me. I remember sitting on the store floor, working on inventory and trying to pump myself up.

"Don't worry about this investor landscape," I told myself. "One day, you'll be the investor you are looking for."

I didn't fully understand what that promise meant, I just needed someone to believe in me. I also imagined helping other entrepreneurs in the start-up phase make their own dreams come true. After a couple years, the stress of the business became overwhelming. On paper, Fabulous Clothing was profitable, but I couldn't see past the obstacles; I closed the store. Looking back with greater maturity, I wasn't failing, I simply wasn't patient enough to weather the retail industry's business cycles. I keep the financial records as a reminder to give myself grace and trust the process.

I graduated from FAMU in 2003. It was the same year the *Grutter v. Bollinger* Supreme Court case upheld the use of race as one of many factors colleges can consider as they attempt to build a diverse student body. This decision also boosted minority enrollment at predominantly white institutions (PWIs). In their decision, the Supreme Court identified that a diverse student body is in the state's interest.[5] Though the Grutter case didn't cause this, it's notable that between 2000 and 2010, 55 percent more white students enrolled at historically Black colleges and universities (HBCUs), which also saw significant gains in the enrollment of other students of color.[6]

Almost twenty years after I closed Fabulous Clothing Store, and not long after the disappointing experience in Gary Vaynerchuk's offices, I sat in my office journaling, my face turned toward the sun.

"I will build a fund that proves that ordinary women of color can build generational wealth and claim our place at the table—a capitalization table," I wrote.

A capitalization, or "cap," table is a spreadsheet or document describing who owns how much equity in a start-up company, early-stage venture, or any other private firm. Created before other business documents, the cap table tracks the company's ownership structure, including founders, investors, employees with stock options—a financial instrument employers grant certain employees to give them the right to buy or sell stock at a fixed price by a certain date or time—and any other stakeholders with equity, as it changes over time. Jay-Z rhymes about them in DJ Khaled's cut "God Did": *I'm at the cap table, what the splits is / Not that cap table, boy, we live this.*[7]

When I first started learning about cap tables, I thought they were just a fancy way of describing who owns how much at any given time. It didn't take long until I learned it's much more than that. A well-maintained cap table contains a company's financial history—who invested, when they invested, and what they got in return. It also helps founders and investors understand the impact of future fundraising rounds upon the company's ownership.[8] For example, if I own 50 percent of my company and I bring on an investor who wants 20 percent, the cap table would show my ownership percentage being diluted by the new investment. But the dilution wouldn't just impact me, it would impact all the owners. A cap table also helps answer questions like "How much of the company do I still own?" or "What happens to current investors' share of the business if I want to raise more money later?" It becomes even more important as a company grows. If I'm planning to raise venture capital or eventually sell my company, investors will want a clear picture of who owns what. A messy cap table can lead to confusion and potential legal issues, so keeping it organized is incredibly important.

I was determined to open the doors of opportunity for women-of-color entrepreneurs, already knowing from experience that we are some of the scrappiest business owners out there. Used to working with less, we have low cash-burn rates and the skills and willingness to bootstrap our companies. We don't lack the talent, the ideas, or the work ethic—we lack access to sufficient capital. During my years running AR PR Marketing, I'd witnessed traditional investors overlook countless brilliant women with innovative ideas. Their businesses had potential, their strategies were sound, but the doors of opportunity stayed shut simply because they didn't fit the traditional mold of what an entrepreneur looks like: a wealthy white man. The fund I envisioned would remedy this problem by creating funding opportunities specifically for women of color, who traditionally struggle to access capital. I also wanted to build support systems to address the unique challenges women-of-color entrepreneurs face. This wasn't about creating another venture capital firm; to me, the mission was personal. I wanted to create a practical solution to a systemic problem. I also vowed to fulfill the promise I'd made to my younger self, when I had great ideas but inadequate financing to run my store. I wanted to help rewrite the narrative so women like me wouldn't have to fight so hard just to be seen, heard, and funded. When we invest in women of color, we're investing in innovation, in our communities, and in the future.

As I looked out my windows, I imagined entrepreneurs pitching their businesses, asking for investments, such as $500,000, in exchange for a percentage of ownership, say 10 percent. I knew that for many of women-of-color founders, the Fearless Fund's investment would be their first time accessing venture capital funds and opportunities to expand their business. Few people have the economic exposure and education to understand what it takes to create a sustainable business that will stand the test of time. I, too, had a lot to learn about venture capital and private equity (PE)—and I had to figure out how to bring my idea to life by developing relationships with people who knew what I didn't.

One of the first strategic connections I made was with Tracy Gray, founder of the 22 Fund, which invests in tech-related United States–based manufacturing companies, intentionally including women- and BIPOC-led firms. Tracy is one of just a handful of Black women in the VC investment space—and one of even fewer who ran her own fund rather than working at a VC firm.

I shared my vision with Tracy about starting a venture fund specifically for women of color. She thought my lofty goals were something of a fantasy.

"I want you to know that there are very few Black women in this space," she told me. "You're going to be going up against a lot of white men who are going to be resistant to what you are trying to do. But if you really want to go for this, I know that you can make an incredible impact."

Because I was so serious, Tracy was willing to help.

She introduced me to a Black female securities attorney who showed me what a fund setup would look like. Securities attorneys are costly. I couldn't afford to hire her yet, but the information she shared was extremely helpful.

When I first started researching the racial disparities in venture capital, what I learned shocked me. Women of color make up nearly 20 percent of the US population, yet only 0.39 percent of venture capital funding is invested in women-of-color-owned businesses. These numbers weren't just disappointing, they infuriated me. Though Black women comprise 7 percent of the US population and start more companies than any other demographic, we obtain less than 0.35 percent of VC funding across all sectors.[9] And though we comprise over 50 percent of the US population, women of all races combined obtain less than 2 percent of all VC funding.[10] The other 98 percent is awarded to male founders.

The more I dug, the more infuriating the story became.

I learned that the vast majority of dollars venture capitalists invest come from public employees' retirement funds—their pension funds. Public employees are very diverse. In the federal workforce alone, 44 percent of workers are women; 18 percent are Black; 10 percent are Latino; 7 percent are Asian American; 2 percent are Native American; less than 2 percent are Alaska Natives; and Native Hawaiian and Pacific Islanders make up less than 1 percent.[11]

Hold up!

White men are investing the money of women and Black and brown people, yet they direct just a pittance of those funds back to Black people, brown people, or women of any race. In other words, the money flows from the pension funds of diverse people to a PE/VC industry comprised of 92 percent white men. Not surprisingly, more than 90 percent of VC money is invested in white-owned start-up businesses. Very rarely does that money get invested into people serving the communities where the money was made.

Whoa!

The injustice made my head spin. So not only were Black people not paid for their labor beginning in 1619, when enslavement began, and continuing until the 1860s, they were also underpaid and economically exploited for another hundred years after Jim Crow laws began to be imposed upon Black people during the late 1870s. Yet even today their savings fund the descendants of many wealthy white landowners.

One hundred fifty years after Emancipation, Black people are still underwriting the accumulation of white wealth.

My head spun with this reality, though another part of me wasn't the least bit surprised to discover yet another dimension of racial economic injustice and inequity.

Right then and there, I knew I had to help ensure that retirement fund investments reflect the diversity of the people contributing to them. The challenge was huge, yet I felt undaunted. If I wanted to see change, I had to be a part of making it happen. I'd need to roll up my sleeves and join people like Jay-Z, Gwyneth Paltrow, Nas, and Serena Williams, as well as various activists, bringing their energy and resources into the venture capital space.

I was more aware of the upside possibilities that came with shifting these assets to Black and brown women than almost any white man working in the VC space. Having grown up in and having moved professionally within racially diverse contexts, I knew that the spaces wealthy white people inhabit are overwhelmingly monochrome. Their narrow lens not only leaves them with a colossal blind spot, it also makes our national and global economy incredibly vulnerable to various cognitive biases and distortions, denial, groupthink, unexamined assumptions, and the homogeneity that results when diverse perspectives are lacking—not to mention the reality that we miss out on billions of people's God-given gifts, talents, and skill sets.

I met businessman Rodney Sampson next, in Atlanta.

In 1999, Rodney became one of the first Black men to enjoy a profitable tech exit when he sold his business Streaming Faith for

$27 million. Rodney agreed to become our leading advisor. He also played an important role in naming the fund. Originally, I wanted to call it the Collective WOC Fund; I even filed documents with that name. Rodney knew I'd once run a magazine called *Fearless* and had seen the success of several events I'd thrown.

"You already have the Fearless brand up and running and have an active audience. You need to keep your fund on brand," he advised me.

With that, the Fearless Fund was born—the first venture capital fund built by women of color for women of color.

I decided the Fearless Fund would focus on early-stage investments: pre-seed, seed, and series A. *Early-stage* means when the business is just starting out; pre-seed investments are made before a company has significant revenue; seed investments occur once there is some revenue and traction. I envisioned investing in businesses already demonstrating momentum and significant potential for growth. The fund would provide catalytic capital to help them advance to the next stage; it would also improve the founders' access to resources in the ecosystem as a whole. Many women entrepreneurs also needed to learn how to design a pitch deck, set up corporate governance for selling equity, prepare a company to get ready for venture dollars, and so on. We created the Fearless Foundation to provide them with these types of educational resources as well as grants.

Rodney and Tracy were instrumental in helping me get the Fearless Fund off the ground. They didn't just believe in my vision, they helped me believe in it, too. They also reminded me that we weren't just looking for funding; we were looking for partners who could help us create a movement. The Fearless Fund would be disruptive, rewrite the rules, and ensure women-of-color entrepreneurs had the opportunities that they deserved. I needed to take charge of my future so my vision of economic freedom for women of color would come to fruition. Through prayer, walking in faith, researching and studying, seeking assistance, running the numbers, writing my plan, and applying untold hours of elbow grease, I prepared myself to embody what I saw in my mind's eye. I moved forward as though what we envisioned was already complete.

> **The world moves out of the way for people who know where they're going.**

The Playbook

The Cure for Venture Capital and Private Equity Firms

Venture capital and private equity firms play a significant role in reinforcing global financial exclusion. These firms pride themselves on innovation and disruption, yet their funding models consistently uphold the same racial and economic hierarchies that have existed for centuries. Investors talk about risk, return, and market potential, yet time and again, they dismiss Black entrepreneurs—not because Black businesspeople's ideas aren't profitable, but because these executives, merchants, and whiz kids don't fit the image of who VCs and PE firms have historically backed.

In this industry, it's also time to acknowledge the fact that the demographics of pension fund contributors are far more diverse than the demographics of those making the investment decisions. If we are serious about inclusivity and justice, we must ensure the people benefiting from these massive pools of capital reflect the communities that fund them. This is not just about fairness; it's about recognizing the power and potential of every community and ensuring that no one is left out.

Private equity and venture capital firms need to:

- Adopt a "share the wealth" mindset. There's plenty of money to go around—no one is burning it. The financial opportunities in private equity and venture capital can transform communities, create jobs, and drive positive change.
- Rethink how we approach investment and work together to create a more equitable landscape.

- Align the demographics of our investments with the people whose pensions fund them, so we can build a future where everyone benefits from the collective power of our economy.

Chapter 5

Raised for This

> Historic discrimination and systemic inequities have limited opportunities for Black entrepreneurs—especially Black women. . . . "America's racist history has negatively impacted African Americans' opportunities for generational wealth. From slavery to Jim Crow, formal institutional barriers and discrimination have made it difficult for African Americans to gain upward economic mobility. . . ." Contrary to outmoded and prejudiced notions that Black Americans "have lower levels of wealth because of poor decisions or a culture of poverty," recent scholarship proves that "racial wealth inequality has been structured over many generations through systematic barriers that have hampered Blacks throughout history—slavery, Jim Crow, so called de jure discrimination, and institutionalized racism. . . ." At the same time, "historical government policies have helped Whites acquire the assets which are the source of today's racial wealth gap."
>
> —Black Economic Alliance Foundation, brief of amicus curiae in *American Alliance for Equal Rights v. Fearless Fund Management, LLC* in support of the Fearless Fund's opposition to the AAER's motion for preliminary injunction

SEPTEMBER 26, 2023

This was the day of the preliminary injunction hearing to determine whether our Fearless Strivers Grant program would have to cease operations. The judge would also determine whether the fund could continue its work while Blum's reverse-discrimination case wound its way through the courts. This was a pivotal moment in what was shaping up to be a protracted legal battle for the Fearless Fund's future and the entrepreneurial aspirations of women of color.

My team and I arrived at the Martin Luther King Jr. Federal Building in Atlanta. I wore a black suit to reflect both the seriousness of the occasion and the court's conservatism.

Our Fearless Fund employees met us at the courthouse. Both my parents and sisters flew into town for the occasion, and my cousins who live in Atlanta attended as well. Pastor Danielle Murphy was there to support me, as were other members of our dReam Center Church of Atlanta family. Her husband, Bishop Murphy, had not only written a sermon about AAER's attack upon the Fearless Fund, he'd delivered it wearing a T-shirt reading, "I Am Fearless." As he educated our congregation about the lawsuit, Bishop Murphy explained, "The goal is to stop Black folks from helping Black folks. The Fearless Fund doesn't just help Black women, they help women of color—they help Asian and Latina—not just Black women. They were intentional to go after Black women, in particular."

I was incredibly grateful for the bishop's support. He asked the intercessory prayer team to pray for me all day, and our congregation fasted every Tuesday to support me.

Also congregating in front of the courthouse were Atlanta's fifty-ninth mayor, Kasim Reed; Reverend Al Sharpton and local members of the National Action Network; Reverend Dr. Jamal Bryant, the senior pastor of Atlanta's New Birth megachurch; members of Atlanta's civil rights community; and interested citizens from the ATL and beyond. Everyone knew what was on the line—constitutional law that would impact the lives of all Black Americans. I felt both moved and empowered to experience so much support during this difficult time.

Mayor Reed encouraged the crowd and spoke to the large gathering of local and national press outlets present. "All of us wonder what we would have done if we could have walked with Malcolm X. Well, ladies and gentlemen, I submit to you, this is your moment!"

"We will not bend, we will not bow, we will not break, we will fight on! If I can do it for sixty years, you can!" another speaker declared.

"It was said by a fearless Black woman, 'If you don't have a seat at the table, then you are on the menu,'" Dr. Bryant reminded the crowd, citing a well-known quote often repeated by renowned political strategist Donna Brazile. "Come on, let's fight, Atlanta, until justice is won."

At one point I looked over and saw two children who couldn't have been older than seven—a girl holding a sign that said, "I am a future Black female entrepreneur," and a boy waving one that said, "We demand racial equity." They reminded me why I was doing what I was doing—so they could have a more inclusive society.

By this point, Edward Blum had made his case in one court of public opinion. AAER had raised $1.5 billion to support his cause, including $500 million on the day the case was announced. People like the Koch brothers, employees of Goldman Sachs, and many other notable conservative supporters have donated to AAER.

Over the previous weeks, I'd met with many Black VCs and requested financial support.

"We have to fight this issue," I implored them. "It will become a much bigger problem if we don't."

In a nutshell, I tried to explain how what racist white people did when they burned down two hundred Black-owned businesses along Black Wall Street in Tulsa, Oklahoma, in 1921, was what AAER was trying to do to the Fearless Fund. Though Black businesses in Tulsa's Greenwood District operated next door to one another on a physical street, the Fearless Fund supported Black- and brown-women-owned businesses all over the world. If they stopped the Fearless Fund, they'd stop in their tracks the five hundred or more businesses we funded, as well as thousands of new and soon-to-be business owners we educate, and countless women dreaming of starting their own business who would be in the pipeline behind them.

I was heartbroken to discover that many Black business owners either didn't understand or didn't believe how much was at stake. Either that or they didn't believe that supporting the movement to create racial equity is part of their role. Some did support us, but not as many as I hoped. Our encouragement in terms of physical presence largely came from civil rights leaders and clergy.

Fortunately, we had multiple law firms on the case, with the law firm of Gibson Dunn in the lead, and Ben Crump Law and Alphonso David as co-counsel. (Dennis Ellis would later join the team as co-counsel.) Additional firms provided strategic counsel.

My attorneys and I ascended the steps and strode through the front door of the imposing building.

Everyone placed their jackets and electronic devices on the belt of the X-ray scanner. I couldn't afford to trust many people, including those who worked for the courts. I'd left my phone in the black Suburban I'd arrived in.

We walked down the corridor and turned into a large room overflowing with Fearless Fund supporters, and I felt empowered to see so many familiar faces. A bright yellow dress caught my eye—it belonged to an African woman to whom we'd awarded a grant and who lived in Atlanta. Her presence lifted my spirits even higher. We then entered the courtroom, a small room with only a few rows of seats behind the attorneys' benches on each side.

"All rise," the bailiff announced as senior US District Court judge Thomas Thrash entered wearing his black robe. I stood before this distinguished-looking older white gentleman whom my team had told me President Bill Clinton appointed.

"The judge may not rule from the bench, we may have to wait," Attorney David whispered to me.

"It's a high-profile case," I replied. "I bet you he rules the day of."

Either way, I felt like he'd treat us fairly. I knew this case wasn't just about legal technicalities; this was about real women, real communities, and real business and wealth-building opportunities that would be lost if the opposition prevailed. The opposing counsel looked ready for battle; I steeled myself for whatever they would throw at us. I saw no sign of Ed Blum himself. My team told me he only shows up when his cases reach the Supreme Court.

How cowardly.

As oral arguments from the plaintiff's attorney began, you could have cut the tension with a knife.

Ed Blum's lawyer started off.

". . . Section 1981 prohibits racial discrimination in contracting. Its protection extends to all persons and gives them an equal right to form and enforce contracts, and it protects the would-be contractor as much as it protects those who have already entered contracts.

"Defendants flaunt Section 1981. They repeatedly and expressly confirm that they engage in racial discrimination. Just look to the official rules per the contest at issue in this case. They explicitly state that the contest is open only to Black women. That's confirmed in the briefing here, where they also confirm that the contest is open only to Black women.

"So they boast that they have enacted an express racial bar. They won't even consider applications from Hispanic and Native American women, nor will they consider applications from Asian and white women, like the members of the Alliance who have filed declarations here."

I took several deep breaths as the attorney basically accused me of being racist.

I noticed that as Blum's lawyer laid out his argument, he insisted that Blum wanted to live in a world where race doesn't matter.

The attorney kept talking about how Owners A, B, and C had been "harmed" and "injured," like they had been dramatically or traumatically impacted. I was astounded he would use such words without even proving these people existed.

After Blum's people made their argument, our attorneys responded.

"Section 1981, as the Court knows, was enacted after the Civil War to help ensure that the formerly enslaved would have the same right to make and enforce contracts as is enjoyed by white citizens. The plaintiff is attempting to turn this seminal civil rights law on its head, and the plaintiff is trying to stop the Fearless Fund from providing charitable grants to Black women entrepreneurs who run small businesses.

"Those grants are provided so those Black women can grow their businesses and achieve the American Dream. The foundation does this because it recognizes the incredible disparity in access to capital that Black women entrepreneurs face."

My legal team argued this truth: The colorblind world Blum purported to want didn't exist yet, and before we could claim it did, we had to acknowledge the harm that had already been done—and rectify it. In theory, I want the same thing as Blum does: I dream of a world where opportunity isn't shaped by the color of my skin, where Black and brown people don't work twice as hard to receive half as much, and where fairness is already baked into the system and institutions don't need diversity, equity, and inclusion initiatives. For generations, race has mattered in ways that have excluded, disadvantaged, and erased entire communities. Race has determined who gets the loan, who gets the promotion, who gets admitted, and who gets ignored. To pretend otherwise is to gaslight people about an entire history of inequity. Affirmative action, DEI programs, and policies that acknowledge systemic disparities weren't created to give people of color an unfair advantage; they were created to counteract barriers to their progress that have existed for centuries. So no, I don't want race to matter. But until we right the wrongs of the past, we can't pretend they don't exist. And I refuse to let anyone erase that truth.

The very idea that my work—rooted in empowerment, access, and equity—could be challenged in such a way felt surreal. I had spent years building something meant to fill the gaps left by traditional funding structures that had long overlooked women who looked like me. Yet I was being told that my attempt to build something to address a disparity was, in fact, unfair. Clearly, we were caught up in someone's personal political agenda, whether a Trump agenda or an agenda of his supporters.

My attorneys continued, "Owners A, B, and C do not provide sufficient information about themselves or their businesses in their anonymous declarations, which are secret, to show that they have experienced or will experience injury in fact by virtue of this grant program. . . .

"There's no opportunity for the Court to verify any of this information, and there certainly is zero opportunity for the defendants to do so, yet it is their burden.

"They also don't claim to have suffered any emotional or stigmatic harm. . . .

"And, again, because Owners A and B and C are anonymous, there is no way for the foundation to test their unproven assertions, yet the foundation, the Fearless Foundation, doesn't even carry the burden of proof. It's their burden."

At one point the judge asked the plaintiff's attorney, "Let's say you've got a theater company that wants to put on a production of *Othello,* and the director says, 'Well, I'm not going to consider anybody to play the role of Desdemona except a white woman.' I mean, has that director violated [Section] 1981 twice and can't exercise his or her artistic judgment to say Othello has to be played by a Black man, Desdemona has to be played by a white woman? I mean, that's discrimination."

The judge's use of this particular Shakespeare classic, a play with a Black male lead character, signaled to us that the judge was leaning toward our arguments. But my team and I weren't certain, and we didn't want to get too excited.

About halfway through the proceeding, the judge called for us to take a break. As I headed to the bathroom, I passed some of the plaintiffs' counsel.

You are not the first person in your family to walk amid people trying to destroy everything you've built. Hold your head high.

I intentionally stared at them, wanting to look in their eyes. I was ready to speak if spoken to, but they avoided eye contact. I carried myself in a way I believed my ancestors, my parents, and my people back home in Detroit would feel proud of.

In 1981, when I was born, the United States was a lot more equitable than it had been during my ancestors' lifetimes, though persistent racial disparities remained.

My parents raised me and my sister, Ashley, who's five years younger, in Indian Village, one of Detroit's richest neighborhoods. Detroit is full of beautiful houses: Tudor, Victorian, Colonial, Foursquare with a central dormer. Homes with beautiful crown molding, hardwood floors, stained-glass windows, ballrooms, and basement bars. With so many ornate details, the level of craftsmanship is unmatched. Our family home was a historic dark brick Tudor with a large yard, a long straight brick walkway from the sidewalk to the front door, and nine bedrooms. Six were in the main house; three, including the maid's quarters, were located over the garage. Our backyard had an in-ground swimming pool and a deck.

There was Black art all over the walls of our home as well as African wood carvings, masks, and figurines. Just two blocks away, my aunt housed refugees, so I grew up with both her children and young people from Ghana, Nigeria, Senegal, and other sub-Saharan nations. My father had been to the continent and my uncle had, too. During an era when the media portrayed the place I knew as the "Motherland" as the "third world"—represented by starving children asking for donations and other limited images of both the continent and its people—we knew better. Three times the size of the United States, the continent consists of fifty-four distinct nations. Rarely did we see images of its huge urban centers, seemingly limitless natural resources, or wholesome paradise of stunning landscapes and wildlife. In our family we took as much pride in being of African descent as we did in being American. But I felt proud of being African American also. I grew up watching the award-winning documentary series *Eyes on the Prize: America's Civil Rights Movement*. Empowering information about Black people was ever present in our world.

My parents emphasized economic self-sufficiency, and so did members of our community. Mom and Dad went out of their way to patronize Black businesses, grocery stores, and gas stations just as Asian American, Asian Indian, Hispanic, Jewish, and other racial and ethnic communities support their members. I learned it was important to make the effort even if it was inconvenient. Driving to the Black-owned gas station wasn't always easy, but everybody still did it. Ours was that kind of household; I lived in that kind of community.

During the years when I grew up, decades of civil rights protests and pressure had opened opportunities in the automotive and other industries, helping a huge number of Black people finally become middle-class. But the deindustrialization that began during the 1950s was compounded by white flight, reducing Detroit's population and changing the racial demographics to 88 percent Black. The Detroit of my childhood was Black on Black on Black. Still, the city was socioeconomically integrated. As I grew up, I experienced a blend of economic backgrounds. We may have lived in Indian Village, but a low-income neighborhood began on the block behind us. The richest kids and the poorest kids all went to the same schools. In high school, when I walked to the corner store, I'd see the kids of doctors and lawyers and factory workers strolling past prostitutes and crackheads. The experience taught us balance and humility. It also made the possibilities on both sides clear. Ashley and I were well aware that life was about choices—and the wrong one could land you on the other side of our block.

We learned to be comfortable with people of wide-ranging socioeconomic backgrounds. If someone was poor, you didn't judge them; you helped them. Whether I was candy-striping at a hospital or serving at the soup kitchen, I learned always to assist those less fortunate; to work collectively to support everyone to be in the best situation possible; to look out for others. If you needed a ride home, somebody's mother would come get you. We never exhibited a mindset of trying to keep another person down. The fellowship of it all, the community of it, the looking out for, the village raising one another's kids—it was so beautiful.

I attended Montessori preschool and elementary school at Grosse Pointe Academy. Each school level had its own building—one for the Montessori, one for the elementary, and a wing for the middle school, all on the same sprawling green campus. The grounds also featured outdoor tennis courts, a running track, and other amenities few Detroit public schools offered. All the positive racial affirmation my family and Detroit community provided prepared me to feel free in this racially integrated environment.

When I was three my teacher, who was white, spoke with my father.

"Your daughter is empowered," she told my dad.

"I know that," Dad answered. "But what makes you say it?"

"I had all the kids draw themselves," the teacher responded. "She's the only Black child who drew herself with a brown crayon."

A long line of research, including the famous "doll test" by Kenneth and Mamie Clark, has identified that children—especially Black children—often internalize the racial biases they experience in their environment. This can lead to low self-esteem and even self-hatred, and a preference for white people's characteristics, an issue I clearly didn't have. I grew up with plenty of positive representation in my community. Beyond that, I had been a model for Lord & Taylor, Crowley's, and Saks Fifth Avenue as a toddler. I not only felt empowered, I felt celebrated.

But the fact that I had high self-esteem in a predominately white environment didn't mean the school always valued Black and brown children. When I was ten, the academy published a book to be sold for the school's largest fundraiser, the Action Auction. The volume's cover art consisted of facial caricatures meant to represent the student body. But there was a big problem: I didn't see any brown faces—the school was about 30 percent Black and brown. I felt disappointed, both due to the school's misrepresentation of its students and because I had been helping the school raise a lot of money. I created a petition to end the printing of this book that did not accurately represent the student body. Students and even teachers signed it. Though I was in elementary school, the middle school principal rewarded my strong persuasive skills and organizing abilities by calling me into her office and asking me to please cease this petition because I was causing disruption.

This woman hasn't seen disruption.

I called the local news station. The book was never seen again.

Going to Grosse Pointe Academy not only gave me a top-flight education from preschool through seventh grade, I learned how to navigate racial diversity. I became a vital member of the student body, playing piano and participating in dance, cheerleading, tennis, and track from primary school through high school. In eighth grade I attended Golightly Education Center, a premier Detroit public magnet school that was 85 to 90 percent Black. I graduated as valedictorian.

In addition to being the descendant of affluent ancestors and growing up in a middle-class family where I didn't experience the financial trauma so many people do, I received a very positive financial socialization in conjunction with my church. Unlike in many spiritual communities, where people are taught "money is the root of all evil" or other misinterpretations of the Bible—which says "the *love* of money is the root of all evil"—my family attended a church that proactively taught responsible financial stewardship.

Greater Christ Baptist Church was an African American congregation of about five hundred whose leadership believed in teaching its members, including children, how to handle money. The church had a credit union. My parents opened an account there for me when I was a toddler. By the time I was four, I had my own bank ledger. At least once a month, adults in the church would give us a dollar or two. After service I would deposit my money and then update my ledger. When I was a teenager, our church came out with a debit card. My mother would put $20 on my account each month to teach me how to use it. I was an adult before I learned most other churches don't engage in these types of activities. In my family and church community, people openly talked about money; it wasn't taboo.

We also talked about our future in a very precocious manner. By the time I was nine, my father had us setting goals and working toward them. My sister and I had goal journals. He also taught us how to time-manage our days using adult planners.

"Time is your most valuable asset," he taught us. "You can't go back to recover any moment; you have to seize them as they are given."

I was very entrepreneurial and ran a lemonade stand from the front of our house. Like my mother, who was a savvy shopper, I also loved fashion. I would sketch malls and promise myself that one day I would own one. A tech person, my mom knew the internet was coming; I had an email address before anyone else I knew. My parents also taught me the importance of participating in civic organizations. I have been a member of the NAACP—an organization founded in 1909 to help Black Americans obtain their constitutional rights—since I was three or four. I also participated in the civic activities of social groups like Jack and Jill, the Girl Scouts, Delteens, and others. Our weekends always included service activities. That's where my first exposure to fundraising occurred.

Most parents carry the weight of raising money for their kids' organizations. Not my mom. She would equip me with her address book and—whether I was selling Girl Scout cookies, or candy, or T-shirts—have me call her network of friends, coworkers, and community members. Because my parents' friends almost always said yes, I never felt awkward asking for money. By age ten, I was the number one fundraiser for both the local United Negro College Fund Bike-A-Thon and the local NAACP—distinctions I held multiple years in a row. I also became the top fundraiser for all the other civic organizations I belonged to. This gave me a tremendous amount of confidence. I felt comfortable asking anyone for money, whether I reached the person by phone or in person. It's how I developed my fundraising chops.

By the time I was raising money for my senior prom, I had more than fourteen years of experience. By then the Benjamins that vex so many people had become just numbers to me.

Now, Arian, if you could make a career fundraising for a great cause, you would feel fulfilled, I once said to myself while sitting in my car at the corner of Broadway and Gratiot after collecting from yet another donor. To this day, when my friends text me asking for money for their kid's fundraiser, I tell them I will give, but only if the child calls me directly to ask.

In ninth grade I enrolled in one of Detroit's premier public educational institutions—Cass Technical High School. Cass Tech offered a variety of educational tracks—architecture, engineering, arts and sciences, and business among them. It was like declaring a major in high school. I enrolled in the business program, which included a co-op, the equivalent of a half-day internship each day during my junior and senior years. This solidified my passion for business long before I reached college. I found something incredibly empowering about having a vision, seeing it through, and then witnessing its impact on other people. I also felt motivated to earn my own money and the empowerment having your own financial resources brings.

After I turned sixteen and got my driver's license, my mother offered to get me a car at a Honda dealership. I was very excited until I noticed she was walking toward the used-car section outside.

"Mom, why are we going there?" I asked.

"To pick out your car."

"But that's the one I want," I told her, pointing to a shiny red Accord sitting in the middle of the new-car showroom.

"That's wonderful," she replied, smiling. "You can have it, but you're going to pay for it."

I didn't back down from my mother's challenge. I worked two jobs so I'd have enough money for the car, clothes, and anything else I desired. I worked at the clothing store Express and broke regional sales records; I also worked at Jacobson's department store. Clothes were a big deal in our household. In addition to my mom's love of fashion, my great-aunt was the first Black salesperson Hudson's department store hired in downtown Detroit. I benefited from my great-aunt's discount; we also used the discounts of my mom's friends who worked at Neiman Marcus. The salesladies would hold what we wanted, we'd wait for the clearance sale, and they'd add the discount to that price. I would also buy Versace and Moschino from the high-end Black-owned store Broadway. By high school, I was best dressed at Cass Tech, though it looked like we spent a lot more money than we did. My mother was very savvy. She may have had a $100,000 closet that she spent $5,000 on, literally. My mom could also sew. I also leveled up to start my own Mary Kay business, selling makeup to my large network of family and friends.

I found the possibility of having choices, and earning money that allowed me to make them, incredibly fulfilling.

By senior year I had a 3.93 GPA and was near the top of my class and ready to apply to college. Between my grades, my leadership in multiple school organizations, and my civic involvement, I was qualified to go almost anywhere. I knew I wanted to attend the best business school possible. My parents had attended a predominately white institution (PWI), Michigan State, where they received a great education but experienced many racist incidents. They strongly encouraged me to go to an HBCU, knowing that the culturally rich and nurturing environment would have a generational impact on my life. Created as parallel institutions when white people refused to admit Black people to PWIs, HBCUs, which admit students of all races, maintain a tradition of excellence while offering Black students a supportive campus community, a stellar and affordable education, and a strong alumni network.

Buttressing my academic excellence and extracurricular achievements, the affirmative action policies of the era increased the likelihood predominantly white universities would consider me seriously as a candidate. The policies ensured a holistic admissions process that considered race as one of many factors in a student's portfolio, allowing members of underrepresented groups to access the higher education many PWIs had historically denied them. Two years earlier, California had enacted Proposition 209, which banned the state's public universities from including race among many other factors in their admissions decisions. Studies show that minority enrollment at PWIs drops by 10 to 20 percent in the years following such bans. We learn time and again that when race-conscious programs are nonexistent, people of color get left behind—Black people in particular. Though they're not members of a racial minority group, research shows that white women have benefited most from affirmative action in both higher education and the workplace. They've also been the biggest beneficiaries of DEI, a fascinating reality that for some reason white people who believe in their superiority—and often accuse Black people of needing a "handout"—conveniently leave out of their narratives.[1]

I received multiple acceptances, from leading HBCUs like Howard as well as Ivy League schools, earning full rides to some of the country's top universities. In addition to that, I was named a Coca-Cola Scholar, a very elite opportunity my counselor told me would be game-changing if I earned it. Not only did it afford me the opportunity to write a check for any school I pleased, it placed me in some very powerful networks I participate in even today.

Both during their own educational experiences and back in Detroit, my parents always stood up for justice and demonstrated a constant concern for the welfare of our community.

A little under six feet tall, caramel-colored, and with a part on the left side of his short natural hair, my father trained as a tax attorney, but he most enjoyed entertainment law. His practice included negotiating contracts for athletes and entertainers. In fact, he became one of the founders of the Black Entertainment and Sports Lawyers Association, which helped African American entertainers and sports figures obtain fair and equitable treatment. Many famous people and civil rights leaders would visit our family because of his work. Heavyweight boxing champion Tommy "the Hit Man" Hearns was a client of my father's and would come by our home. Bill Brooks, a Detroit civic leader and the highest-ranking Black person at General Motors, who also served in three presidential administrations and ran several large companies, was also a frequent guest.[2]

A creative at heart, my father also spent a lot of time at Detroit's famous Music Hall producing plays about Black history. Actor John Amos, the father on the television show *Good Times,* would hang out with my dad and starred in a play he produced. My dad and jazz violinist Noel Pointer were involved in the Detroit fundraising event to make Martin Luther King Jr. Day a national holiday. Actors LaTanya Richardson Jackson and S. Epatha Merkerson visited us. There was Alex Haley's son. Fellow lawyer and "uncle" Johnnie Cochran's picture hung on the wall of our home. I could go on.

My father's commitment to justice included attending auctions where Ku Klux Klan members sold KKK memorabilia.

"Dad, why do you want to be around those people?" I asked during my teen years.

"Arian, I am going to buy back any Black people's belongings they have in their possession."

"Is it safe? You are probably the only Black person there," I said.

"A few of us from my office are going, but the Klan members are probably more scared by the boldness we show just by being there," he told me. "And, no, we aren't scared of them. I am going to see if they have any of our stuff."

I come by my backbone honestly.

My mother, slim, always dressed to the nines, and usually wearing a bob or a huge French roll, was a computer engineer with Detroit Edison. She was part of the first generation of Black people and women breaking down barriers in STEM disciplines and in the corporate workplace.

When I was a teenager, my mother's department at Detroit Edison underwent a major reorganization. After the dust settled, it became clear that the company had demoted all the African Americans in management. Every. Single. One. The white employees had been either kept at the same level or promoted, including men with no college degree. In other words, the white guys were the "DEI hires," not her. Though I saw my mom every day, I never knew she was being mistreated at work because she refused to allow it to impact our family. Mom suffered in silence. Later I learned she'd often cry in her car. I call her a quiet storm.

Once the Black workers figured out what had happened, they concluded that the situation couldn't be normal, particularly in the case of my mother, who had both high academic credentials and clearly documented stellar performance. In fact, an outside consultant had recently witnessed her rave performance review. A group of seven or eight Black employees decided to file a class-action lawsuit. Each night after she got home from work, I watched my mother organize memos, reports, notes, and other documentation into three-inch binders the attorney gave each lawsuit participant.

"You've got enough documentation to win the whole thing," the lawyer told my mother, seeing the strength of her evidence.

"No, I don't want to do it," my mother said, afraid of both the unknown and of how this huge corporation might attack or even blackball her professionally, jeopardizing our family.

"Well, that makes no sense," the lawyer told her. "Your case alone can win the whole case."

"I've got to pray about it," my mother responded. I come from a family of spiritual warriors. Very little happens that we don't pray or seek God's guidance about.

God's answer to my mother took a while in coming.

"Are you ready to sue them yet?" the lawyer asked more than once.

"Not yet," my mother would answer. "I haven't heard from God."

"Well, when you hear from God, let us know," he'd respond.

My mother was sitting at her desk one day when the telephone rang. It was someone from the government.

"We think you've been discriminated against," the man told her.

"What?!" my mother responded.

"We had to audit your department and based on your records alone—without even talking to you—we know you've been discriminated against," the voice said. "We will help you."

"Thank you, Jesus!"

Mom's answer had finally come.

As the discovery phase of the lawsuit began, Detroit Edison removed my mother from her normal position. The company also gave her attorneys what they thought was junk data the plaintiffs couldn't use. My brilliant mother, with her master's in engineering, analyzed the numbers. They showed that every single Black person in the entire company—not just those in management—was lower ranking than every single white person in every single department. No matter what job, no matter what position, if you were Black and worked for Detroit Edison during that era, you were at the bottom. The Black employees were also the lowest paid.

My father, Ashley, and I witnessed our mother stand up to this major corporation by suing them for race, sex, and age discrimination. Everyone in the Motor City followed the case; it was all over the newspapers. The outside consultant testified in court that my mother's performance review was the best he'd seen. For her suffering, my mother won what had been the largest financial settlement for a discrimination lawsuit in the state of Michigan at the time: $750,000. That would be about $1.5 million today.

My mother's daughter, I knew how to stand up to the powers that be.

Chapter 6

The Movement

> Congress enacted § 1981 as a remedial law designed to secure the rights of newly emancipated Black citizens who were historically deprived of the rights to make and enforce economic contracts during Reconstruction. The freedom to contract and participate in the economy on equal terms "as is enjoyed by white citizens" was central to overcoming the legacy of slavery and anti-Black economic oppression. The Act's remedial purpose squarely aimed to benefit Black people. It is that remedial purpose, which is at the very heart of § 1981, that is under attack in this case.
>
> In the face of our country's history of racism, its pervasive structural discrimination, and the pernicious effects of both, Plaintiff attempts to upend the spirit and the purpose of § 1981 to further entrench the status quo of inequitable market access. Plaintiff's challenge to the Fearless Foundation's Fearless Strivers Grant program, a remedial program that awards grants to Black women-owned small businesses which historically have been disadvantaged in their ability to obtain funding, is contrary to § 1981's congressional purpose and intent and should not succeed.
>
> —Lawyers' Committee for Civil Rights Under Law, the Leadership Conference on Civil and Human Rights, National Action Network,

National Association for the Advancement of Colored People ("NAACP"), National Urban League, National Coalition of Black Civil Participation, and LatinoJustice PRLDEF, brief of amicus curiae in *American Alliance for Equal Rights v. Fearless Fund Management, LLC* in support of the Fearless Fund

SEPTEMBER 26, 2023

Back in Atlanta, the restroom break ended, we returned to the courtroom, and our case resumed. As the day went on, my team and I developed the strong sense that the judge was favoring us, and this provided some relief.

At one point the judge said, "Well, let me ask you this. So Byron Allen is probably one of the richest Black men in the United States, and his company, Black Entertainment Network, I think, annually does a TV program, and he calls it Black Entertainment Awards. And on the website, it says the winners are limited in all these different categories to Black entertainers and other minority entertainers.

"Now, am I supposed to tell Byron Allen he has to start giving awards to white people?"

I could hear a couple people in the gallery snicker.

"Well, as I understand—I'm not familiar with the particular program, but as I understand the Court's description of it, much like in the Claybrooks case that's been discussed, the final product that Mr. Allen is trying to produce is a television show," AAER's counsel replied.

"Well, he's trying to send a message supporting Black entertainers," the judge responded.

When oral arguments were done, Judge Thrash ruled orally in our favor.

"I'm going to deny the plaintiff's motion for a preliminary injunction for these reasons: I don't think the plaintiff has shown sufficient likelihood of success on the merits to grant the extraordinary relief of a preliminary injunction," he said.

He later issued a written statement, writing that AAER's attorneys failed to make its case either based on merit or by proving that Owners A, B, and C had been irreparably harmed.

The Fearless Fund had won round one. Our Fearless Strivers Grant program could continue—at least for the time being. Outside, our supporters cheered, we all rejoiced, and I, who had never seen my dad cry in my life, witnessed my father shed a tear.

"We will continue to run the nation's first venture capital fund built by women of color for women of color," I told the crowd from the podium.

Afterward our team headed across town to Morehouse College, where Vice President Kamala Harris was on a tour, speaking about freedom and diversity. By the time we entered the auditorium, the news of our victory had traveled across Atlanta. I was greeted left and right with congratulations and thanks. From former mayor Keisha Lance Bottoms to Senator Reverend Raphael Warnock, all of the city was cheering for us. Though I knew this battle wasn't over, the entire day felt victorious.

I woke up the following morning to the sunshine streaming through my bedroom windows. I rolled over and smiled, the warmth of our victory spreading over me. I enjoyed my morning devotional, thanking God for all my blessings. Then I reached for my phone and turned it on. It immediately began buzzing with news alerts and texts. Overnight, AAER had filed both an appeal on Judge Thrash's ruling and an emergency motion for an injunction intended to stop us either from closing the application window for the Fearless Strivers Grant Contest or from selecting a winner until the judge ruled upon the appeal. I felt my heart sink, my stomach turn, and my heart rate increase.

Two days later my team responded to the emergency motion; AAER then responded to that. A legal chess match was in full effect—and I found myself on the front lines of the civil rights movement's version 2.0.

Lord, help me! I know I have backup! My Calhoun ancestors, Mrs. Parks, and more are walking with me. With You in control, even in unprecedented challenges, I know I can do all things through Christ who strengthens me.

My parents grew up during the height of the civil rights era. My dad was born in Detroit in 1948, the same year President Harry

Truman issued Executive Order 9981, which laid the groundwork for desegregation throughout American society by ending racial discrimination in the military.[1] Segregation was widely practiced in Detroit and other Northern cities, limiting opportunities for Black people to work, receive a quality education, and live in integrated communities, though racial discrimination is not often discussed within the context of the North. Dad was born without a penny, as he puts it, though Detroit had long been a global powerhouse.

My mom entered the world, also in Detroit, in 1950, the year the city's population peaked at 1.85 million, making it the fourth-largest city in the United States.[2] During my lifetime, rapper and fellow Detroit native Eminem opened his video for "Beautiful" with an infographic that contained these words:

> In 1950, Michigan was 1 of 8 states in America that collectively produced 36% of the world's GNP. . . .
>
> Detroit was the greatest manufacturing city in the world.[3]

My parents witnessed this.

My mom's people migrated to Detroit during the early 1940s, seeking both the jobs the Motor City seemed to promise and safety from the economic oppression and white supremacist violence of the South. Though the Calhoun family had prospered in Macon, Georgia, the family's good financial fortunes declined, as happened in many Black entrepreneurial families. Though the civil rights laws of the 1960s required white-owned companies to open their doors to African Americans and Black people began shopping in white-owned establishments, very few white people patronized Black-owned shops. Foot traffic in Black businesses declined, including in Macon. African American business owners were also forced to deal with government policies like urban renewal, which tore down many Black communities, often destroying historic Black business districts. They had to navigate eminent domain strategies that seized Black people's land to build highways and other public works without fairly compensating them. Policies like these undermined more thriving Black communities than anyone can count. Practices like racial redlining limited Black people to living in certain communities. Many Northern Black neighborhoods became overcrowded as increasing numbers of Black Southerners fled to them, some contending with racial violence and intimidation tactics into the 1970s.

As my relatives migrated to Detroit, one family member would find a job, then send for the next. During the 1950s and '60s, my grandmother Naunny worked as a domestic, cleaning middle-class white people's houses, one of the few jobs available to Black women during that era. One day while cleaning for a wealthy white family, she observed them meeting with a financial advisor. Having been born into a family of means, my grandmother understood exactly why this meeting was taking place.

"I may not have as much money as they have, but please invest our money where you invest theirs," she told the financial planner; he did.

Naunny's husband, my grandfather Roger Flournoy, worked for Ford, the only car manufacturer employing significant numbers of Black people at all levels of its manufacturing operations. In those days General Motors only employed a handful of African Americans; Chrysler hired Black people only to work menial jobs.[4] My grandparents lived modestly, raising my mother and her siblings. When Mom was in high school, my grandmother noticed her applying for college scholarships.

"Why do you need to do that?" my grandmother asked.

"I need scholarship money," my mother replied.

"Pick your school," my grandmother told her. "We have enough money to send any of our kids to college—cash!"

Between 1950 and 1965, the stock market went up by roughly four times,[5] and my grandparents ended up owning an extensive portfolio of stocks and bonds as well as three houses. Their experience was highly unusual. During this era fewer than 10 percent of Americans of any background owned stocks. Black people comprised 10 percent of the population during this time period, but after slavery and Jim Crow segregation, they owned less than 2 percent of the nation's wealth. They owned 0.1 percent of the wealth accumulated in stocks. Structurally, the ability to accumulate wealth was possible for very few Black people.[6] The rich were getting richer; so were the middle class. Both were overwhelmingly white.

Indeed, life in the North came with its own set of racist challenges.

In Detroit, Black people were discriminated against when they applied for municipal jobs. Overt racism in hiring and in the workplace were common. Black people encountered discrimination when looking for a home or apartment. The schools they attended had fewer resources and were overcrowded compared to predominately white schools. Adding insult to injury, since the days when my great-grandparents arrived in the Motor City, Black people had been complaining about the Detroit police's racial profiling and notorious head-busting tactics. The Detroit PD constantly picked up and arrested innocent Black people, including respected members of the community, often beating them. I should also mention that compounding the shift in social climate, during the midsixties the United States entered the Vietnam War and drafted mostly poor young men and sent them overseas to fight. The military often intentionally sent Black soldiers to the front lines. As many neighborhoods nationwide experienced, when those soldiers returned home, some suffered from debilitating injuries, PTSD and other wartime trauma, and/or substance abuse disorders, contributing to both the breakdown of families and the deterioration of conditions in the community.

White Southerners migrated to Detroit as well, but they could make their home within any part of the city they chose. Unlike Black people, their options for what neighborhoods they lived in were not limited by racial violence and intimidation, or by racist banking practices like redlining, which denied loans for mortgages, home improvements, businesses, college, and other investments to qualified Black people, or by the predatory interest rates banks offered Black people, or the racially restrictive covenants, racial steering, and block busting in the real estate industry that confined Black people to all-Black neighborhoods. White Americans also benefited from the New Deal during the Great Depression and the GI Bill following World War II. Devised to appease Southern whites, both federal government programs were designed to exclude as many Black people as possible. White people, including those who had recently immigrated from Europe and didn't speak English, qualified for government benefits Uncle Sam denied African Americans. This included low-interest mortgages that allowed white people to buy houses in growing suburban communities that were appreciating in value. White people invested in stocks in industries Black people weren't allowed to participate in. The ability to take out loans and leverage accumulated wealth funded the college tuition of generations of white Americans.

One of my grandmother's first cousins, Emory Calhoun, whose father was the dentist in Macon I referred to earlier, lived in New York. I remember visiting Cousin Emory as a child. Like most people in our family, he lived modestly, but I remember walking around with him picking up envelopes throughout his apartment building.

"Why are we collecting the mail?" I asked.

"I own this building," he answered.

Turns out not only did Cousin Emory own the building, he also built a construction business, a taxi service, a dry cleaner's, and more. One of my friends gasped in surprise when she overheard him recounting business deals he'd made during the 1970s and '80s for seven million and eight million dollars—the equivalent of $43 million to $50 million today.

"Arian, you and your generation are going to get us back on track," Cousin Emory once told me.

Feeling empowered, unafraid, and financially savvy was both my legacy and my spiritual destiny.

When my parents met at Michigan State University during the late 1960s, they were part of the first cohort of Black students who benefited from federal government policies attempting to rectify past racial discrimination through "affirmative action," where people who'd been discriminated against were finally offered an opportunity equal to what was available to white people in education, employment, and the workplace itself—in theory at least. My parents rushed through these newly open doors. The ability to go to college helped my dad overcome his economic disadvantages and graduate from law school; my mother earned her master's degree.

The civil rights laws of the sixties set Black people on more firm footing for the future, but white backlash against these advances started right away. And after they had worked for 246 years without being paid and experienced economic exploitation for a century after that, nothing had been done to compensate Black people for the racial intimidation and economic oppression they continued to face. Many Black people remained painfully poor. In both the North and South, leaders and communities desperately explored a wide range of options to help Black people win the rights the Constitution, the Declaration of Independence, and other founding documents promise.

Mainstream civil rights leaders and organizations, such as the Southern Christian Leadership Conference, headed by Dr. Martin Luther King Jr., advocated peaceful steps taken in the modest increments white leaders insisted would make white people feel most comfortable. Black nationalists and those participating in the Black Power movement were often less concerned about white people's comfort and more concerned about how to help Black people become economically self-sufficient and thrive.

During the decade before my parents met, civil rights icon Malcolm X did important movement work in and around Detroit. In Lansing, Michigan, where Malcolm spent some of his early childhood, he and his family were terrorized by white supremacists, who were also widely believed to have murdered Malcolm's father. Eventually, Malcolm relocated to the East Coast to live with his half sister.[7]

During his twenties, Malcolm experienced a phase of self-enlightenment, when he changed his last name to X, converted to

Islam, and joined the Nation of Islam, a Black nationalist religious organization. Before long, he became one of the Nation of Islam's leading ministers and spokespeople.

Malcolm X conducted some of his early ministry in Detroit, sharing his anger about the glacial pace of racial change and becoming known for his scathing critiques of white supremacy. In 1963, he delivered his famous address "Message to the Grass Roots" at the historic King Solomon Baptist Church on 14th Avenue in Detroit, the same place Dr. King had spoken several weeks earlier.[8]

> America has a very serious problem. Not only does America have a very serious problem, but our people have a very serious problem. America's problem is us. We're her problem. The only reason she has a problem is she doesn't want us here. And every time you look at yourself, be you black, brown, red, or yellow—a so-called Negro—you represent a person who poses such a serious problem for America because you're not wanted. Once you face this as a fact, then you can start plotting a course that will make you appear intelligent, instead of unintelligent.[9]

Malcolm X respected Martin Luther King as a leader; however, he sharply criticized Dr. King's nonviolent and multiracial approach.[10]

Comparable movements to achieve freedom and justice took place across Africa and in the Caribbean, where various European colonial powers had oppressed and exploited Black people since the transatlantic slave trade began. In the 1950s, Libya, Sudan, Morocco, Tunisia, Ghana, and Guinea won their independence. Nineteen sixty became known as the "Year of Africa," as seventeen African nations ran foreign governments out, transforming themselves into independent states.[11] These newly formed nations and many Caribbean countries began to take control over their natural resources, establish fair governments, and build institutions that served their own citizens rather than European economic interests.

A lot of cross-pollination occurred between the African, African American, and Caribbean movements. The fact many African countries gained independence in the 1950s helped catalyze the civil rights movement in the United States. Malcolm X actively participated in pan-African conversations, aware that the issues impacting African Americans were part of a global problem. To help African Americans gain more international support, he urged leaders to frame the movement not as an issue of civil rights but as an issue of human rights. *Civil rights* is defined as "the rights of citizens to political and social freedom and equality." *Human rights* includes the fundamental freedoms and rights all people have because they are human and are based on the principles of respect, equality, and dignity. Economic equality is a human right.

As he traveled and spoke in the United States, Malcolm X challenged the US government to note the progress of African states. In 1964, he also petitioned the United Nations, imploring it to view America's racism as a global issue. If South African apartheid and domestic disputes could be brought to the UN as a global issue, why not American racial discrimination and racial cruelty, he argued.

In the early morning of February 14, 1965, his home was firebombed. He; his wife, Betty; and their four daughters fled. Despite the horrific tragedy, Malcolm kept his commitment to return to Detroit, where he spoke that very night. Here's an excerpt of what he shared:

> After 1959 the spirit of African nationalism was fanned to a high flame, and we then began to witness the complete collapse of colonialism. France began to get out of French West Africa; Belgium began to make moves to get out of the Congo; Britain began to make moves to get out of Kenya, Tanganyika, Uganda, Nigeria, and some of these other places. And although it looked like they were getting out, they pulled a trick that was colossal.
>
> In that—when you're playing basketball and they get you trapped, you don't throw the ball away, you throw it to one of

> your teammates who's in the clear. And this is what the European powers did. They were trapped on the African continent, they couldn't stay there; they were looked upon as colonial, imperialist. So they had to pass the ball to someone whose image was different, and they passed the ball to Uncle Sam. And he picked it up and has been running it for a touchdown ever since. He was in the clear, he was not looked upon as one who had colonized the African continent. But at that time, the Africans couldn't see that though the United States hadn't colonized the African continent, he had colonized twenty-two million Blacks here on this continent. Because we are just as thoroughly colonized as anybody else.[12]

A week later, on February 21, 1965, assassins killed Malcolm X.

Though he's often portrayed as being the opposite of Malcolm X—and though he focused far more attention on desegregation and voting rights—Dr. King understood that Black people and other low-income Americans would never enjoy full citizenship until they were secure economically, as well.

"I fear I may have integrated my people into a burning house," Dr. King is said to have told singer and activist Harry Belafonte about his efforts to incorporate African Americans into a deeply flawed system rather than attempting to root out economic injustice and inequity. In fact, one of Dr. King's greatest regrets was that he didn't begin fighting for Black people's economic rights first.

In November 1967, Dr. King addressed this reality by launching the Poor People's Campaign, which demanded jobs, unemployment insurance, a fair minimum wage, and education for low-income children and adults[13] in order to create genuine equality. As part of the campaign, he and other civil rights leaders attempted to persuade Congress and President Johnson about the need for economic justice and to pass an economic bill of rights. This bill of rights would guarantee work for those who were able, an income for those who were unable, and decent housing for low-income Americans of all racial and ethnic backgrounds, including poor white people.

On March 14, 1968, Dr. King delivered a speech, titled "The Other America," to 2,700 people in the same town of Grosse Pointe where I would later attend school. The speech Dr. King delivered was one for the ages.

> There are literally two Americas. One America is flowing with the milk of prosperity and the honey of equality. That America is the habitat of millions of people who have food and material necessities for their bodies, culture and education for their minds, freedom and human dignity for their spirits. That America is made up of millions of young people who grow up in the sunlight of opportunity.
>
> Now, what we've got to do . . . is to attack the problem of poverty and really mobilize the forces of our country to have an all-out war against poverty, because what we have now is not even a good skirmish against poverty. I need not remind you that poverty, the gaps in our society, the gulfs between inordinate superfluous wealth and abject deadening poverty have brought about a great deal of despair, a great deal of tension, a great deal of bitterness. We've seen this bitterness expressed over the last few summers in the violent explosions in our cities.
>
> And the great tragedy is that the nation continues in its national policy to ignore the conditions that brought the riots or the rebellions into being. For in the final analysis, the riot is the language of the unheard. And what is it that America's failed to hear? It's failed to hear that the plight of the Negro poor has worsened over the last few years. It has failed to hear that the promises of justice and freedom have not been met. It has failed to hear that large segments of white

> society are more concerned about tranquility and the status quo than about justice, humanity, and equality, and it is still true. It is still true that these things are being ignored.

As he spoke, Dr. King also asserted, "It's much easier to integrate a lunch counter than it is to guarantee a livable income and a good solid job."[14]

Three weeks after his Grosse Pointe speech, Dr. King was gunned down, in Memphis, Tennessee, on the balcony of the Lorraine Motel.

After all he'd done, and done nonviolently, Black Americans felt hopeless and traumatized. Uprisings occurred in more than two hundred cities,[15] including Detroit. Already white residents had been leaving major cities; with the outbreak of civic unrest, they fled even more quickly. As a result of white flight, the percentage of Detroit's population that Black people comprised increased from about 25 percent to 43 percent by 1970.

Also during this time frame, increasing numbers of Black people began demanding reparations. Political activist James Forman developed a "Black Manifesto" and read it as he commandeered the pulpit at Riverside Church in New York. In it he demanded $500 million from white churches and synagogues for their roles in slavery and subsequent injustices to African Americans.[16]

Though reparations were debated, including in elite circles, little progress was made.

Economic freedom and economic justice run hand in hand.

Despite the many threats and challenges they faced, civil rights leaders were very good at focusing on one issue at a time in a concentrated effort and getting it done.

In 1955 and 1956, the Montgomery Bus Boycott forced the city's public transportation system to desegregate. Civil rights leaders fought for the Civil Rights Act and the Voting Rights Act, and President Johnson signed them in 1964 and 1965. Though leaders like Dr. King, Malcolm X, and other stalwarts of the civil rights era championed these principles, our nation never passed an economic justice act. Almost sixty years after the start of the Poor People's Campaign, issues of economic inequity remain unresolved.

Rather than creating economic freedom and justice, our leaders were murdered.

Similar to how the Israelites of the biblical Old Testament spent forty years wandering through the desert after God freed them from Egyptian captivity, our nation has experienced a sixty-year "wilderness," between 1965 and 2025, where little progress toward reducing economic inequality has been made. Though people who believe in white supremacy deny racism of any type motivates them, the reality is: helping Black people helps everyone, and hurting Black people hurts everyone. As I write these words, Black and brown Americans are moving backward economically under President Donald Trump's second administration. Political activists are upset about countless issues: free speech, abortion rights, healthcare, immigration, Medicaid—there's no end to the list of legitimate problems. But I believe we must focus our fight on achieving economic justice. After economic justice is achieved, everything else will fall into place.

In the Old Testament, the scripture Ecclesiastes 10:19 tells us that money answers all things. Powerful people know that money talks. Money creates the leverage needed to handle everything else. When you're economically empowered, other issues no longer become fights. This is why I believe we have to handle economic issues first. It's important that we be able to discern the times and the seasons. Doing the right thing at the wrong time is not effective. That's why it's important we all get in accord, and it's important we get in accord globally.

Rather than leaving issues of economic justice to be fought over in the courts, as I was experiencing, governments should resolve them.

Our civil rights leaders did the very best they knew how to do while working under conditions more oppressive and dangerous than many people today can imagine. They did the best they could with the knowledge they had; however, in this one particular area, they may have fallen short. This shouldn't surprise us; most were ministers, not businesspeople, after all. If they had been businesspeople, they would have had the experience to understand the leverage money creates to handle other issues. The Civil Rights Movement 2.0 must address and create economic justice.

Working in the space of venture capital, as I do, also means working in the areas of racial equity, job creation, wealth creation, and generational wealth. Some of the more politically inclined venture capitalists are among the new leaders and driving forces of Civil Rights 2.0. Though the civil rights era of the 1960s focused on equality, the civil rights era today is all about equity. The difference between equality and equity is a subtle but crucial one. *Equality* means giving everyone the same thing, while *equity* means treating people justly according to their circumstances—giving them what they actually *need* to succeed. Creating financial equity often involves providing funding, mentorship, and support to people historically excluded from systems of economic empowerment. It involves opening doors and breaking down the walls that have kept so many people out. It's about leveling the playing field so that success isn't reserved for a select few but accessible to everyone willing to work for it. Because even now, when Black people try to break through barriers, they're met with gatekeeping hidden behind words like *creditworthiness, investor confidence,* and *risk assessment.* But what is "risk" except the same biases wrapped in financial jargon? The current worldwide financial systems were never designed to work for Black, brown, and Indigenous communities; they were designed to keep us out.

After waking up one morning with the spiritual download that we must pick up where Dr. King left off by passing some kind of economic justice act or policy, I discussed this revelation with my pastor, who often preaches conscious messages tied to current events through a justice lens, similar to Jeremiah Wright or Raphael Warnock. The idea resonated so much, he was in awe of what I was saying and added the Fearless Fund to the church's intercessory prayer list.

I became obsessed with trying to piece together where things left off in Dr. King's movement. I participated in the King Historic District Tour, taking in the locations, stories, and documents with adult eyes. I visited Dr. King's house, and I sat by his grave and journaled. I also toured both Atlanta's National Center for Civil and Human Rights and the Birmingham Civil Rights Institute, where I served on the board of directors. I gathered information from Dr. King's journals on how he leveraged the power of the Black church, leaders of national civic organizations, politicians, celebrities, attorneys, businessmen, and the media to mobilize people to create change. I realized a lot of his strategies are still relevant and can be applied today.

Dr. King told Americans that the road to economic justice would be far longer than the road to the Civil Rights Act, the Voting Rights Act, and other significant accomplishments had been. For he observed that when he shifted his message toward economic justice, the civil rights movement lost some white supporters, numerically and financially. Economic justice would require billions of dollars to be deployed to Black people. He knew it would take time and action for white people to digest that idea. Still, Dr. King's final interviews, speeches, and talks drew attention to economic justice.

"I feel that we are in the midst of the most critical period of our nation, and the economic problem is probably the most serious problem confronting the Negro community and, I might say, the most serious problem confronting poor people generally, and I don't want to be narrow about this, talking only about the Black poor in our country, because I must be concerned about Puerto Ricans who are poor, Mexican Americans, American Indians, and Appalachian whites," he stated in 1968 while leading the Poor People's Campaign.

Today we still struggle with many of the problems Dr. King aspired to address.

The more research I engaged in, the more I felt the weight of Dr. King's life and legacy. Progress has been made in some areas, but not nearly enough. Though almost sixty years have passed since his death, in the United States alone creating economic justice would require allocating trillions of dollars to Black people. But if the lawsuit facing the Fearless Fund showed me nothing else, it demonstrated that changing systems is an uphill battle. Some days, working in Civil Rights 2.0 makes me feel like I should be wearing combat fatigues. Nonetheless, I remain motivated to pick up where Dr. King left off, and inspired and committed to resolve systemic economic issues.

The Playbook

The Cure for Government Policy

As I write this book, our team is developing the Fearless Freedom Economic Justice Act. Through this act, we provide comprehensive model legal guidance offering clear and actionable guidelines for allocating funding fairly from a variety of sources. These guidelines were designed to be adaptable everywhere. They can be customized to reflect the legislative processes of any country, state, province, or municipality, while upholding the core principle: Public funding, contracts, and services should be allocated in proportion to the demographic composition of the population served.

The Fearless Freedom Economic Justice Act aims to level the playing field by ensuring that funding decisions are made transparently and without bias, no matter whether large manufacturers, small businesses, nonprofits, or businesses run by individuals are involved. We have designed the act so it can be customized to cover a wide variety of entities—contractors, subcontractors, manufacturers, service companies, corporations—that maintain their principal place of business within the jurisdiction described. Here I summarize a few key points for federal, state, and local governments. The exact model legislation as well as its terms are located in the Appendix:

1. Federal-Level Contracts

This model was created for national governments, specifically the US federal government, to ensure that contracts, goods, and services are distributed equitably according to the nation's demographic composition. It serves as a foundation for any national-level effort to rectify economic disparities rooted in colonial or systemic exclusion. Some of the key points include:

- The United States's policy is to balance the distribution of federal contracts purchasing goods and services, public works contracts, and contracts for projects among individuals and businesses so that they reflect the demographic characteristics of the United States.
- The head of each federal agency that awards these contracts may establish targets for individuals or businesses demonstrating a specified racial characteristic, on the basis of competitive bidding procedures, for contracts for constructing, reconstructing or rehabilitating public buildings, constructing and maintaining highways, and purchasing goods and services (including pension fund management contracts and other services contracts).
- For each specific racial characteristic, the awards target should approximate the percentage of people of that background in the general population of the United States. If an agency establishes a target for a specified racial characteristic, it must establish a target for every specified racial characteristic.
- Any contractor, subcontractor, manufacturer, service company, or corporation engaged in interstate commerce in the United States is qualified to compete; however, any contract that conflicts with a federal law or regulation is excluded.

2. State-Level Contracts and Contracts for Quasi-Public Agencies

Our recommendations for US state legislatures, such as General Assemblies and State Senates, can be adapted by provinces, territories, or regions in other nations that have similar governing structures. They direct state governments to establish benchmarks for achieving demographic equity in awarding contracts and public projects.

- The state's policy is to balance the distribution of its contracts purchasing goods and services, public works contracts, municipal public works contracts and contracts for quasi-public agency projects among individuals and businesses to reflect the demographic characteristics of the state.
- Based on competitive bidding procedures, the head of each award-granting state agency may establish targets for individuals or businesses with a specified characteristic, for contracts or portions of contracts that cover the construction, reconstruction or rehabilitation of public buildings, the construction and maintenance of highways, and goods and services (including state pension fund management contracts and other services contracts).
- The targets for contract awards shall approximate the percentage of individuals with each specific racial characteristic residing in the state. If a state agency establishes a target for any specified characteristic, it must establish a target for every specified racial characteristic.
- The legislation would cover contractors, subcontractors, manufacturers, service companies, or corporations that maintain their principal place of business in the state; however, any contract that conflicts with a federal law or regulation is excluded.

3. Local-Municipal Contracts for City or County Governments

Our recommendations for municipal legislative bodies, such as city councils or county commissions, empower local governments to align their public funding, procurement, and contracting with the demographic realities of their jurisdiction. The model is replicable across cities globally and can be customized to local charters or codes.

- This city's policy is to distribute its contracts purchasing goods and services, public works contracts, municipal public works contracts, and contracts for quasi-public-agency projects among individuals and businesses so that they reflect the demographic characteristics of the city.
- On the basis of competitive bidding procedures, when awarding municipal public works contracts, the head of each agency or department may establish targets for awards to individuals or businesses with a specified racial characteristic, for contracts or portions of contracts for the construction, reconstruction or rehabilitation of public buildings, the construction and maintenance of streets and highways, and the purchase of goods and services (including city pension fund management contracts and other services contracts).
- For each specified characteristic, the agency's contract award target shall approximate the percentage of individuals with the specified characteristics in the city's general population.
- If a city agency or department establishes a target for any specified characteristic in the general population, it must establish a target for every specified characteristic in the general population.

- The legislation would cover any contractor, subcontractor, manufacturer, service company, or corporation that maintains its principal place of business in the city; however, any contract that conflicts with a federal or state law or regulation is excluded.

Chapter 7

Knowledge Is Power

Market access is not equal among racial groups in today's America. Venture capital provides a stark example. Black businesses face a funding rejection rate three times higher than their white counterparts. Black women are the fastest growing group of entrepreneurs. But the job isn't easy. . . . Black women businessowners' lack of access is even worse. Black women receive less than 0.35% of all venture capital funding, despite Black people making up 14.2% of the US population. . . . Applying § 1981 to prohibit private, remedial grantmaking programs that increase Black women's access to venture capital is inconsistent with its purpose and history. Black women currently have access to a mere sliver of venture capital compared to other demographic groups. Finding a program that increases Black women's access to funding unlawful under § 1981 would exacerbate inequitable economic access currently faced by Black communities.

—Lawyers' Committee for Civil Rights Under Law, Leadership Conference on Civil and Human Rights, National Action Network, National Association for the Advancement of Colored People ("NAACP"), National Urban League, National Coalition on Black Civic Participation, and LatinoJustice PRLDEF, brief of amicus curiae in *American Alliance for Equal Rights v. Fearless Fund Management, LLC* in support of the Fearless Fund

SEPTEMBER 30, 2023

Just two days after AAER filed their emergency motion, the court granted the injunction blocking the contest, pending our appeal, in a closed panel meeting, in a 2–1 vote, with only the Clinton-appointed judge, Charles Wilson, ruling in our favor. The other two judges were Trump-appointed judges.

What in the world?!

I was in shock.

I remember the silence on the phone when attorneys Alphonso David and Ben Crump spoke with me about the decision.

My head spun.

I'd known losing was possible, but I hadn't thought losing was likely. I'd assumed that just as the district court had found Blum's argument foolish, the circuit court would also see it was wrong. At that time, I didn't know who our judges would be. Once we'd discovered we'd have two Trump appointees, my lawyers had begun preparing for the possibility that they might rule against us. I had not, and the reality of our loss crashed down all around me.

Our legal team had worked very hard and I was very grateful for their efforts, but I suddenly found myself questioning our approach, our arguments, our everything. I was used to winning as a matter of course. Any time I didn't, my practice was to try to figure out what I could have done differently that would have gotten the desired outcome. In this particular situation, so much was on the line, a postmortem was essential. In the days afterward, various experts and talking heads discussed how Trump had appointed 234 federal judges, including three Supreme Court justices, six US Court of Appeals judges, and fourteen at the US District Court level.[1]

Now here I was—a real live case study proving that elections have consequences. In one quick moment, I discovered that leaders implement systems that outlive them. It was like Donald Trump was still in office even though he had been voted out. This fact cemented in my mind the reality that, though we were living under President Biden's administration, we were still ensnared in the Trump agenda.

In the coming days, as I went on walks, practiced deep breathing, and engaged in other practices to regulate my nervous system, both my shock and the swirl of my thoughts calmed down. Emotionally, I recovered from our loss. I didn't know yet what path forward we would take, but I still had hope. I was committed to moving forward to achieve economic justice.

We're going to have to fight! Civil Rights 2.0 is on!

In addition to racially socializing us to appreciate Black life, arts, culture, and community, my parents taught us the importance of looking out for the well-being of Black businesspeople, ministers, politicians, and other leaders who stood on the front lines of racial progress.

Frequently, notable people from both within and outside Detroit would visit us, including famous elders from the civil rights era. Sometimes they came for meetings, fellowship, or a meal; other times they stayed with us for days, even weeks, if there was a big event going on.

"Dad, why are we housing this person today?" I'd ask regarding whatever prominent individual we were sharing our spacious home with.

"Arian, we have to take care of our leaders," he'd say. "They are out there protesting on our behalf, so they shouldn't have a moment where they don't have a place to sleep, or can't buy a meal, or can't enjoy the regular amenities of life. These people need to be provided for."

In 1990, my father hosted South Africa's president Nelson Mandela when he appeared in Detroit. President Mandela gifted my father a bottle of wine, which my dad waited to open until Mandela's death in 2013. My parents also taught Ashley and me that if we wanted to effect change, we had to contribute financially to the people and causes that support it.

"Things have to be funded," my mother taught me, whether it was the NAACP, the UNCF, or Grosse Pointe Academy.

One consistent presence in my life was the civil rights icon Rosa Parks. Mrs. Parks and her husband moved to Detroit in 1957, shortly after she refused to give up her seat near the front of a Montgomery, Alabama, bus to a white man, as Jim Crow segregation laws required. After her courageous stand launched the Montgomery Bus Boycott, she not only lost her job as a seamstress, she and her husband also experienced racist threats and intimidation. They fled to Detroit, where she already had family.

In 1987, my father began praying for the opportunity to help her. My father prayed for three years, even writing down his prayer. In 1990, Rosa Parks walked into his office and asked him to represent her. She was struggling financially at the time. Dad wrote a list of twenty things they were going to do together; they would go on to accomplish nineteen of them. Mrs. Parks became a fixture in my life, like family. She and her husband, Raymond, who died before I was born, had long been very active in Detroit's civil rights movement, hosting salons and participating in various meetings and organizations. She always said she would have loved for her husband to meet our family. For years, she worked as the secretary to Michigan congressman John Conyers.[2]

Mrs. Parks played an essential role in cultivating my appreciation of Black history, pouring wisdom into me as a grandmother would and telling stories the history books left out. Whether we were sharing a meal, talking about life, or simply sitting in comfortable silence, spending time with Rosa Parks was a gift; I felt the impact of her presence. She carried the history of a movement on her shoulders, yet she moved through life with humility, grace, and quiet strength. I was blessed to experience this firsthand.

When I was fourteen, I traveled to a California church with Mrs. Parks. While there, we came across a young white boy who was just learning who Mrs. Parks was. After hearing that she'd been arrested during the civil rights movement, he'd assumed she'd remained in jail for many years since no one mentioned that she'd been released. This note from one of the authors of Mrs. Parks's memoir captures the scene. (Typos are part of the original note.)

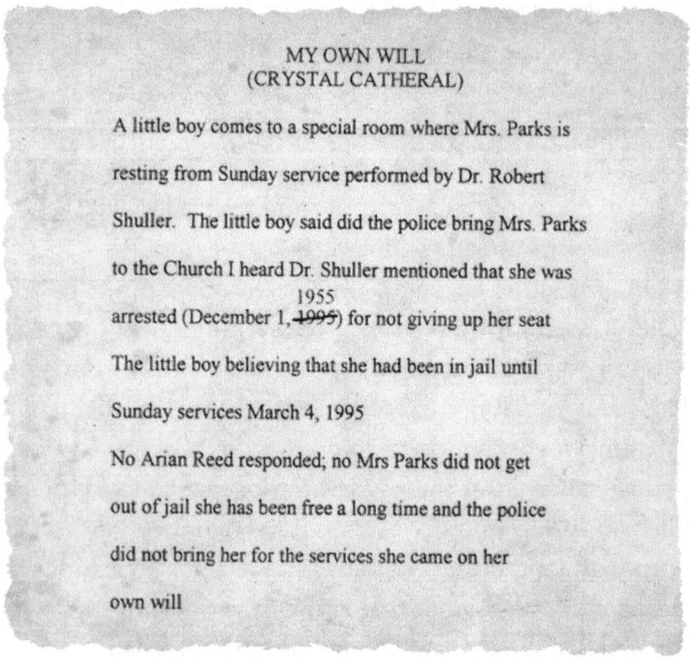

MY OWN WILL
(CRYSTAL CATHERAL)

A little boy comes to a special room where Mrs. Parks is resting from Sunday service performed by Dr. Robert Shuller. The little boy said did the police bring Mrs. Parks to the Church I heard Dr. Shuller mentioned that she was arrested (December 1, ~~1995~~ 1955) for not giving up her seat The little boy believing that she had been in jail until Sunday services March 4, 1995

No Arian Reed responded; no Mrs Parks did not get out of jail she has been free a long time and the police did not bring her for the services she came on her own will

Feeling that I was like Mrs. Parks's granddaughter, I took it upon myself to defend her honor.

Through my parents' education and Mrs. Parks's mentorship, I became familiar with all sorts of leaders in the civil rights movement. Sometimes a little too familiar. In December of that same year, my parents arranged for Ashley and me to fly to Alabama to attend the fortieth anniversary of the Montgomery Bus Boycott. My parents had to travel ahead, so it was also the first time they trusted Ashley and me to fly by ourselves.

Before the trip, I started having all these terrible thoughts. I had never been to Alabama; all I knew about it was the horrible stories Mrs. Parks shared—about the Ku Klux Klan, the cross burnings, the beatings, the hangings. Not once had anyone shared the great stories of all the adversity Black people had overcome there. Plus, I was a teenager and would have rather hung out with my friends. Having fun with them seemed way better than being around people I believed didn't mean me any good.

Why would anyone want to go to that place? I sure don't.

"What do you mean you aren't going?" my mother replied when I told her I wasn't coming.

"There are evil people there and I don't want any part of it," I told her, asking, "Do you have a gun with you?" Naunny didn't take anything from anybody. I knew she would've carried her "nine" to someplace like that.

"Arian, I am down here now and things are just fine," my mother said calmly. "Rosa Parks, Coretta Scott King, and Juanita Abernathy are all waiting on you," she continued, running down the names of other icons of the civil rights movement.

"Mom, I can see those old ladies anytime!" I replied.

"Arian Simone Reed, you are getting on the plane with your sister and we will see you soon!"

Needless to say, I got on the plane, and when Ashley and I landed, we were greeted with so much love. All was well in Alabama. The trip was amazing and a celebration. I got to sit at the feet of and learn from these amazing women of the civil rights movement, including Mrs. Abernathy, whose husband, the Reverend Ralph Abernathy, was Reverend King's closest friend and advisor, and after his death, his successor as the head of the Southern Christian Leadership Conference, which he also cofounded.[3] This trip I was almost afraid to go on would lay the foundation for my lifelong admiration and respect for the civil rights movement and our leaders, and in particular Dr. Martin Luther King Jr.'s efforts toward the end of his life to help Black people achieve economic justice.

Beginning that year and continuing until I was sixteen, I participated in Mrs. Parks's Pathways to Freedom youth development program. During summers she would lead busloads of young people to visit and learn about Underground Railroad and civil rights sites and monuments. The tours would begin down south—we'd travel through Alabama; Georgia; Virginia; Washington, DC; and other locales—and end in the North, where we visited places like First Congregational Church and Second Baptist Church in Detroit. These were among the final and most critical stops for Black people escaping slavery by crossing the Detroit River to Canada, where slavery was prohibited. Detroit's code name on the Underground Railroad was "midnight." Our city played a vital role in helping Black people evade the fugitive-slave laws that allowed bounty hunters to capture and return to their enslavers Black people who successfully escaped to Northern states that prohibited enslavement.[4] Once we also traveled to historic sites in New York State.

> Whether from my own personal experiences or from listening to my parents, Mrs. Parks, or some of our nation's greatest leaders, I learned it's important to commit to moving forward even when you're afraid.

One of the greatest lessons that I learned as a young person was how to value and honor Black people's efforts in a world that constantly diminishes and disparages our achievements.

My father often took me with him when he traveled around the world for work, which expanded my horizons greatly. My dad taught me very directly that knowledge is power. He taught that knowledge has a worth—one that all too often has been ignored when it comes to Black leaders and creatives.

He also understood something that many people overlook: the value of Black stories.

Not just the value of our struggles or our triumphs, but the tangible, intellectual, and monetary value of Black thought, Black writing, and Black resistance. My father knew our history was not just something to be remembered; it was something to be owned, protected, and honored.

Dad put his literal money where his mouth was. After the death of Alex Haley, the coauthor of *The Autobiography of Malcolm X,* my father discovered that several of Malcolm X's personal papers were being put up for auction as part of the Haley estate. Immediately, he knew he had to be present.

I'd heard about Malcolm X as a young person. His philosophy had meaning in our home and his teachings on Black people being self-reliant and self-sufficient inspired me. Additionally, Detroit was a city where you had to be street-smart and look out for yourself. Having a grandmother who took no trash from anyone and carried a gun, I learned not to initiate any type of conflict with anybody. I also learned you defend yourself, in the words of Malcolm X, "by any means necessary." If someone picks a fight with you, you definitely finish it. I was a hardcore Malcolm X girl and didn't yet comprehend Dr. King or why various civil rights leaders didn't fight back. As a child, that ideology wasn't easy to grasp. I didn't understand the discipline required to have a nonviolent movement.

Before Malcolm X's writings went up for auction, the most anyone had ever spent on papers or an original manuscript from a Black author was around $5,000, about $12,000 today. Rumor had it Malcolm X's papers would sell for millions. Word on the street was that these rumors were being circulated to deter Black people from attending. During those days some white authors' works were selling for upwards of one million dollars. My father saw the huge racial disparity and refused to accept the devaluing of Black life. He didn't just want to celebrate Black literature and history; he wanted to invest in, protect, and preserve it. He also wanted to make a statement to the world that our intellectual property was just as valuable as anyone else's.

"In the face of attempts to erase or diminish our worth, we can still take ownership of our own narrative," he told me.

My father was determined to ensure that these invaluable pieces of history ended up in Black hands. At the auction itself, he discovered that among Haley's papers were chapters not included in the published version of Malcolm X's autobiography—representing missing pieces of one of the most significant autobiographies ever written. My father not only participated in the auction, he stretched himself financially in order to place the highest bid—quickly making national news. He was featured in *Time* magazine, on our local NBC-TV affiliate, and in many other national publications. And people weren't just talking about the contents of the papers themselves, they were talking about the importance of preserving Black history in Black hands.

> It's important to see past the surface obstacles when you're on the verge of liberating yourself from a constraint and experiencing a breakthrough.

Not long afterward, Malcom's widow, Dr. Betty Shabazz, reached out to my dad. A civil rights activist and college professor who raised their six children alone after her husband's murder, Dr. Shabazz understood, better than anyone, what those papers meant. They weren't just old manuscripts or historical documents; they were part of her husband's written legacy—now protected for generations to come. My father had ensured that these drafts weren't lost or exploited—and for that, she was grateful.

Over the years, their connection deepened and Dr. Shabazz sought my dad's counsel. I remember coming home from school one day and finding Sister Betty sitting on our steps. Dr. Shabazz trusted him, not just because he invested in Malcolm X's work but because he moved with an unwavering belief in the power of Black intellectual property. Through his commitment to honoring Malcolm X's truth, ensuring his words remained in Black hands, Dr. Shabazz became part of the community of esteemed elders that encircled me. I could feel the spirit of those elders as I stood up to AAER's unexpected legal attack.

Denise Woodard, Founder, Partake
(African American woman)

At Partake Foods, our goal is to provide delicious, allergy-friendly snacks that everyone can enjoy. Building a company from the ground up requires not just passion but also strategic partnerships and financial backing. Fearless Fund has been instrumental in empowering entrepreneurs like me, ensuring that underrepresented founders receive the resources they need to scale and succeed.

Fearless Fund's work extends far beyond funding—it's about fostering a community of like-minded individuals who uplift and support one another. Their commitment to breaking barriers and championing diverse voices in the business world is something I deeply admire. I am grateful to be a part of their mission and to contribute to the broader goal of creating a more inclusive entrepreneurial ecosystem.

Chapter 8

Backlash

When venture capital thrives, the US economy grows. And venture capital thrives most when it promotes innovation from businesses from all parts of the country. Too often, however, venture financing goes to companies on the coasts, founded and run disproportionately by non-minority entrepreneurs. This stifles growth—for example, companies with all-male founding teams perform, on average, worse than counterparts with at least one female founder. . . .

Just as with the economy as a whole, the promise of a more robust venture capital industry lies in diversifying its reach, so that the best ideas, not immutable characteristics, determine the direction of the country's growth. Grant programs like Fearless Fund's that aim to redirect investment to Black-women-owned businesses are critical to realizing this goal. The Court should not sanction Plaintiff's campaign against them, and the motion for a preliminary injunction should be denied.

—National Venture Capital Association and the Venture Capital Foundation, amicus brief in *American Alliance for Equal Rights v. Fearless Fund Management, LLC* in support of the Fearless Fund

Who doesn't remember where they were in March 2020, when various governments began implementing Covid shutdowns?

What I recall most about that time, when I hunkered down in my home like everyone else, is the widespread empathy. We were all scared of this deadly virus killing our loved ones and neighbors, sending people to the hospital struggling to breathe, causing people to lose jobs, to lose income, to lose their sense of safety and security. For once, much of the world seemed to be on one accord, caring for one another. This wasn't just an Atlanta experience or an American experience. It wasn't an urban experience or a rural experience. It wasn't a national experience. So many lives were lost and so much devastation was taking place; all of us were having a global experience. The fact everybody was having similar things happen to them at the same time created so much understanding and community. Though the situation was extremely tragic, there was also something beautiful in the entire world coming together to solve a life-threatening problem. We were all learning care and compassion and empathy at once.

There is another day that year that is equally important: May 25, 2020. The date when George Floyd was murdered at the hands of Minneapolis police officer Derek Chauvin, who, along with several coworkers, engaged in a horrific act of police brutality. I had the privilege of working from home on the day George Floyd was murdered. I can't tell you how many people sent me the video seventeen-year-old Darnella Frazier took documenting Derek Chauvin choking the life out of George Floyd, a human being with gifts and talents, whose existence mattered to God, his children, and his loved ones. I never watched the video; I couldn't. I'd seen far too much Black death as a result of police brutality and had heard far too many Black people cry out, "I can't breathe!" I remember having two sets of thoughts:

This is finally a time when the world can see and feel what the Black American experience is like. And . . . *This is what it took for you to understand? Well, thank God you're listening now.*

The video of George Floyd's murder ricocheted beyond the

United States. Protests unfolded all around the world as other people of color, those with marginalized identities, and white allies joined Black Americans on the front lines calling for racial justice. None of us had ever seen anything like the surge of compassion and support for Black people's cries that our lives matter.

We're finally going to get justice served!

As sickened and sad as I was, a part of me also felt hopeful that change might finally take place. Fearless had a team create an amazing video compilation of protests from all over the world, including in places you might not expect: Japan, Germany, Australia, New Zealand, Italy, London, France, and South Korea. The rapidly growing calls for racial justice pushed many US corporations to announce sweeping commitments to diversity, equity, and inclusion (DEI). Corporations put their black squares up on Instagram. Feeling hopeful that some economic justice might be served, one of our advisors texted: "It's reparations time."

I vividly remember when the trickle of emails started, asking me to schedule a meeting.

"We have this initiative. . . ."

"We'd like to schedule a Zoom. . . ."

With all of us locked inside and meetings including my own suddenly unfolding online, I wish I'd been smart enough to own Zoom stock at that time.

By this point the Fearless Fund had been fundraising for more than two years. We had already raised more than $1 million and passed the rigorous diligence required to secure institutional investors—we were making a name for ourselves. By now I'd presented our fund to rooms of potential investors 150 to 200 times. Thousands of people knew who we were; we'd received some press. The fund had also secured several big-name partners; however, almost all the investors we'd pitched to had passed on the chance to support women-of-color entrepreneurs.

For years, Black entrepreneurs had been fighting for funding tooth and nail. We'd watched some of our white counterparts secure million-dollar rounds of funding with nothing more than an idea on the back of a napkin. We, on the other hand, were asked to "prove" ourselves ten times over.

But after the world witnessed the horror of George Floyd's death, something shifted.

A collective rage developed that appeared to ignite a long-overdue racial reckoning in our country. Conversations about systemic racism, inequities in business, and the lack of access to capital for Black and brown entrepreneurs took center stage in ways we hadn't seen before. Suddenly, people—especially investors—started paying attention, and not just in words, but in action. In the VC/PE world, a number of significant publications began documenting the inequities everyone already knew existed. A new reality began to take shape, and it was clear corporate America and the venture capital world were scrambling to be on the right side of history.

The trickle of emails turned into a steady stream, then a deluge.

For the first time, it felt like the doors that had been shut to Black entrepreneurs for so long were being kicked open. Money was flowing in ways I had never seen before, and for a moment, it seemed like things were finally going to be different. As it turned out, those first couple hundred meetings had been more than just pitches, they'd been building blocks. The fact we already had several big names on board helped us once massive numbers of calls began pouring in. We were the right people doing the right thing at the right time.

One day, I was grinding, hustling, trying to make my way, and the next, everybody was reaching out to me as some of the world's largest companies—Walmart, Microsoft, Verizon, Amazon, Meta, and more—made steadfast commitments to diversify their leadership ranks, engage in minority supplier programs, and pledge philanthropic commitments to end persistent racial gaps in wealth, education, health, and more. The Fearless Fund began taking meetings with investors who had previously ignored our emails. The shift to Zoom allowed us to secure investments without extensive travel, making it easier to obtain significant commitments. And for the first time, we weren't walking into rooms as underdogs—we were the ones being courted. Investment firms that had never even glanced in our direction were now actively seeking us out. Everyone wanted to align with our mission, to be seen as a champion of diversity, equity, and inclusion.

All of the calls went about the same way.

"We have a commitment," they'd begin, never mentioning George Floyd or the nation's history of racial injustice. "We understand the work you do and who some of your investors are. We would like to talk about what partnership might look like."

"I'm not sure I understand what you're saying," I'd reply, wanting them to state clearly exactly what they meant. "Are you calling to invest? What's happening here? I need clarity."

From childhood I'd been taught my time is precious. These people were taking it up and I needed to understand what they were talking about.

People in the same rooms that once closed their doors to us were now calling, asking how they could help. The same investors who'd once hesitated were suddenly ready to put their money where their values were, or rather, to put their money where their values had shifted. Suddenly corporate diversity initiatives started pledging real sums of money and rolling out multimillion-dollar funds dedicated to minority founders. Everyone wanted to be a part of the "solution" and announced their new Black-focused funds, women-focused funds, Latinx funds, accelerator programs, and pledges to close the racial wealth gap. More money meant that we could now fund more women-of-color entrepreneurs, invest in more ideas, and provide more pathways to success.

In addition to what was happening with the fund, I became the DEI "poster girl."

Corporations wanted my face on their corporate websites—I was front and center on Bank of America's home page for about six months. I was featured in national commercials, including in a nationwide ad for a Fortune 100 company that ran for about eighteen months. My phone began blowing up with friends, family members, and strangers saying, "We see you on TV." I was being tagged in social media posts: "I logged in to check my bank account and there is @ArianSimone on the home page." Brands were paying me $25,000 just to put up one social media post, and partnership deals around a half a million dollars were rolling in. I would sit there staring at my phone, looking at the contract details, and just shake my head in disbelief. I couldn't believe the kind of money companies were offering. My name began being mentioned in rooms I had never even stepped foot in. People were discussing our work, our impact, our influence—all without me having to say a word. For years I'd sown the seeds; now it was time for the harvest. I spoke on panels, sat on advisory boards, asked to help craft initiatives that—allegedly—would reshape the workplace into a more just and equitable space. It felt like we were making real progress—like finally, the world was shifting in a way that could create lasting impact.

My most memorable Zoom meeting took place with a gentleman from PayPal. I gave him my whole spiel about what the Fearless Fund was building, A to Z.

"What would it do for you if I cut you a ten-million-dollar check?" he asked, very directly. Basically, he had a problem, and we had the solution.

"Well, any one institution can only be at 20 percent of our fund," I responded, "so that would transform us into a fifty-million-dollar fund."

I was ready to accept the money right then, but since being a $50 million fund would mark a turning point for the Fearless Fund, I consulted with my partners before saying yes.

They wanted to stick with the original $5 million target.

"Are we serious right now?" I asked.

What is this?

"Let's just start with the five and then go from there."

"We're being given a gift here," I responded. "The floodgates are open. We don't know how long this opportunity's going to last!"

"We want to make sure we can manage it," they said.

WHAT??!!

"Do we not believe in ourselves?" I replied.

I thought my partners were making a gigantic mistake, so I reached out to our advisors for help; they're veterans in the space and have been in it for years.

"Do you know how long Black venture capitalists have been waiting to participate in the call you just had?" the advisors responded, feeling frustrated. They understood the challenges of fundraising as a Black founder, recognized this rare opportunity, and urged my partners to take advantage of it. More funds could be deployed to support Black and brown businesses!

"How dare you ever stop any capital from getting to our community!"

My partners were scared and wanted to make sure we could handle it. I believe in democratic leadership, so I agreed to raise funds to a level where everyone was comfortable. We settled upon $20 million but oversubscribed to $25.8 million.

Two things can be true at once:

We'd benefited from a great opportunity!

And . . .

We'd missed the moment.

It was a lesson to me. Fund I could easily have been $100 million or more—and if life offered me a do-over, I would go for it. After PayPal invested, they imposed a "key man policy" on me, the sole full-time partner, to ensure the millions they'd invested were going to someone who was fully committed. I couldn't work elsewhere; I let go of my other businesses.

Finally receiving the funding and acknowledgment we deserved felt like justice, or at least a piece of it. We had spent so many years trying to prove our fund was worthy of investment, and now, suddenly, people were seeing what we had always known to be true: Black and brown female entrepreneurs are brilliant, innovative, and more than deserving of the same opportunities as everyone else.

Though women of color represent 47 percent of entrepreneurs in the United States, as of 2024 they represented 57 percent of women taking steps to start a business.[1] Black women, in particular, are the fastest-growing entrepreneurial demographic. Prior to the Fearless Fund's existence, the average fundraise by an African American female was about $30,000. Only thirty-four Black female entrepreneurs had ever raised over $1 million for their business. The Fearless Fund came on the scene cutting seven-figure checks. We received 5 to 10 percent equity in each firm for our investment. When the next list of Black women who'd raised $1 million for their start-up was published, more than ninety companies were on the list—a lot of them funded by us. I don't make light of the Fearless Fund's achievements, but though $1 million may sound like a lot, it is an extremely small number in VC/PE. Individuals raise millions upon millions for some start-ups—and depending on your perspective, that reality could be extremely disturbing, no matter what round it's awarded in. In the context of raising VC funds, anything under $150 million is considered a micro fundraise. For example, a $50 million fund typically deploys 50 percent of its funds, or $25 million, as first-time investments into start-ups. They distribute the other 50 percent ($25 million) as follow-on investments in the start-ups that are doing well; they don't invest it into new companies. The average check size of an early-on investment by a $50 million fund is anywhere from $500,000 to $1 million. So, $25 million in initial checks means funding anywhere from 25 to 50 companies, maximum. The remaining $25 million allocation would be for follow-on checks. There are, of course, fees and other financial details. Bottom line: that $50 million is only reaching about 50 companies.

My team and I also knew that writing checks is only one part of the equation. Yes, capital is critical, but money alone isn't enough. Factors like knowledge, mentorship, and community allow businesses not just to exist but also to thrive. So when we started deploying those first checks from the Fearless Fund, I could feel that something monumental was happening. The mark we were making disrupted business as usual.

As all this was unfolding, the United States government began directing massive funding to a social safety net to help Americans weather the Covid pandemic. The Trump administration's Coronavirus Aid, Relief, and Economic Security (CARES) Act became the largest economic stimulus package in US history. It, along with the Biden administration's American Rescue Plan Act, helped countless working people and business owners weather the economic storm. Among other benefits, these historic pieces of legislation expanded the social safety net, providing food and housing assistance for parents and people who were unemployed. Though the stimulus wasn't perfect, it showcased what could happen when greater economic justice was extended to low-income people—and not just those living in inner cities but also those living in suburbs and rural communities.[2]

These measures also fueled a rapid recovery as employment surged and the economy grew far more quickly than it had after the Great Recession. The strengthening labor market also helped improve the pay of low-wage workers of all races, who are disproportionately Black and Hispanic. The subsequent economic recovery drove the Black unemployment rate to historic lows and helped create wage growth among many lower-wage workers, who are also more likely to be Black and Latino.

In other words, everybody benefited.

Major corporations such as Apple, Walmart, Target, Costco, and JPMorgan Chase began to publicly support diversity, equity, and inclusion (DEI) initiatives as essential to their corporate values, workplace culture, and bottom line. The conclusions of the McKinsey report were proving true: making money and building an inclusive workplace and economy aren't mutually exclusive, as many leaders had long told Black civil rights leaders and activists. Companies with diverse employees were performing better, demonstrating higher-quality decision making and greater innovation, and attracting employees who aligned with their values.[3] Bottom line: DEI programs and policies were not only helping companies fulfill their shareholder responsibilities; by treating all people fairly, they were building a more inclusive economy.

But not everyone felt comfortable with that.

We completed our fundraising and closed on Fund I in 2021. As I raised money for Fund II, the rise of the Black Lives Matter movement, the increasing visibility of minority entrepreneurs, corporate commitments to DEI efforts, the sudden surge of racial diversity in advertisements—some featuring me!—and the growing presence of people of color in high-profile industries, including Black media experts suddenly being called on to share their knowledge, seemed to contribute to some white people's anxiety. A number expressed displeasure with Black and brown people's progress. Others complained about activists' demands that we create greater racial and economic justice. The conversation about white people allegedly "losing jobs" grew louder. So did complaints about "the changing face of America," a phrase used to describe the reality that as our society becomes less white, greater numbers of Black and brown people enjoy the American Dream just as generations of people of European descent did.

Activists began naming the obvious elephants in the room that many had been too afraid to confront, mention, or address. They pointed out how the privilege of some white people, in particular, was acquired by oppressing other human beings. Some white people squirmed because their unsavory past (or even present) now was being clearly articulated for all to understand. Other people felt uncomfortable about the use of words like *privilege* and *racism*.

Clearly, the nation's economic and cultural narratives were no longer being solely written by those historically in power. To some this reality felt like a threat.

Through my own research, during various personal conversations, and from the media, as well as by participating in a wide variety of public appearances, I learned that much of the fear is not just about losing political control or the fading of white cultural dominance; it's also about losing the economic power that's been hoarded by a select few for centuries. Though it goes unspoken, some white people worry that minorities—specifically Black, Latino, Indigenous, and other marginalized groups—will gain economic influence and destabilize the existing order. In the minds of those who have profited from historical inequities, the idea that minority groups, especially Black people, could not only demand but also achieve economic independence and influence threatens the very ideas America was built upon, including the genocide of Native Americans and enslavement of Black people for economic gain. To them, economic independence for marginalized groups isn't just a matter of fairness; it's a matter of alarm.

For many people who hold these beliefs, the rising population of people of color is seen not as a sign of progress or a chance for greater diversity and growth, but as a direct threat to their power. When you have held power for so long, the thought of that power slipping away can create deep, unsettling fear. That fear is not just about politics or social change—it's about the fundamental belief that a shift in the demographic balance could undermine the structure of society as they know it. It's a fear that runs deep in the hearts and minds of those who believe in white supremacy, and it has shaped much of the history of this country. The desire to oppress people of color is rooted both in the desire to reap the benefits of economic exploitation and in the fear of losing power and control.

Contextualizing my present-day experience in the lessons from freedom-fighter icons in my family and home communities, it becomes clear that white people who believe in white supremacy are terrified of losing their perceived place at the top of the country. They fear their children won't inherit the same privileges as they did and that wealth that had been passed down through generations could eventually be redistributed to those historically shut out of opportunities. To call a spade a spade: white people who believe in white supremacy are fearful of the minority becoming the majority. Some of them also fear that once we become the majority, Black and brown people will treat them as poorly as they've treated us.

As these conversations unfolded, many powerful people worked their networks and back channels. Negative press and threats of boycotts by conservative organizations led several companies to take a pause. By 2022, firms that had pledged millions to Black founders quietly stopped talking about those initiatives. Published reports began showing that the actual dollars distributed to Black entrepreneurs were minimal compared to the grand promises made. Companies' bold statements about making systemic change faded into the background, replaced by excuses about economic downturns, shifting priorities, and the need to return to "business as usual."

Deepica Mutyla, Founder, Live Tinted
(South Asian woman)

As a female founder and a woman of color, going to raise capital is, hands down, one of the most difficult things I've ever had to do. All the stats and stuff are not in our favor, and it's a pretty defeating feeling going into these rooms and sharing your story and constantly hearing no.

So to hear that there is an entire fund dedicated to changing those stats and changing that percentage for women is incredible and inspiring, and it helps me, as a woman-of-color founder, feel supported and seen, and I think specifically with Fearless, it's one of the few funds that I've experienced that has not just talked the talk.

Fearless does truly walk the walk, and Arian is always trying to get me into the right rooms. Which is so important as a woman-of-color founder, when you're not necessarily always invited into those rooms. And she's also always trying to look for opportunities for us—paid opportunities, by the way—which, again, is unheard of. Any resource that Fearless is able to give you guys, always try to do.

The Playbook

The Cure for Global Economies

In January 2022, I had the opportunity to meet with the prime minister of Belize, His Excellency Johnny Briceño, a very kind head of state who was willing to listen to my findings on the struggles of women-of-color entrepreneurs in his country. The day prior we'd hosted a dinner with local women-of-color entrepreneurs to hear their pain points. Not surprisingly, access to capital was their number one challenge. Well-known Belizean entrepreneur Khadija Assale of Kaj Expressions, a jewelry designer, shared her frustrations with their credit system, where even if you pay off your credit card balance the day after you use it, you have to wait until the next month's cycle to access even a small line of credit again. This causes inventory delays and makes it almost impossible to scale and grow at all, much less at massive rates. But we didn't just meet with these women and hear their problems. After we documented these women's findings to present them to the prime minister, we surprised the women with grants to help support their growth. Luckily Khadija and her colleagues live in a country where the prime minister is sensitive to their needs. Many new programs for female entrepreneurs now exist in Belize.

Consider what happens when a promising entrepreneur in Brazil is denied funding simply because they are Black. They don't just lose out on an opportunity—their community does too. That business, which could have created jobs, generated wealth, and contributed to local economic growth, never gets off the ground. That lost potential isn't just a personal setback, it's an economic loss for the region and, ultimately, for the world. Now multiply that story by millions. Imagine the impact of countless businesses never being started, inventions never being developed, and markets never expanding because funding is hoarded by a privileged few. The world doesn't just lose individual success stories—it loses entire industries, solutions to pressing global issues, and the economic mobility that fuels long-term stability.

When economic stagnation takes hold in one region, people are often forced to look elsewhere for opportunities. And yet, the same countries that deny investment to these regions often treat migrants who leave their home for economic reasons as a problem rather than a symptom of a broken system. If capital were distributed more equitably, if businesses in emerging markets had the same access to funding as those in wealthy nations, we wouldn't see as much economic displacement. People wouldn't have to uproot their lives in search of survival because they would have the ability to thrive where they are.

We know that in the United States, Black and brown communities have been systematically denied access to capital for generations, with financial institutions creating a cycle where Black wealth cannot accumulate at the same rate as white wealth. The result? Black businesses are underfunded, Black homeowners face higher mortgage rates, and Black communities remain economically vulnerable. Now zoom out and consider the global stage. The same forces that keep Black communities in the United States economically disadvantaged are at play in African, Caribbean, and Latin American nations. The banks that deny loans to Black business owners in America are often the same ones setting the financial policies that keep African economies from flourishing. There's a reason Black entrepreneurs globally face the same struggle for funding—and it's not just about location, it's about race. The global financial system wasn't designed to support Black wealth, whether in Detroit or Dakar, Atlanta or Accra. And that means addressing these disparities requires more than just local solutions—it demands a rethinking of how the entire economic system operates.

If we want to close the racial wealth gap in the United States, we need to look at how capital flows globally. We need to recognize that financial institutions that disadvantage Black Americans are part of the same structures that underdevelop the Global South. And if we truly want to support Black economic empowerment, we need to push for reforms not just at home, but across the world. So how do we move from a world where financial exclusion is the norm to one where access to capital is truly equitable?

The first step is changing how we think about economies. Too often, we focus on local solutions without recognizing the larger forces at play. Governments, investors, and financial institutions need to stop treating economic disparity as isolated incidents and start seeing the bigger picture. This means:

1. Investing in Black and brown entrepreneurs globally. Venture capital, private equity, and banking institutions need to actively fund businesses led by people of color—not as charity, but as smart economic policy. These businesses are engines of growth that benefit everyone.

2. Rethinking economic aid. Instead of loans that trap countries in cycles of debt, we need models of economic support that empower nations to build self-sufficient industries. Wealthy nations should be funding innovation, education, and infrastructure globally, not hoarding resources while expecting economic stability.

3. Holding financial institutions accountable. Banks and investment firms must be transparent about who they fund, where their money goes, and how their policies contribute to inequality. Change won't happen unless these institutions are forced to confront their role in global economic disparities.

Most important, we need to shift our mindset. Economic justice isn't just about numbers on a spreadsheet; it's about human lives. It's about ensuring that someone born in Lagos has the same shot at success as someone born in London. That a Black entrepreneur in the United States has the same funding opportunities as their white counterpart. We cannot afford to see financial exclusion as just a local issue; it is a global problem. Malcolm X was way ahead of his time, seeing during the 1960s that it requires global solutions.

In today's world, which is more connected through technology than ever, the sooner we recognize this fact, the sooner we can start building an economy that works for everyone. Just as America needs to pick up where Dr. King left off, the global movement with all its interconnectedness needs to pick up where Malcolm X left off.

Solutions were already in motion decades ago and it's up to us to pick up the ball, race down the field, and score.

Chapter 9

The African Queen

Section 1981's history and purpose demonstrate that it is a remedial statute meant to ensure and equalize Black citizens' economic market access. The long history of private, remedial grantmaking is consistent with this purpose and necessary to rid the United States of the vestiges of "badges and incidents" of slavery that the 13th Amendment meant to purge from the market. Plaintiff's efforts to weaponize the very provision that was enacted to address the economic inequities that persist from slavery and the Black Codes, and more modern-day discrimination, is wholly misguided. The effects of years of systemic anti-Black discrimination persist across many sectors of American society. Private efforts to remediate such "manifest imbalances," such as the grantmaking here, should be upheld as lawful under § 1981.

—Lawyers' Committee for Civil Rights Under Law, Leadership Conference on Civil and Human Rights, National Action Network, National Association for the Advancement of Colored People ("NAACP"), National Urban League, National Coalition on Black Civic Participation, and LatinoJustice PRLDEF, brief of amicus curiae in *American Alliance for Equal Rights v. Fearless Fund Management, LLC* in support of the Fearless Fund

Back in 2021, I hosted my friends His Imperial Highness (HIH) Prince Yoel Makonnen and Her Imperial Highness (HIH) Princess Ariana Makonnen in Atlanta, Georgia. Prince Makonnen is the great-grandson of Emperor Haile Selassie I, the last ruling emperor of Ethiopia, the only nation on the African continent never colonized by the European colonial powers: the British, Dutch, French, Germans, Italians, Portuguese, and Spanish. Ethiopia is the cradle of civilization, home to the oldest human beings archaeologists have ever discovered. In part because of its strategic location in the Horn of Africa—and sharing boundary lines with Djibouti, Eritrea, and Somalia, all of which border the strategic Gulf of Aden or the Red Sea—one nation or another is always trying to gain control of it.

As a person who was raised to appreciate Africa's greatness, I wanted my peer group in Atlanta to learn more about African royalty. So often in the United States, where there are no kings and queens, our nation's experience of royal families is limited to the highly publicized British monarchy. But much royalty exists among Africa's fifty-four countries, many of whom are home to multiple ethnic groups—anywhere between twenty and more than two hundred, depending on the country. Many of these ethnicities have royal families; the most well-known tend to come from the larger ethnic tribes. Out of all of the nations with multiple lines of royalty, only Morocco, Lesotho, and Eswatini continue to be sovereign ruled. Since the end of colonialism, most have shifted to governmental approaches to leadership. That said, even when African royal families are not sovereign rulers, they retain influence within their tribal group and over tribal lands. They are acknowledged and celebrated, and their traditions and lines of succession are upheld. In many places governments protect royal tribal lands, write both the rulers and the lands into their constitutions, and involve traditional leaders in resolving disputes.

Prince Makonnen's royal family descends from the House of Solomon, the same Solomonic dynasty that originates from King Solomon—yes, the one in the Bible—who was at one time the wealthiest man in the world. The Makonnen family's recorded lineage dates back thousands of years—far longer than the British monarchy. I wanted to expose my friends to this history and tradition. The crowd was receptive and intrigued.

Fast-forward to the spring of 2022. I took a "bucket list" trip to Egypt to see the newly restored Avenue of the Sphinxes shortly after it was opened to the public. As I always do when I visit the continent, I clothed myself in large African gowns, dresses, and elaborate head wraps embodying our rich culture. During the trip I toured the pyramids throughout Cairo and Luxor. I saw the mummies of many kings and queens. I'd seen them in movies and on television; I'd seen them in books with hieroglyph images. Seeing them in person was completely different. The drawings in books left me with the impression that they had one tuft of hair. In person, I could see they had full manes of hair that looked just like mine. Walking around Egypt, I could also gain a sense of these rulers' skin color, which looked a lot more like mine than that of the actress Elizabeth Taylor, who played Cleopatra in the movies back in the day.

One queen whose story impressed me was Queen Tiye. We hear about Nefertiti, Nefertari, and Cleopatra in the commercial media, but Queen Tiye was the first queen recorded on official Egyptian documents. A global leader, she negotiated with many other heads of state—unheard of for a woman during that era. Queen Tiye bore many children. Her son Akhenaten later ascended to king and she became his advisor. He is the king who married Nefertiti. I remember standing over Queen Tiye's sarcophagus with such admiration as she lay in all her glory and beauty—yes, she remained pretty, though she was thousands of years old, her skin walnut brown and hair curly. Though the mainstream media often portrays ancient Egyptians as racially ambiguous or perhaps Arab in appearance, in reality the Arab invasion didn't occur until six hundred years after the death of Christ. Ancient Nubia was populated and led by dark-complexioned human beings.

I left Egypt feeling extremely empowered and very motivated to do more work on the continent to give back to Africa in a meaningful way, commensurate with what I'd learned through my travels. After searching the internet and finding nothing that inspired me, I called my sorority sister Heidi Stampley, who also happens to be a Ghanaian princess and visits the continent many times a year, for advice on how to give back.

"My sister Sabrina married a man from the Ivory Coast, Ghislain Dadie," she told me. "They are building schools in the Ivory Coast."

I called Sabrina right away.

"Our mission at ProSeed Foundation involves building schools to help eradicate poverty," she told me. "Agriculture is big business in Africa. If children don't receive an education by the time they're eleven, they are forced to work in the fields and have very little chance at upward mobility." Sabrina went on to explain that the small group of children able to attend school in one community often crossed a dangerous river to get to their classes. "Depending on the river currents, these children are literally risking their lives to get a good education."

"You had me at eradicating poverty," I responded. "How do I partner with you to build a school?"

Understanding the importance of economic justice, it didn't take much to convince me this was a great opportunity to invest in and create new futures for children. Sabrina and her husband synced my team and me with their foundation, and within three weeks we were breaking ground on what would become the Arian Simone Fearless Leadership Academy. I scheduled a trip to attend the ribbon cutting about six months later, in the fall of 2022.

In the meantime, I learned about the state of education in Africa, where four out of five ten-year-olds struggle with literacy. In 2030, the African continent will be home to 42 percent of the world's youth. Countries like Ghana and Rwanda are investing heavily in education—secondary schooling and IT training—and preparing their children for the global economy.

About a month before my trip to the Ivory Coast, I had a phone meeting with Marita, my chief of staff.

"Arian, when you arrive in Africa, a stylist will meet you," she told me.

"No one in Africa will need to touch my hair," I replied. "I'm going with my hair naturally curly."

"Oh, no, it's for your wardrobe," she responded.

"I'm wearing jeans and a polo shirt with the school logo on it."

"Oh gosh, you don't know!"

"Know what?"

"Arian, they are crowning you queen!"

"I think you're confused," I responded. "I'm traveling to Côte d'Ivoire for a ribbon-cutting ceremony," using the Ivory Coast's name in French.

We laughed and ended the call.

Surely this is an honorary title. I'll be given a plaque or some other type of award.

About a week before my departure, Ghislain sent a formal email detailing the importance of the event, stating that it would be "all hands on deck"—the governor, the senators, the mayor, and other elected officials would all be in attendance for my coronation. The letter included a quote from the village chief describing how they'd prayed to God for a queen and God had answered their prayer. In that moment I realized Marita wasn't kidding. The Ivorians were so grateful to me for creating a new school that they'd chosen to crown me the queen of Dawa. There was a note at the bottom of the email that read, "The Queen will address her people."

I was stunned!

"This is not like a Disney queen," Ghislain told me by phone. "We take this seriously and you are already a big deal in Côte d'Ivoire. Many people are awaiting your arrival!"

When we hung up, I was astonished and self-conscious. Since

most royal titles came through bloodline or marriage, I wondered how HIH Prince Makonnen, whose royal bloodline dates back over three thousand years, would react. I felt relieved when Princess Makonnen told me that her husband was excited for me. Afterward I watched other African coronations online, noting that parts of the ceremony seemed to be conducted in secret, and prepared my body, soul, and spirit for the experience. I wanted to fully embody my impending queendom. I also had to learn government protocol overnight—how and in what order of rank to address people. There were cultural traditions to study, tribal practices, traditions of the heritage. I was very excited my territory's official religion would be Christian, my faith.

I arrived in Abidjan, the economic capital of the Ivory Coast, in October 2022. I was accompanied by Fearless team members Christina and Brianna, Trell, our videographer, and Pastor Danielle Murphy, my church's first lady.

As I stepped off the plane onto the jet bridge, my phone received an Apple News alert—an article titled "5 Royal Tribes Who Were Captured in the Slave Trade." My mind began racing with a thousand thoughts.

I am a descendant of the slave trade, and the ancestors are calling me home to claim my rightful place.

We were greeted by security officers wearing black suits and white shirts. When I turned the corner to baggage claim, I began to understand why: a huge crowd of people and paparazzi waited to greet me, their new queen. People handed me flowers of all types, including the beautiful bird-of-paradise plants that grow throughout the region.

I was blown away as we drove through the city. Prosperous, cosmopolitan, and the largest French speaking city in West Africa, Abidjan is known as the Paris of the West. Everywhere I went, people knew who I was. And everywhere I went, I was greeted with flowers. In that moment I certainly received my flowers while I was living, as the saying goes.

I arrived at my hotel expecting to take the next day slowly; the journey had taken twenty hours.

"I will be having a spa day," I said.

"Not exactly," they replied. "Makeup will arrive at six a.m., the head wrap lady will arrive at six thirty, and you will appear on national television at eight a.m."

"Oh, okay!" I had tons of questions but decided to surrender to the once-in-a-lifetime experience.

Just flow with the trip and truly embrace it.

The next several days unfolded wonderfully, from media appearances, to city tours, to dinners. The next day we flew to the village of Dawa, where I was checked into a resort and greeted with dancers, an elaborately decorated dinner on the beach, and more flowers. They served the best-tasting lobster I'd ever had in my life. I learned there is nothing like a lobster from the Ivory Coast.

The night before my coronation, Ghislain prepared me for what I should expect.

"It is an incredible honor to be welcomed into this village," he told me. "The coronation should be honored as sacred moment for you and these beautiful people."

I nodded.

"Tomorrow, you have a culture briefing," he told me.

"Huh?"

"Once you are queen, the people will have requests," he stated.

"Uhh, what requests?"

"As soon as you become queen, you have influence."

"Okay."

"You are going to say, 'I will take this back to my counsel and we will review it.'"

I nodded.

"Don't go in trying to answer and make things happen in the moment."

"Got it!"

"There is also a moment in the ceremony where they can accept you or reject you," he continued.

"Accept me or reject me, what do you mean?!" I responded. "I came all this way, and this was their idea, not mine. Now you're telling me—"

"Arian, they take this very seriously," he interrupted. "After the ceremonial kola nut presentation, they have this option. You are becoming their people."

"I am their people—I am Black and they are Black."

"Arian, it doesn't work like that."

"Okay," I said. All I could think of was the scene from *Game of Thrones* where Daenerys Targaryen had to eat a raw stallion heart. "At least they're not asking me to do that; I'll surrender."

Lord, you are in charge!

The next afternoon we drove to Dawa, and I took in the beautiful fields. As we pulled up, I saw two long rows of children wearing orange T-shirts, chanting, "Fearless! Fearless! Fearless!" I couldn't hold back the happy tears now running down my face.

When I got out of the car, a beautiful teenage girl handed me flowers. I walked down an aisle surrounded on both sides by children chanting. I sat on the dais for the next five hours as both the school opening ceremony and the coronation took place. One of the chiefs poured libations; a kola nut ceremony representing friendship and hospitality was held; two sermons were preached, one by the French-speaking pastor, the other by Pastor Danielle Murphy, who brought the house down. There were addresses by chiefs and government officials, then I took some questions. Let's just say that my team and I made some bloopers.

Before the coronation, the village women took me to the back to change me into the traditional clothing royalty wears for the ceremony. When I returned to the dais, the village elders stated they would anoint and revere me as their new queen, crowning me Queen Wa. (I later learned *wa* means "the blessing" in Kroumen, one of the languages spoken by the Kroumen people of Liberia and the Ivory

Coast.) The crowd cheered and I struggled to hold back my tears. It was so overwhelming to recognize that little ol' me—a girl from Detroit who just wanted to own her own business and make her family proud—was now an African queen. I held it together long enough to finish my initial address, speaking in English, with Ghislain translating. I felt high off adrenaline. It was a moment that I will never forget. I promised myself I'd brush up on the French I'd learned way back as a student at Grosse Pointe, so the villagers could understand when I spoke in the future.

Many people made an offering before making their petition—handcrafted clothing, hand-carved wooden art, a crate full of fresh lobster, even a live ram. After I listened to people's requests, I'd say, "I will take this back to my counsel, and we will review it." It felt a bit awkward at first, but I knew it was the cultural protocol. Before long, I got the hang of things and recited it expertly, as the villagers opened their hearts and souls to me in ways I hadn't expected.

There was one request I knew I wanted to grant in the moment. The women living in Dawa have an entrepreneurial coop. They needed a business grant to buy taxis, a machine that grinds and breaks down cassava root, and other materials so they could scale—and I knew exactly what to do! In that moment, I realized being queen was not just a title but a responsibility. I had the opportunity to use my influence and experience working with the government and other supporting entities, organizations, and so on to help improve people's welfare. This was similar to the Fearless Fund's work in the United States, but I was on the other side of the planet.

What an awesome blessing and responsibility!

I was so incredibly overwhelmed; I knew I was experiencing my spiritual destiny.

Afterward I had the opportunity to speak with one of the chief leaders of Dawa.

"We prayed to God to tell us who our queen would be, and he said it was going to be YOU."

Now, I knew that God would open up doors that would defy my

expectations, but I certainly hadn't expected anyone to literally put me on a throne.

Not long after the ceremony, I heard some people saying, "She is our savior!" I was definitely not comfortable, though I understood what they meant and how excited they were about the possibilities for the school. We were escorted to the beach by a second-line band. Though a feast awaited us, I asked for a moment to myself just to walk the shore and feel the water run over my feet. I wanted to be alone with God to thank Him for using me in such a mighty way. I felt the cool water rush over my feet and dug my toes into the Ivorian sand. I imagined my ancestors living in this setting and acknowledged what a miracle it was that I was standing in the place they'd left. I couldn't even begin to take in what they might have been thinking about me.

After a while, I heard some giggles behind me, and I turned to see a crowd of children watching. I moved to hug them but could tell from how they reacted that they'd been instructed not to touch me. I asked and received approval for the instructions to be relaxed because I love children so much; these were my village's babies.

About a month after returning to Atlanta, we awarded the women's business co-op a $10,000 grant.

Shortly thereafter, I heard a staff member speaking French on Zoom with a group of men.

"Ooh, this is interesting! What's going on?" I asked.

"This is your pitch committee," he responded.

"What pitch committee? I was only brainstorming aloud," I said, recalling a conversation I had on my previous trip to Cote d'Ivoire, when I thought I was just tossing ideas around.

In that moment the weight of my responsibility sank in and almost took my breath away. In my role as queen, when I speak, some people interpret my words as an order.

Oh, Arian, you need to be extremely careful—even more thoughtful than usual—when you speak!

I stumbled into the fact that a new international pitch committee had been preparing to kick off its first competition in Abidjan. I discovered the Ivory Coast was paving the way for itself to become a digital hub in West Africa to drive social and economic growth, including start-ups led by young people and women, and focusing on equity and economic development. As I learned more about the economic situation, I realized this type of transformation is occurring all across the planet as young people demand inclusion and challenge governments that have allowed traditional colonial powers to exploit their resources while leaving the nation economically dependent and their people impoverished. In Sudan, youth played a pivotal role in ousting its longtime ruler Omar al-Bashir and have otherwise been a powerful force for political change. With over 60 percent of the population under thirty, Sudan exemplifies how young Africans are shaping their nations politically and socially.

In May 2023 I returned to Dawa to inaugurate the school's expansion. We had built housing for teachers, a house for the pastor, and a playground for the children, and provided Wi-Fi for the whole village. It was my first time coming back as queen, and I was greeted with an even larger welcome than during the previous trip; there were people everywhere. They even secured a military escort for the ride from the airport to Dawa—it was unreal! My duties as queen kicked in immediately. The villagers and leaders were waiting with requests for me to begin taking back to the government leaders for action.

I could see how thrilled these entrepreneurs were to have equipment to develop and sustain their cassava business and to further enhance their financial well-being. Acknowledging how excited the villagers were about expanding and innovating their small businesses, on this trip we were also hosting a Fearless Fund pitch competition in Abidjan. I knew how much Fearless Fund entrepreneurs in the United States benefited from this kind of healthy competition.

During the school expansion ceremony, there was a moment where the entire audience said, "Wow!" and became very excited. I was curious what this "Wow!" was for, but the moment passed quickly. Before I could even ask, the program moved on. I soon discovered I'd been gifted with land in the village. I was floored! I discovered it was beachfront property with an amazing view of the ocean and shoreline—imagine palm trees and greenery even more spectacular than in the Caribbean. When I arrived at the land, I dropped to my knees in tears and began praising God.

"No, no!" said the chief. Apparently, I was unknowingly violating some sort of royal protocol by being so emotional in public—for having what appeared to be a breakdown. "C'est bon! C'est bon!" he said, lifting me up by my arm, telling me something good was happening to me, and suggesting I need not cry.

"C'est bon!" I said in response, nodding and assuring him that I was okay.

During those moments I recalled the prayer I'd been saying for months: "God, increase my belief." I truly believed in the promise that God gives us house and cities, but I never could've imagined this. This was living proof that when you do God's work, you receive His promises.

Ghislain, my chief of protocol, asked if I could have a few minutes to reflect.

"But she's the queen," the chief responded. "People are still watching her."

Though I was only accompanied by five or six people, to the chief it was too many for me to be having what he viewed as a breakdown, though I was just awestruck.

I walked along the clean sand and allowed the ocean to wash over my feet.

What?!

I struggled to make sense of what I was experiencing.

I have the deed but no taxes? Is this my spiritual inheritance?

I stood in pure gratitude, beginning to understand that being queen wasn't going to be just a title but a divine opportunity and responsibility to provide the village with genuine leadership, wisdom, and strategy to improve people's welfare and stability. Later I described my experience on social media:

> TESTIMONY—I stood in tears of gratitude as the water from the ocean covered my feet on the shore. I was standing on land that was gifted to me as Queen, beautiful beachfront/oceanfront land that I now own!
>
> In many African traditions when the title of Queen is bestowed you receive land. During my ceremony this trip when it was presented everyone said wow, I fought hard to hold the tears back cause I knew I had to make an address but once the ceremony was over I had a moment to walk to the shore and I released them.
>
> I always knew God gives houses and cities we didn't build and land we didn't labor for but I never could've imagined this!
>
> This is living proof that when you do God's work you receive God's promises!
>
> I am living in a generational blessing.
>
> Joshua 24:13
>
> I gave you a land on which you had not labored and cities that you had not built
>
> #ToGodBeTheGlory #blessed #grateful
>
> #GenerationalBlessings

Shortly after I returned to the United States, Missouri and Joshua Calhoun's descendants held our annual family reunion in Macon. We conducted DNA testing as a family. I'd been tested before, so I already knew that plenty of African nations populate my DNA map. I have been quite intrigued to learn that 35 percent of my DNA is East African and 35 percent is West African. Most African Americans' genes lean heavily toward West Africa due to the transatlantic slave trade.

"Do you know we have Ivorian in us?" a cousin asked, aware of the title recently bestowed upon me. The moment really resonated with me. Not long ago I'd been concerned about being bestowed the position of queen in a way that did not involve either marriage or bloodline, but now I was discovering I have both Ivorian and Ghanaian blood. It felt like proof that I was being called back to take my rightful place.

"Wow . . . ," I responded, not having remembered or connected the dots.

On the final night of our gathering, our family strode around the hotel wearing the year's theme colors, white and gold, as we prepared for our traditional banquet. Many of us had befriended the receptionist, Porsha, a friendly and very talented café-au-lait-colored sister who sported a warm Southern personality and a curly weave.

"Ever since you all stepped in here, you have reminded me of royalty," she told a group of us. "But now that you are dressed in this white and gold, you truly look like royalty."

One of my relatives told her I'd been crowned an African queen.

"I heard you're a queen; I love African queens!" she exclaimed to me. "I am all about the warrior queens: Queen Nzinga, Yaa Asantewaa, Amina, and everyone."

To my surprise, Porsha then recounted how, throughout history, many African queens demonstrated tremendous leadership on issues involving justice. From Nigeria's Amina, queen of Zaria, who controlled trade routes and was an accomplished military strategist;[1] to Queen Nzinga, who led a thirty-year war to counter Portugal's expanding slave trade;[2] to Ghana's Yaa Asantewaa, who led a war against the occupying British, African queens demonstrated tremendous heroism in the fight against colonial rule.

"Baby, I know what you've read in the books. I am African royalty, but I'm not a warrior queen," I responded. "You won't find me leading any army or out on anybody's battlefield."

Porsha frowned and a serious look fell over her face.

"Ma'am, not to offend you, but all battles are not physical," she stated. "Get ready."

Though in the moment I froze, I had no idea that less than six weeks later I would find myself in the biggest legal battle of my life.

Chapter 10

What's a War Without Soldiers?

The Alliance's unprecedented interpretation of § 1981 would pervert the statute's text, history, and purpose, turning it against the very class of persons it was designed to protect. The district court did not abuse its discretion in refusing the Alliance's request for extraordinary relief.

Enjoining the Grant Program would violate the First Amendment per se, and even if strict scrutiny applies, Appellant cannot satisfy its burden of identifying a compelling interest that would justify the injunction it seeks. Prohibiting the Foundation from using its private funds to help the same underserved group that Section 1981 was enacted to protect would not serve any government interest. The Court should reject Appellant's effort to interfere with the Foundation's charitable grants and affirm the District Court's decision protecting the First Amendment right of foundations and nonprofits to express their missions and ideals through philanthropy.

Conclusion

This Court should affirm the District Court's decision to protect the First Amendment right of an organization to express a message or point of view through grantmaking, and reject Plaintiff's attempt to use Section 1981 to prevent Fearless from expressing a mission that is consistent with its history and purpose.

—Gibson Dunn, amicus brief filed in *American Alliance for Equal Rights v. Fearless Fund Management, LLC* in support of the Fearless Fund

DECEMBER 12, 2023

While we waited on a date for appeals court, there were deadlines for briefs that we had to meet. In addition, people and organizations by the drove had filed petitions and amicus briefs on our behalf, the prestigious Ford Foundation among them. Our attorneys at Gibson Dunn, one of the leading law firms in the world, filed a brief supporting the Fearless Fund with the court.

The Council on Foundations, a nonprofit membership organization that helps grantmaking foundations and corporations with their philanthropic work, filed an amicus brief on our behalf. Even Letitia James, the attorney general for the state of New York, and nineteen additional attorneys general from across the nation weighed in, requesting that the case be dismissed.

Given all the madness swirling around me, it meant the world to receive so much support from these powerful organizations. The briefs fortified me, strengthened my fight, and helped me endure what had become an overwhelming workload and spending so much time isolated from so many people I love. I tried my best to compartmentalize the case so it didn't take over my life any more than it already had.

As I awaited the court date for our preliminary-injunction appeal, scheduled for January 31, 2024, I found myself not only fighting the preliminary injunction but also preparing for what could be a major court case against the Fearless Fund and Fearless Foundation. I was incredulous the fund was being sued for reverse discrimination. The nation's racial climate had shifted so quickly it almost gave me whiplash.

How did this happen?

I'm a very peaceful person; I could hardly believe this life was my own.

Then, adding insult to injury, each morning, people I knew—Fearless Fund investors and donors, members of my church, my alma mater, my sorority, the board of directors of the Steve Madden company (of which I'm a member), and key business contacts—began forwarding me crazy and slanderous emails sent from a protected, encrypted, anonymous email address.

Increasing numbers of racist people and white supremacists commented on my social media. Many of our investors began received threatening and often anti-DEI messages from conservatives and politicians, warning them not to fund our work. By God's grace, everyone who received the messages forwarded them to me, so I'd know right away what was going on and what rumors were being spread about me.

Then, shockingly, in addition to the case itself, I experienced unexpected challenges from within my inner circle. This was certainly painful. I'm certainly not one to question God, but I do know that when God elevates you, He will do anything and everything necessary to clear out the people you need to leave behind. It's not personal, but that doesn't mean that it's painless.

And yet, even grounded in my spiritual framework and understanding, this multipronged assault wasn't easy to wake up to. I felt defenseless. Half the time, I wanted to cry. Day after day, my stomach balled up in knots.

Coming from a large extended family and community, being cut off felt very isolating. But with the Fearless Fund facing such a vicious attack, I had to consider the worst aspects of humanity; it wasn't easy. "Get very small very quickly," one of my closest friends advised me. "Your circle needs to get very small, very fast. Conserve your energy for the case. It could be the biggest fight of your life."

Contrasting the attacks, my phone also rang nonstop with offers of support—and among family members, friends, business colleagues, and acquaintances, I was getting about a thousand text messages a day. But the volume was too great to assimilate and everyone who was reaching out to me wasn't in a position to help me. Beyond that, I knew I'd best not allow others to attempt to do so. If I wasn't careful, I might take on some of their thoughts, which ran the gamut from my church family saying, "We're praying for you," to guys back in Detroit saying, "We'll handle it for you."

People can project their fears and concerns onto you—plus, energy is contagious. During a crisis, only spend time with the people who can solve your problem.

"To protect yourself from being deposed, your attorneys are going to tell you to stop texting and emailing," my friend advised me as the battle in my inner circle raged. To minimize my risk of legal exposure, I cut off communications with many people I love. This was incredibly painful. And my physical safety was also compromised. In addition to receiving random threatening messages and social media comments, private investigators, members of the press, and random people suddenly began breaching my personal space.

One afternoon, I was sitting on my porch when a white guy with a foreign accent rode up on a bicycle.

"Can I take a picture of your trees?" he asked.

"I'd appreciate it if you wouldn't."

He took pictures anyway. Later, my attorney and I reviewed the footage from my Ring security camera. Clearly, this man had been casing my house.

"You should move out," some people told me.

"These people aren't running me off my block or out of my home!" I exclaimed. Among many great lessons I had learned growing up in Detroit, street sense was one of them; I was always aware of my surroundings. That said, I was responsible for the health of the Fearless Fund. If anything happened to me, the fund's prospective backers might withdraw their support. I took steps to make sure I was physically safe, including but not limited to hiring an off-duty cop to watch my house.

Some of my other senses started tingling.

I had to be mindful of people in my space, what I said in public, conversations with seatmates on airplanes. Once after I got off a flight to Los Angeles, I heard a voice saying, "Arian Simone, tell me about the court case."

What?!

A reporter from TMZ had been waiting for me to arrive!

Who could be planted near me to listen to what I'm saying?

I couldn't risk something from everyday life being used out of context against me. I looked to the right and to the left, suspicious, wherever I went.

If there hadn't been so many things going on at once, I could have slowed down and strategized. I would have gone on walks and carved out time to be intentional in my practice of cleansing breaths, getting my nervous system in alignment, and engaging in other calming techniques to settle myself and clear out the fear. But so much was happening I couldn't keep up. So I just went into tunnel vision and put one foot in front of the other. I took whatever steps I needed to take to go through the process.

> And if there's another thing growing up in Detroit taught me, it's when you believe in something, you stand firm, fearless and free, and you don't back down.

It was also essential to keep the fund running properly. Even when business is operating as usual, most traditional venture capital firms do one thing at a time: they raise funds first before they invest. Once they've closed their fundraising round, they focus solely on the success of the companies in their portfolio. However, as part of our everyday activities, the Fearless Fund faced the challenge of fundraising and investing simultaneously. We did double duty because fundraising typically takes longer for women-of-color firms.

I spent days participating in investor meetings, portfolio company meetings, and staff meetings, and otherwise running the fund full-time, as well as meeting daily with our legal and communications teams. Nights, I read through the legal briefs, word by word, as my mother had, sending my feedback to the lawyers representing us. I never questioned that we'd be victorious, though I couldn't see exactly how at that moment. I knew the adversity would bring new opportunities for our business and imagined that with this newly elevated media exposure, more money would flow into the Fearless Fund, just as it had after George Floyd's murder. Boy, was I wrong. . . .

The Playbook

The Cure for Modeling Global Solutions

Both my work at the Fearless Fund and my work as an African queen are driven by a mission to advance global economic inclusion. I meet with presidents, dignitaries, and entrepreneurs all over the world, discussing economic justice, visiting business cooperatives and regional tech hubs, and participating in focus groups with businesspeople and pitch contests throughout the African Diaspora. I also perform research on economic justice. From London to various African countries, to Canada, to the Caribbean, and beyond, racial funding disparities are a worldwide issue. Racial economic inequities aren't confined to the United States.

The challenges are structural.

When European powers carved up Africa, the Caribbean, South America, and large parts of Asia, they didn't just take land; they also extracted wealth, controlled trade routes, and designed economies that benefited them at the expense of the people they colonized. Colonized people weren't allowed to own land, start banks, or accumulate wealth in ways they could pass down. Instead, their labor was used to fuel the colonizers' economies. When these nations finally gained independence, colonizers left them with broken financial infrastructures, exploitative trade agreements, and economies still dependent on the very systems that robbed them. Not to mention that even today, a number of African countries still pay a "colonial tax" to France in the billions per year, though they are so-called independent countries now.[1]

Countries rich in natural resources—gold, diamonds, oil, precious minerals, and fertile soil—remain poor because their economic systems were built to benefit their colonizers, not to benefit them. International financial institutions like the International Monetary Fund and World Bank, largely controlled by Western nations, continue to impose restrictive economic policies that prioritize debt repayment over economic development. Former colonies are still playing by rules they never wrote, and the consequences are clear in the disparities we see today.

Even in countries that pride themselves on being "developed" and "progressive," as the United States and many European nations do, systemic biases are baked into every level of the financial industry. Banks, venture capital firms, and loan officers make decisions based on patterns they claim are neutral but that were shaped by centuries of exclusion. When Black entrepreneurs are denied loans at higher rates, when Black homeowners are given higher mortgage interest rates than their white counterparts with the same credit score, when Black-led businesses receive only a fraction of venture capital funding, as is the case, these aren't isolated incidents, they're symptoms of a much larger problem.

Though they are becoming louder and louder, the claims about Black people undermining white people's opportunities don't add up, whether in the United States, Europe, or elsewhere around the world. As I raise funds and disburse awards to founders, participate in focus groups with businesspeople, and meet with and learn about the Black economic experience and entrepreneurship globally, I've learned that the oppressive economic conditions that African Americans face also plague Black and brown founders and entrepreneurs all over the world. In Brazil, for instance, where 55 percent of the population is Black, venture capitalists only award 0.5 percent of their funding to Black residents of their nation. In South Africa, where 80 percent of the population is Black, Black people receive only 1 percent of venture capital / private equity funding. In France,

Germany, and Canada, where the Black populations are 4, 1, and 4 percent respectively, less than 0.5 percent of such dollars are allocated to Black people. I was stunned to discover that economic injustice and oppression that happens to Black people anywhere happens to Black people everywhere.

All the news isn't dismal, though.

I remember being awestruck when I first read that in Ghana, women found a greater proportion of their nation's businesses than women anywhere else globally. More than 46 percent of Ghanaian women found companies. I am also impressed by promising signs like the continent's youthful population; the rise of tech hubs in Nairobi, Lagos, and other African cities; and the abundant minerals and natural resources. That's not to mention the groundbreaking technology and innovations African tech founders are launching.

Silicon Valley is yesterday's news. The future of venture capital lies in Africa.

Chapter 11

Back in Court

The American Alliance for Equal Rights is not entitled to a preliminary injunction prohibiting Fearless Foundation from implementing its grant program for Black women entrepreneurs because . . . U.S.C. § 1981 cannot be read to prohibit charitable grants to historically excluded populations. Indeed, § 1981 should not be interpreted to apply to charitable giving at all. This argument, although rejected by the district court, provides an alternative ground for affirming the decision of the district court, and makes it unnecessary to consider, as the district court did, whether, if the statute prohibits such grants, the Foundation nevertheless would have a First Amendment right to make them.

First, § 1981 cannot be read to prohibit these grants because at the time of its enactment, similar grant programs were widespread and there is no indication that anyone believed those grant programs were put in jeopardy by this statute. This country has a long and well-established tradition of charitable giving to provide economic assistance to racial and ethnic communities that have historically been excluded from full participation in the marketplace. These grant programs trace their origins to the founding era, and became more formal, and more prevalent, during the nineteenth century, when philanthropic organizations and charitable trusts were formed under state laws to endow schools and hospitals and to provide financial assistance and other forms of aid to African Americans and new immigrants—populations often barred from established institutions. This tradition continued through the twentieth century and continues to this day to remedy the persistent effects of historic discrimination. It would be contrary to the purpose of § 1981, which was passed to enforce the Thirteenth Amendment, to interpret it to prohibit relief aimed at the very population that Congress was trying to help in the statute.

—Brief of amici curiae filed by the states of New York, Colorado, Connecticut, Delaware, Hawai'i, Illinois, Maine, Maryland, Massachusetts, Minnesota, Nevada, New Jersey, Oregon, Pennsylvania, Rhode Island, Vermont, Washington, and Wisconsin, and the District of Columbia, in *American Alliance for Equal Rights v. Fearless Fund Management, LLC* in support of the Fearless Fund

JANUARY 31, 2024

A lottery had already taken place to determine which judges would hear our case at the Eleventh Circuit US Court of Appeals. Our three-judge panel consisted of two Trump appointees and one judge appointed by President Obama. Considering that our original court proceedings had taken place in Atlanta, I was disappointed to learn the appeals case would take place in Miami. When I arrived a day before the trial, I found myself in Ron DeSantis land, a conservative state where the governor demonstrated a political combativeness similar to Donald Trump's, taking on what DeSantis labeled "woke" ideology.[1] DeSantis also opposed government lockdowns, protective face masks, and vaccine mandates very early during the Covid-19 pandemic, long before vaccines were available, when people were still being hospitalized and even dying of the disease. And between disparaging undocumented immigrants and challenging diverse curricula in schools, he'd stoked bigotry and racism by tapping into some white Floridians' fears of the so-called browning of America.[2]

Over the past several years, Florida had transformed into a place where the shifting tides of the judiciary were evident, and the consequences of the 2016 presidential election felt real. Though Governor DeSantis hadn't become the Republican Party's presidential nominee as he'd hoped, his campaign and landslide gubernatorial win in 2022 helped swing Florida from politically purple to scarlet red.

As we prepared to argue our case, the state's political climate loomed over us.

I added conservative-leaning attorney Dennis Ellis of Ellis George Cipollone to our legal team. Not only would he provide a more diverse set of perspectives for this stage of our fight, Dennis and Ben had worked together on cases before. I felt good about this move.

It is essential to know when to ask for help.

Here I was back in the Sunshine State, my collegiate stomping grounds, a region that had helped shape me into the powerful businesswoman I'd become. The weight of the moment pressed upon the shoulders of my cream-colored pantsuit as I stepped out of the car and addressed the crowd of supporters gathered out front. My mother had flown in from Detroit to support me. The Fearless Fund staff and the board of the Fearless Foundation stood by me as well. Unfortunately, my father couldn't make it this time.

Our team then strode into the modern concrete building with ocean-blue windows.

> I knew my purpose and conviction together were my antidote to fear.

Once in the courtroom, I was overcome with the reality that three individuals held the power to decide the fate of millions as they ruled in this preliminary injunction. The Republican judges were seated on either side of the Democratic judge, and we sat before them bracing for what was to come. Would the panel overturn Judge Thrash's ruling? Would they confirm it? Either way, our team knew the judges probably wouldn't rule in person. Given the situation's complexity, they'd need to discuss the proceedings afterward among themselves.

Edward Blum's attorney stood, buttoned his gray suit jacket, and purposefully approached the bench.

"Gilbert Dickey on behalf of appellant, American Alliance for Equal Rights," the opposing counsel began his argument. "Section 1981 prohibits racial discrimination in contracting. The Supreme Court has already said that this prohibition doesn't violate the First Amendment. It regulates conduct, not speech. Even if a discriminator intends to send some message through their racial discrimination, it's still conduct, not speech. This case calls for a mine-run application of Section 1981, not some strange exception. After all, Fearless boasts that it engages in racial discrimination. . . ."[3]

Starting their arguments this way—saying I was a "discriminator," essentially calling me a racist—was a more aggressive approach than they'd undertaken earlier. Moments later, they stated I was running an operation equivalent to a WHITES ONLY sign outside a restaurant during segregation.

Oh, no, they didn't!

Though in everyday conversation the term "racist" is used in a wide variety of ways, often to describe people who behave in a bigoted manner, the definition I ascribe to is that being racist generally requires both harboring prejudice and being in a position of institutional power. Though one Black individual can certainly discriminate against other human beings in this country, African Americans don't possess the societal authority or national domination required to be racist. Second, the WHITES ONLY signs that were displayed by a wide variety of institutions and were so prevalent throughout the Jim Crow South were intended both to oppress African American people and to offer white people better conditions than those offered to Blacks. There was and is nothing racist or oppressive going on at the Fearless Fund or the Fearless Foundation. In fact, we were being sued for attempting to address an imbalance and close the gap between the capital white and Black women founders have access to. We were not trying to give Black women founders some advantage that white founders don't already enjoy (the way those WHITES ONLY signs were intended to advantage white people over Black people). Still, the plaintiff's counsel kept asking in various ways, "What message is it sending? What message is it sending?"

Our counsel countered sharply, presenting our arguments with the same conviction that had brought us this far. They laid out our case, emphasizing the legality and necessity of our actions. As our lawyers presented each point, the plaintiffs objected. Our team countered with facts and precedents that supported our position.

I carefully watched the three judges' reactions, which varied from nodding to remaining expressionless, with all three asking tough questions of both sides. Their queries seemed very unbiased and even-handed. No one on our team could make out which way any of them were leaning. That day we left court not knowing the fate of the program.

Once we were outside, a television reporter approached me.

"When you heard the opposing counsel use the phrase that this is the equivalent of 'Whites Only' signs, what was going through your mind?" she asked.

"What was going through my mind at that moment as the founder of the foundation is we are reaching a disparity. I'm not sure what disparity he's addressing with the mission of his argument, but we are reaching a disparity. Unfortunately, Black women have received very little funding. Black and Brown women receive about 0.39 percent of venture capital funding. We are, again, meeting a disparity and a need. And honestly, I actually have the same belief as the plaintiff. I would like a world where race-based things do not matter. But guess what? We live in America, and there are disparities that have to be solved for us to get to that point."

The grant program was not only lawful but also necessary for the communities it served.

Oddly, the very next day, some guy who resides in a correctional facility in South Carolina filed a case saying the Fearless Fund had negatively affected his rights.

Are you kidding me?!

We still don't know who this man is, or who involved him, or under what pretenses, but he filed, and it was quickly dismissed.

We awaited the ruling, praying and holding on to hope.

I knew the Eleventh Circuit appeals court usually announced its rulings around the three-month mark, suggesting we wouldn't know anything before the end of March. Until then, we had to keep up the community's awareness and momentum. With Black people's economic freedom on the line, I urged anyone and everyone to sound the alarm as we awaited the judges' decision.

That March, I stood on the steps of the US Supreme Court alongside two hundred women participating in a pro-DEI rally and protest organized by Melanie Campbell, president and CEO of the National Coalition on Black Civic Participation. Melanie also convenes the Black Women's Roundtable, where some of the nation's most influential leaders from across many disciplines strategize and organize to expand and strengthen the power of Black women's leadership and move a Black-woman-focused policy agenda forward. I also made the rounds on Capitol Hill, discussing the case and its implications with members of Congress in both the House of Representatives and the Senate. I felt honored when Congresswoman Maxine Waters invited me to participate in her Women's History Month roundtable at the US Capitol. But when the month ended, the court hadn't issued a decision.

To counter the unbelievable levels of stress while awaiting the outcome, I took a sabbatical—an intentional period of rest and rejuvenation. I am big on wellness centers, which are now an industry, though I gained my exposure to Deepak Chopra, Marianne Williamson, and other people in the wellness space when I was a child.

I decided to go to Miraval, a spa in Arizona, to engage in self-care that would embolden and prepare me—mind, body, and soul—for the battle to come.

In addition to all sorts of delicious body treatments, one of the first things I signed up for was a stress reduction class. I knew I would need every skill, tool, and strategy available to stand lion-hearted in the face of the attacks coming at me—I was determined both to remain fearless and to win.

"Our thoughts create our feelings, so if we want to feel more peaceful, relaxed, and at ease, we need to begin with our thoughts," the handout from our instructor, Michelle, read. A clinical counselor and holistic life coach, Michelle taught a number of different strategies to manage worry and stress.

Spiritual disciplines and years of coaching and personal development work had familiarized me with the power of affirmations and practicing gratitude, focusing on aspects of life I am thankful for. I knew the human brain naturally turns its attention to any potential risks and negativity it perceives in any environment. A survival mechanism, this tendency allowed our ancestors to evade predators and other threats. It remains active today—often overly active—though most of us don't experience the threat to life and limb many of our forebears did. Michelle reminded us that just because our brain has a thought, it doesn't mean that thought is true. By intentionally focusing on things we appreciate, we can ward off fear and negativity, get our brain out of doom-and-gloom loops, and imagine new possibilities to create for our future. I thought about the discipline I'd need to continue to practice in order to courageously create the results I wanted in the midst of an onslaught. I also considered how the human tendency to imagine disaster scenarios might fuel some of the demographic anxiety white people who believe in their supremacy have, as they assume bad things will happen to them as America's population becomes more Black and brown.

Michelle also led us through a conversation about neuroplasticity, the brain's ability to rewire itself over and over during the course of a person's lifetime, allowing humans to grow, develop, and evolve, even during old age. The reality that we can reinvent ourselves wasn't new to me. In my own life, I'd done it several times already, and I was in the process of reinventing myself again. If I could do it, I knew other people could too.

> Doing novel things increases our capacity to take on the responsibilities and demands associated with our new elevated place. I also find the unknown exciting.

At Miraval, I intentionally selected activities I'd never tried before—like beekeeping.

"You're coming at a very unique time," the instructor, Noel, told me. "We're in the middle of a super bloom; it's magical!"

Where typically, a honeycomb is orange and yellow, when I looked inside this honeycomb it was also turquoise, purple, and pink. When the pollen is different colors, the honeycomb is different colors and the honey especially flavorful. I reflected upon how this principle applies to human beings as well. More diverse people create a wider range of beautiful and delectable possibilities.

I also took a course called Manifesting Joy and Harmony, where we learned about the power of spring.

"You really want to come alive during this season," the instructor, Richard, told us. "Otherwise, you will lie dormant for the year."

In that moment I thought about my garden, my mother's garden, and my friend Kellie's garden.

"You've gotta come over now," Kellie would implore me almost every spring.

"Why now?"

"So we don't miss the date," she'd say. "If we don't plant now, the garden's not gonna bloom until next year."

Essentially my instructor was telling me the same thing.

"April Fool's Day used to be the start of the new year," he explained. "Many people set their fitness and nutritional goals in January, when the body is supposed to be hibernating. They don't fail because they lack discipline; the sun isn't out long enough to give them sufficient energy. It's no wonder their plans fall apart by the end of the month and 80 percent of them fail by March."

I realized I needed to plant the ideas I'd been incubating soon.

After leaving Miraval, I traveled to San Diego, where my cousin Joy runs Avocado House, a no-phone, no-television resort designed for you to listen deeply to your inner child. Joy teaches that we arrive on earth with wisdom and need to unlearn some of the information we've subsequently adopted and believe we know. This frees us to engage in the practice of deliberate creation.

When I arrived, I was in the thick of the court case and I needed to stay unplugged.

"We are going to expand the universe," she told me as we embarked upon the process of deliberate creation.

"Okay, cousin," I replied, knowing Joy is always helping people break through their obstacles and limit lines to create audacious new possibilities for themselves.

I journaled; I meditated; I enjoyed salt baths.

Most important, I dreamed big and boldly. I saw the Fearless Fund impacting women globally and Black and brown women changing the world to create racial economic justice and freedom.

April and even May went by without the Eleventh Circuit Court issuing a decision. In the meantime, speculation about whether President Biden would run again during the 2024 presidential campaign rose to a fever pitch.

The political climate also became quite aggressive as white supremacists, white nationalists, Christian nationalists, and anti-government groups moved into the mainstream, bringing anti-Black and anti-immigrant language with them. Increasingly, Black and brown people found themselves bearing the brunt of new portrayals of age-old threats to white people's economic security, both in the United States as well as around the world. Misinformation and disinformation campaigns to sow discord among and discourage Black Americans from voting increased.[4] Many Black women online came under vicious attacks. The FBI reported a rise in hate crimes, with Black people being the most targeted group in both online and offline spaces.[5] Nationwide, we also witnessed educators, courses, and books about African American history or racism increasingly be censored, whitewashed, and/or banned. With the outbreak of terrorism and war in the Middle East, violence against Arabs, Jews, and Muslims also began to rise.[6]

BACK IN COURT

One evening, I was scrolling through Netflix and typed in "African queens," looking for something inspirational to watch. Ironically, one of the movies the algorithm served me was *On the Basis of Sex,* a biopic on the life and cases of the second female Supreme Court justice, Ruth Bader Ginsburg. Now deceased, Justice Ginsburg was affectionately known as RBG. I watched.

"The court should never be influenced by the weather of the day, but inevitably they will be influenced by the climate of the era," the actor playing Harvard professor and constitutional scholar Paul Freund said during the film.

The comment took my breath away.

That's exactly what happened to me!

Had our case been heard post–George Floyd in 2020, when corporations were making significant reparative commitments to the Black community, I believed it highly likely the suit would have been dismissed immediately. However, given the 2023 Supreme Court ruling ending affirmative action in higher education, the climate in which our case was being tried couldn't have been more different. Just as I had once been the face of DEI, I now found myself embroiled in one of the defining lawsuits of the anti-DEI movement. I was experiencing firsthand how the era's climate—perhaps even more than the strict judgment of the law—was influencing the outcome of our case. How ironic: the exact same quote could describe the advancement of the movement for gender equality during an era when women were gaining rights *and* how Black women's rights were now being suppressed, as more judges issued rulings reflecting the current anti-DEI mood. The speed of the backlash was headspinning.

Chapter 12

Crowned for This

> Black women face disproportionate barriers—including racial discrimination—in accessing funding to grow their businesses. . . . The Alliance below never questioned the stark inequalities in access to funding—with only 0.13% of funds going to the 2% of small businesses owned by Black women. . . . These massive disparities far outstrip the minimum necessary for a valid remedial program. . . . The Foundation also satisfies the second requirement because its grant program does not "unnecessarily trammel" the interests of non-Black women who own small businesses. . . . Nor has the Alliance shown its members face an "absolute bar" to obtaining capital from other sources—99.87% of which goes to people other than Black women. The Foundation's modest grants don't limit the Alliance members' access to funding in any meaningful way and are instead "designed to break down old patterns of racial segregation and hierarchy" in a capital market that has "been traditionally closed" to Black women. And if the Alliance were to succeed in enjoining the Foundation's grants, the likely result is that the program would end—a contraction, rather than an expansion, of available funds.
>
> —Gibson Dunn, amicus brief filed in *American Alliance for Equal Rights v. Fearless Fund Management, LLC* in support of the Fearless Fund

JUNE 2024

Eager to expand my universe, create my future, and continue my adventure into the new season unfolding around me, I traveled to Ghana invited on an official visit as Queen of Dawa, a guest of President Nana Akufo-Addo.

This was the first time I'd spent any meaningful interval in this nation of thirty-five million people so intimately linked to the human trafficking of Black Africans to the Americas. About 15 percent of African Americans trace their genes to Ghana, one of the first African nations to gain its independence from European colonialism. In 1957, Kwame Nkrumah became the nation's president, which also sparked tremendous excitement in the civil rights movement in the United States. On this trip, I was particularly excited to learn more about the incredible 46 percent rate of entrepreneurship among Ghanaian women—the highest rate on the entire planet.

As my flight circled Accra, I could see the city's colorful buildings and billboards the closer we came to landing. When the plane touched down, the fact that many passengers cheered and clapped made me feel even more excited by the incredible opportunity to meet with President Akufo-Addo, who is known for igniting the Year of Return, inviting Africans, especially African Americans, back to the continent, in 2019. I looked forward to learning more about the nation's economic opportunities and tech scene, as well as meeting the Ghanaian people and touring the country.

> The unknown is exciting to me
> and full of new opportunities.
> Exploring it makes you more intrepid.

I'd been told many times that Ghanaians take very seriously the reality that many Black Americans' ancestors were stolen from their nation and are sensitive to giving African Americans a "welcome home" experience. In fact, media personality Steve Harvey always tells people to visit Ghana before other parts of Africa. Several friends had told me they'd participated in renaming ceremonies intended to indoctrinate them into the culture. I'd heard stories of their visits to the Cape Coast, home of the infamous slave castles, where millions of kidnapped Africans were held captive before being herded, shackled together, and packed into the bowels of slave ships for the inhumane months-long Middle Passage of the transatlantic slave trade that built the economic system we know as capitalism.

Though visiting the slave castles is part of many African Americans' return experience, I honestly wasn't sure how I felt about it. I've studied African history back to the 1100s, so I know Black life is much richer and more dynamic than the enslavement era. Throughout my life I have witnessed the empowering images of African empires and trade and royalty suppressed as slavery images are emphasized. Whether it's done consciously or unconsciously, I believe this reinforces Black oppression. Either way, I knew this was an important part of the experience and my understanding of myself, and emotionally prepared myself for the trip.

After being in Ghana for several days, I took an in-country domestic flight to Tamale, a region in the north of the nation, to check out the supply-chain system of a company we were considering adding to our portfolio. Once we landed, I turned on my phone, expecting a few messages from my team back at the office. Notifications began sounding at an alarming rate. When I saw the first one, my stomach dropped.

CNN: Federal appeals court blocks Fearless Fund from issuing grants to only Black women

The US Court of Appeals for the 11th Circuit has blocked a Black-owned venture capitalist firm from awarding grants exclusively to Black women entrepreneurs.

In an opinion released Monday, the judges ruled that the Fearless Fund's Fearless Strivers Grant Contest is "substantially likely to violate" the provisions of Title 42 of the US

> Code, which ensures equal rights under the law and prohibits the use of race when awarding and enforcing contracts.
>
> In the ruling, the appellate court ordered a federal court in Georgia to enter a preliminary injunction blocking the fund from closing its grant application process while the case continues to be litigated.[1]

I audibly gasped.

The Eleventh Circuit panel had ruled against our appeal in a 2–1 decision, with the two Trump-appointed judges siding with the plaintiffs and the Obama-appointed judge recognizing the validity and importance of the Fearless Fund's work. After making six grants to Black women that year totaling about $120,000, our Fearless Strivers program was now effectively stalled with just one $20,000 grant left unawarded. On the one hand I felt victorious; on the other, I felt furious.

How dare they undermine the dreams and futures of both women of color and entire Black and brown communities? Thank goodness we got the other grants out!

What were the odds I'd receive the news that the Fearless Fund's work is basically a violation of United States law while in Ghana, the ancestral home of so many African American descendants of slaves?

The irony of my geographic location wasn't lost on me.

I am receiving this news while literally in the place where my ancestors were captured and forced into slavery. Those shackles still exist; they just look different today. I cannot believe the evil that's still taking place.

Still reeling as I was greeted by my hosts at the end of the Jetway and ushered through customs, I shared my distress. To my surprise, they already knew what was going on and weren't surprised by American foolishness.

As we exited the building, I was briefly distracted by both the heat, which made me want to wilt, and the tapestry of humanity: a sea of brown faces of varying hues; families laughing, hugging, and reuniting; limo drivers holding signs and looking to connect with their clients; some people dressed in Western clothing, others in safari shirts and slacks, and still others in colorful traditional African garb and head wraps.

A security detail was assigned to me. As my hosts led me to a black Toyota Land Cruiser and we engaged in pleasantries, I furiously started WhatsApp-ing people. I hadn't been doing anything harmful or disturbing anyone when the Fearless Fund and my work were attacked.

I have to address what just took place. I have to go on social media.

I was in such a daze, I barely remember my first glimpses of Tamale. For much of the time, I had my head down, typing a statement into my phone that I could post on social media. We briefly returned to Accra, along the way stopping at the Christie Brown shop, where Ghanaian fashion designer Aisha Ayensu gifted me a very regal gold-and-rose-colored dress. Though people were attempting to oppress me back home, when I looked in the mirror after the dress was put on me, I saw pure African royalty. The song "Firm Foundation (He Won't)" by Chandler Moore and Cody Carnes played in the background.

I've still got joy in chaos
I've got peace that makes no sense
So I won't be going under
I'm not held by my own strength[2]

My eyes welled up and my tears flowed.

We then continued the ride to the UNESCO World Heritage Site Cape Coast Castle. Feeling wary of what I would see, I got out of the car slowly. Chills ran across my body as I stepped through the doors and was led on a tour. I took off my shoes and walked barefoot, reverently traversed the ground on which my ancestors had cried, screamed, bled, vomited, urinated, given birth, and released their bowels. I walked on their DNA, feeling their presence. When I looked out the infamous Door of No Return, the sight of the huge waves and roiling surf—not to mention the fact that tens of thousands of enslaved Africans passed through its doors during the transatlantic slave trade[3]—not only took my breath away, it made me want to drop to my knees and weep. Afterward I went outside and stood and recorded a video for social media:

> I am in Ghana on an invited visit as an African Ivorian queen and guest of the president, representing the Fearless Fund and Foundation. I received the breaking news while here that the US Eleventh Circuit appeals court ruled that our Fearless Strivers Grant program for Black women violates the law.
>
> I am standing at Cape Coast, where our ancestors were taken, beaten, caged, shackled, raped, whipped, separated from their families, stripped of their languages, and taken to foreign lands of South America and the Caribbean. Then they arrived in America and worked for free for hundreds of years in the most brutal conditions while building the great nation of the United States of America.
>
> Slavery was abolished and the government promised a small reconciliation of forty acres and a mule that was never received. Congress passed the Civil Rights Act in 1866, where section 1981 was specifically written to ensure Black people had the fair right to enter contracts with whites. It was meant to deliver some economic freedom. The disgusting irony is that this is the same law the plaintiffs and judges are claiming we are in violation of.
>
> This is beyond business, this is about humanity!
>
> Just because something is legal doesn't mean it is right. There was a time when slavery was legal, but it was not right.
>
> If what I'm doing to fund Black and brown women can be called illegal, then it's not what I'm doing that needs to be changed, it's the law that needs to be changed!
>
> To be clear, I do not believe that Fearless violates the Civil Rights Act of 1866. This venture capital fund and foundation were built to aid the job creation for which that original law was made.

The United States sets the tone for the rest of the world and I believe we need new protections and policy.

Our ask is for an immediate executive order by the president of the United States to protect DEI and the right to fund specific marginalized groups if and when racial disparities exist. And for Congress to issue the Fearless Freedom Economic Civil Rights Act, an act that supports this executive order.

I am the dream and the hope of the slave!

My security detail and I then returned to the vehicle and drove down the road to another UNESCO World Heritage Site, Elmina Castle. Built in 1482 as a trading post used by first the Portuguese and then the Dutch as they trafficked in gold and African human beings, Elmina Castle is the oldest building built by Europeans in sub-Saharan Africa.[4] I walked with the same mix of dread and respect I had when I toured Cape Coast Castle.

Afterward, as we prepared to leave, we encountered a group of French-speaking Black people.

"Queen!" one of them shouted before identifying their group as from Côte d'Ivoire.

"Welcome home," another greeted me.

"How do these people know who you are? They're from Côte d'Ivoire," the tour guide said.

I wept.

Though the Eleventh Circuit court's ruling stated our Fearless Strivers program was "substantially likely to violate" section 1981 of the 1866 Civil Rights Act and "substantially unlikely to enjoy First Amendment protection," it still puzzles me how funding anyone of color could be a civil rights violation. That sounds like an oxymoron in and of itself. In fact, the dissent written by the Obama judge compared the lawsuit to the act of "flopping," when soccer players dramatically feign injury in order to pretend they've been fouled.[5]

At that moment, I knew that I had to think strategically. The impact of this case could extend far beyond our fund—it could set a dangerous precedent for other organizations working to support marginalized communities. I knew that my mission was to protect the money we had raised and were deploying as well as protect the community. This wasn't just about our case, it was about the broader implications for racial and gender justice and equity. Though the amount of money we awarded capable Black women founders was minuscule within the VC world, the fact we were doing it at all clearly generated a tsunami for those who wanted to hoard the sector, its money, and its high socioeconomic status for themselves.

Someone was using us to achieve their larger political agenda. Still, we weren't through fighting. We were prepared to explore every legal avenue, valiantly taking every possible step to keep pushing forward.

> I am the CEO of my own future.

And I *definitely* wasn't backing down right after visiting a slave castle.

As the inaugural defendant in a case that would have tremendous consequences internationally, I knew that I had to get the word out. That evening, I went live on CNN's *NewsNight with Abby Phillip,* from Ghana. Knowing the show would be running live and that CNN has an international audience, I knew I could express myself for all the world to hear without being edited. This would be my moment to summon the president of the United States of America.

"This ruling is part of a long legal journey that the Fearless Fund has been on. What's your reaction to the Eleventh Circuit making this sweeping claim that your fund violates equal protection laws?" the acclaimed CNN host asked me.

"My reaction to the ruling is I'm very disturbed by this," I responded. "Reason why: saying that we are violating the law of Section 1981 of the Civil Rights Act of 1866, which is a law that was clearly put in place so Black people would have the opportunity at economic freedom by giving them the legal right to enter into contracts."

Abby described how laws intended to protect Black people were now being weaponized. I informed her viewers that Black females are the fastest growing entrepreneurial demographic and that women of color are the most founded but the least funded by venture capitalists.

"Right now, I would like to send a signal and a request to the president of the United States of America to issue an executive order to stand up for DEI. We deserve the right to protect the ability to fund marginalized communities and demographics that can be shown that there are clearly racial disparities. We deserve that. We need an executive order; we need a signal to the DOJ. We cannot just rely on the court systems right now; we need elected officials to state and show and put pen to paper to say where they stand on the issue of diversity, equity, and inclusion. Diversity is one of the values this country prides itself on, and we would like to see our elected officials who we have in office take a stand."

I made many television appearances, including another CNN segment the very next day. I tried my best to shout louder than ever to remind people of the power of their vote. We were seeing how choices made at the ballot box don't just affect policies, they determine who sits in judgment over us, who decides our fate, and whether our battles end in victory or defeat. Though Republican judges had ruled against us and the Democratic judge had voted for us, I knew this wasn't an issue of Republicans versus Democrats. Overwhelmingly, Republicans favor capitalism and business owners, and many have supported the Fearless Fund's work. We were clearly caught up in a movement to dismantle DEI, an agenda not all Republicans support. On social media I posted nonstop about the need to sound the alarm, asking anyone who saw my posts to please share them. Some tagged their reposts @potus or @vp.

Though Black Americans struggled to wrap their head around what was taking place, Black Africans understood what was happening right away. Several Ghanaian officials basically told me, "You can move here if you want to. It's not illegal to fund Black women's businesses here—funding Black people isn't a crime." I chose to stay in Ghana longer; I not only felt safe, I also felt protected.

My spirit also knew I needed to rest and to immerse myself in nature to help me return undaunted to all the foolishness back home. I traveled by car to the Safari Valley eco park, a luxury resort. As I watched herds of zebra with their black and white stripes, the packs of wildebeest, the beautiful peacock that kept strutting around my villa, which had a wood interior handcrafted by local artists, I felt my nervous system regulate. I turned my face toward the sun as I enjoyed the outdoor shower and spent hours soaking in the huge indoor wooden tub and splashing around my private pool. At one with the earth as I relaxed in nature's paradise—and particularly safe because I knew I was home and in good hands among African people—I fortified myself for my return to the United States. If these people attacking the Fearless Fund thought they could back me down, they were wrong.

Given my legacy, I was not going to shrink or be silent when Black economic justice was on the line.

Since standing for justice, leveraging the power of unity, and confronting uncomfortable truths can reduce fear, the ruling made me feel even more determined than I already was.

The Playbook

The Cure for Global Economic Inclusion

Imagine a world where the next Silicon Valley isn't in California but in Nairobi, where the new Wall Street isn't in New York but in Johannesburg. In these bustling urban centers, young innovators are launching start-ups that harness digital technology to solve local problems. They are developing fintech solutions that expand access to financial services, creating renewable energy ventures that address the continent's pressing environmental challenges, and building tech hubs that nurture creativity and collaboration. This generation is perfectly positioned to drive the next wave of global economic transformation. It's absolutely thrilling to be involved.

But it's not only Africa that stands at the crossroads of economic change. Across the globe, we see similar patterns of untapped potential in minority populations in countries like Germany, France, Brazil, and beyond. In these nations, vibrant communities rich in culture, talent, and entrepreneurial spirit are often grossly underserved by investment capital. Whether it's the immigrant populations in France, the Afro-Brazilian communities in Brazil, or the minority groups in Germany, these demographic groups often face systemic barriers to financial support and business opportunities. The challenge here is not a lack of talent or ideas; it's a lack of access to the capital that can help turn those ideas into businesses and economic success stories. The global economic equity movement must not focus only on African markets but also broaden its scope to overlooked communities worldwide that can help drive the next wave of global economic transformation. The Middle East has become a major player in the venture capital space, investing at large scale into venture funds and start-ups worldwide.

Some of America's prominent start-up accelerators, like Y

Combinator, see the advantage of global expansion. Though headquartered in the United States, they have a presence and engagement in Nigeria, Germany, Russia, India, Israel, and more. They have seen a significant increase in start-ups in emerging markets like South Asia, Latin America, and Africa.

Venture capital must play a crucial role in supporting this global ecosystem of untapped potential by driving inclusive growth. With our strategic focus on both domestic and international markets, the Fearless Fund is working to bridge the gap by investing in underrepresented women-of-color entrepreneurs globally. With 80 percent of its capital currently being deployed in the United States and 20 percent internationally, the Fearless Fund has already invested millions into American, African, Australian, Canadian, and Caribbean founders and their businesses. We plan to expand this investment as we diversify our portfolio. Particularly in regions where systemic barriers to capital are often overlooked, our goal is to support more minority-led start-ups across the globe. In addition to direct capital investment, the Fearless Foundation has been distributing grants and support to male and female entrepreneurs in Botswana, Ghana, Côte d'Ivoire, Belize, and beyond, and expanding efforts to reach other regions with large minority populations. These populations' economic promise cannot be denied, and the fund must nurture their growth with the same strategic focus that we apply in the United States. Our foundation has a partnership with Trace Academia, educating and mentoring over one million diasporan entrepreneurs, aiming to unlock the full potential of minority communities around the world and foster a new generation of global leaders who can help transform the world's economy.

Especially in fast-growing urban centers, the global demographic dividend presents remarkable opportunities for urban areas. Rapid urban growth is attracting substantial investments in infrastructure, real estate, and technology, laying the groundwork for long-term economic development. These cities will become hubs of innovation, attracting venture capital and enabling talented entrepreneurs to flourish. By investing in urban infrastructure and supporting the entrepreneurial spirit in these regions, we are fostering the growth of vibrant economies that can drive global prosperity.

The immense potential of these minority-led businesses and emerging markets across the globe calls for immediate action from investors and policymakers. By focusing on regions like Africa, Brazil, and Europe, and investing in the youth and minority entrepreneurs leading the charge, we not only help to create opportunities in these local economies but lay the groundwork for a more balanced, diverse, and innovative global economy. These countries and their growing consumer bases, coupled with their progress in digital transformation and infrastructure development, are quickly becoming attractive destinations for international investment. By embracing their potential, we contribute to the reshaping of a global economic system that values diversity and inclusivity.

The transformation unfolding across Africa, Latin America, and Europe represents not only an opportunity for these regions but also a call to action for the global community. By investing in these diverse minority populations, we fuel the creation of a new economic ecosystem—one that values equity, sustainability, and innovation. This shift represents a powerful opportunity to move toward a more just and equitable global economy, where underrepresented communities can drive growth and innovation on a global scale.

Here are three action steps you can take *now* to foster more global economic inclusion.

1. **Explore.** Explore the world and gain a deeper understanding of the planet beyond the community/country

you're most familiar with. Experience different cultures, economies, and systems firsthand. Traveling fosters connections and can inspire innovative solutions to local and global issues.

2. **Petition.** Petition governments and national assemblies to advocate for economic opportunities, policies, and reforms for the global community.
3. **Protest.** Unite, speak out, and demand accountability from governments, corporations, and institutions with the power to effect change. Protests amplify marginalized voices, challenge harmful policies, and push for reforms that promote fair wages, access to resources, and equal opportunities for all. Be a part of a collective movement that shifts public opinion, pressures policymakers, and sparks conversations on a global scale.

Chapter 13

Sound the Alarm

> The district court correctly held that the First Amendment bars the Alliance from weaponizing § 1981 to alter the content of the Fearless Foundation's speech. The Foundation is an expressive association that exists to support and promote women of color entrepreneurs—a group that has been historically discriminated against in the commercial marketplace. The Foundation carries out its mission by providing charitable grants and mentorship to Black women and then publicizing these efforts to bring attention to its cause—activities at the heart of the First Amendment's protection. Although the Alliance attempts to recast this quintessential speech activity as garden-variety "contracting" subject to § 1981, the district court saw the claim for what it is—an attempt to use an antidiscrimination law to "impermissibly 'modify the content of [the Foundation's] expression.'" . . . The First Amendment forbids this ideological interference.
>
> —Gibson Dunn, brief in *American Alliance for Equal Rights v. Fearless Fund Management, LLC* in support of the Fearless Fund

JUNE 20, 2024

At the White House weekly press briefing, a correspondent asked a question of the Biden administration's press secretary, Karine Jean-Pierre, the first Black person to serve as press secretary to an American president.

"The Fearless Fund, a venture capital fund that awards grants to Black-women-owned businesses, had a federal appeals court suspend their grant program due to the claim that it discriminates against white business owners," the outlet's White House reporter, Gerren Keith Gaynor, began. "The cofounder is calling on President Biden to take executive action to, quote, 'safeguard DEI initiatives and funding for marginalized groups.' Given these concerns, does the White House believe it is doing all it can to protect diversity, equity, and inclusion?"[1]

"I'm going to be really mindful here," Jean-Pierre responded. "It's an ongoing litigation, so I don't want to speak to it directly."

As an experienced communications professional, I recognized the canned crisis communications answer she had been prepped to provide, whether it was valid or not. Now I needed to figure out the plan for what we'd do next. It was essential that we think beyond this moment. Beyond this administration. Beyond the headlines and the performative commitments that often amounted to nothing more than PR plays. We had to create something sustainable, something that couldn't be undone with the stroke of a pen or the shifting of a political agenda. We couldn't afford to be on defense anymore. We had to go on offense. We had to stop reacting to crises and start building an infrastructure that protected and empowered us no matter what came next. That meant pivoting our strategy, rethinking how we positioned ourselves, and most important, fighting for policy changes that would outlive any single presidency or corporate initiative.

One thing became crystal clear: we could no longer operate under the assumption that companies or large institutions would always do what was "right." We couldn't allow our success to hinge on whether investing in minority-owned businesses was trending or not. We needed laws, not promises. Policies, not pledges. We had to push for systemic change that ensured Black and brown people weren't just another short-lived moment of focus but an undeniable force in the economy.

That meant getting aggressive about legislative action. It meant working with policymakers, lobbying for changes that would cement economic opportunities for minority entrepreneurs, and ensuring that equity in business wasn't just a choice—it was a requirement. It meant entering rooms where we weren't always welcome, having conversations that would make people uncomfortable, and demanding a level of accountability that some had hoped we wouldn't pursue.

We would pursue it.

It wasn't enough to simply fight back when funding for minority-owned businesses and historically disadvantaged communities was threatened. Undaunted, I knew that we had to be proactive. We had to create a structure that protected these investments long after the public spotlight moved elsewhere. So our first step was to get President Biden's attention. I pursued efforts to get the Biden administration to issue an executive order.

We didn't just want a conversation or a roundtable discussion. We needed concrete action. We needed something that would last. I wasn't going to wait for President Biden, though many of his staff supported an EO on our behalf. I hired lawyers to draft "The Executive Order on the Right to Invest in Historically Disadvantaged Individuals and Businesses, Low-Income Communities, Empowerment Zones, and Opportunity Zones." This way, if the White House decided to act, they'd already have a white paper to refer to so we could move quickly. If we could get this order passed before the new administration took power, we could at least have it on record. We knew we might face a new administration wanting to undo the work of the previous one, but for me it was about at least establishing a paper trail.

We weren't just asking for more investments in these communities—we were demanding a fundamental shift in how the investments were structured. We wanted a commitment, in writing, that would make it clear: Historically disadvantaged businesses and communities aren't charity cases or occasional talking points for election seasons. They are essential pillars of the American economy, and their growth and sustainability should be treated as a national priority.

The executive order laid out bold recommendations: increased investments in low-income communities, and acknowledgment of the ongoing, systemic barriers that kept these communities locked out of funding opportunities. We wanted more than just words about diversity and inclusion—we wanted action that ensured historically marginalized groups had real and sustainable access to capital. This would require federal agencies and community-based organizations to work together in a way they never had before. We pushed for stronger, more intentional partnerships between government agencies and the organizations on the ground that truly understood these communities. The people doing the work—those building businesses, supporting entrepreneurs, and driving innovation in low-income areas—needed to be in the room when decisions were made. Unfortunately, the Biden administration didn't get the EO over the line; however, we didn't let that stop us. We went to work evaluating local, state, and federal DEI legislation and had the Greenberg Traurig law firm craft model laws for various levels of government.

On Juneteenth, I participated in the White House's ceremony with Ben Crump, the first time I'd been on the White House lawn as a guest. (I'd been there on a class trip during my youth and probably with my parents.) Ben and I sat a few rows back on an angle catty-corner from President Biden. At one point we got up from our seats to go say hello. I wanted to introduce myself and I was determined to make my petition in person. That's when I knew there was a serious issue with his health—he stood there looking so frozen.

"Is this even a good idea?" Ben asked, looking at me.

"Yeah, we're going to turn around," I said. "I think we just need to go back to our seats. This isn't going to go over well."

(Before long, George Clooney and others began going public about President Biden's health.)

Though it was clear the Biden administration would have liked nothing better than for me to be quiet, I felt undeterred; I continued to post on social media.

"Y'all, I need you to help me sound the alarm. We need to make sure everyone's aware what's at stake."

Whenever I asked people to send out the SOS, the posts would go viral. One post had five hundred thousand views and nine thousand shares. It didn't take long until I received a telephone call.

"We understand you'd like President Biden to issue an executive order to protect DEI," the caller stated. "We'd like to ask you to lay off that request right now. It isn't a good time given the reelection and the current political climate."

"I will be petitioning the president, whoever he or she is," I responded sharply. "He just happens to be the president now. What's happening is crazy and I don't get caught up in party lines—I sit on the side of right regardless of who is in office."

They were like, "Can somebody calm her down?" and I was like, "Can somebody solve my problem?!"

Once it was clear that I wouldn't surrender, they didn't resist. They were in the middle of an election, and I had been getting a lot of press. The last thing they wanted was to poke the bear, so to speak. They couldn't risk having me on the five o'clock news complaining that the Biden administration was trying to sit me down. The person who called me played nice at that point. The private sector shouldn't even have been dealing with this. We needed lawmakers to get the laws together; this wasn't my role as a citizen.

One of the unexpected blessings of the court case was having the opportunity to meet with so many incredible people. Among many ways we moved from defense to offense was when the Clinton Global Initiative reached out.

I received a letter from President Bill Clinton, former secretary of state Hillary Rodham Clinton, and their author / scholar / Clinton Global Initiative board member daughter, Chelsea Clinton, expressing their support for the Fearless Fund and inviting me to speak at the Clinton Global Initiative annual meeting in September 2024. I also knew they would advise and guide me on strategy for our legislative efforts. Not only did the Clintons want me to speak, they also wanted me to keynote!

Until now, through one experience or another, everyone in my immediate family had met President Clinton except me. Photos of members of my family with him are prominently displayed around our family home. When these opportunities took place, I was a teenager and had other priorities. Later, I regretted missing those historic moments. Now I'd have the opportunity.

I was excited during the days leading up to the event, which would be held at the New York Hilton on Avenue of the Americas between Fifty-Third and Fifty-Fourth Streets, in midtown Manhattan. I dressed appropriately for the occasion in a pink and purple Chanel sweater set. Still, the magnitude of participating in this event didn't sink in until my chief of staff, D'George Hines, and I stepped into the hotel lobby. Between the gleaming marble floors, all the CGI signs, and people from all over the world walking around, the honor and prestige of having been invited suddenly sank in.

"Wait," I exclaimed, stopping in my tracks and looking at D'George. "I am about to keynote for the CLINTONS!"

Immediately before my speech, I reviewed the schedule for the evening with the stagehands. Then, as I stepped into the hallway leading to the stage, I was surprised to see Secretary Clinton walking toward me.

"Hello, Secretary Clinton, I'm Arian Simone," I began.

"Arian, I know exactly who you are, and I hate that you had to go through that terrible lawsuit. But I am so happy you are continuing your work," she said. "Do you mind if I take a photo with you?"

"I don't mind, but I thought *I* would be asking *you* for a photo!"

When I walked onstage toward the podium, I saw Secretary Clinton in her purple suit, standing in the wings, with her arms folded, smiling with pride. I felt awestruck and inspired as I stood on the stage to speak, especially knowing that she was right there watching.

> As someone who has had an entrepreneurial spirit since she came out of the womb—in fact, one of my friends joked that I would have sold my mother's placenta if I knew it had value—I've learned that it all comes down to one thing: capital. That's the difference between making minimum wage and making someone else's dream come true, and building your own business, your own wealth, your own jobs engine.

I ran down the racial disparities in the venture capital space and described the lawsuit Edward Blum had filed against us and AAER's efforts to keep women of color "in their place." I could see people's eyes as I spoke and knew that we were connecting. I concluded by stating:

> We went to court, and won. They appealed, and won the appeals ruling. Our courtroom battle may be over, but we're still punching.

As I absorbed the applause and encouragement, I felt incredibly proud of our work and at peace with myself. That afternoon, I attended an invitation-only roundtable. Only when I walked in the room did I realize Chelsea Clinton was hosting the session.

"I'm Arian Simone . . . ," I began when I saw her.

"Arian, I know who you are," she said, welcoming me enthusiastically. "We invited you—we were waiting to meet you!"

"Well, now that I've been honored to meet both you and your mother, I'm looking forward to meeting your father."

"Arian needs to meet my dad, please arrange it," Chelsea told her chief of staff.

As I took part in the CGI summit, I noticed how it was organized to leverage change. Most conferences empower participants with information to go out into the world and be a changemaker after they leave. The CGI collects commitments from the global leaders, civic changemakers, executives, and others who attend *during* the summit. Participants don't just attend panels and fireside chats; they gather at roundtables, dinners, and luncheons to plan and partner and make commitments about work they will engage in after the gathering. They literally use the summit as a place to convene to create change and make an impact in helping to solve the world's most pressing problems.

The next day, I wore a black Moschino dress with pearls, knowing I'd been invited to a small meet-and-greet President Clinton would host and I'd have the opportunity to take a picture with the president. I gave very Audrey Hepburn and Diahann Carroll vibes. I thought I'd missed out on the opportunity I had to meet the president during my teens, but now God was giving me a second chance.

"Hello, President Clinton," I stated, extending my hand. "I'll be attending the dinner Secretary Clinton and Chelsea are hosting this evening."

"You are who they ditched me for tonight," he exclaimed energetically—he's still charismatic.

That evening, Hillary and Chelsea hosted twenty-five women for dinner; I was the only African American at the table. Despite the vicious portrayals they've received in some media outlets, I experienced each of the Clintons as warm and lovely. Their care and concern for people carried over to every member of their team. I've been around some of the most powerful individuals in the world and their people. By comparison, the Clintons' team is friendly, accommodating, and solutions oriented, conveying a culture of excellence. This said a lot about the Clintons as individuals. Needless to say, I took note. Back home in Atlanta, I sent thank-you flowers. Before long, I received an envelope marked "William Jefferson Clinton." I opened it and read, my heart overflowing.

November 25, 2024

Dear Arian:

Thank you for the beautiful flowers and your kind note—and for your participation in the 2024 Clinton Global Initiative Annual Meeting.

Hillary, Chelsea, and I were glad to have the opportunity to showcase "What's Working" in global philanthropy, and are pleased that the meeting generated more than 175 new Commitments to Action to address urgent challenges around the world.

We're grateful to you and your team at the Fearless Fund for all that you're doing to widen the circle of opportunity. Keep up the good work, and best wishes to you.

Sincerely,
Bill Clinton

Inspired by what I'd learned at CGI, I modified the Fearless VC Summit, as I'd formerly called it. I realized the Fearless Fund could move from defense to offense by using the summit to solve issues related to economic inclusion.

So we continue to push. We continue to organize. We continue to demand accountability.

Because at the end of the day, this fight isn't just about one administration, one policy, or one executive order. It's about ensuring that economic opportunity in this country is truly equitable—and that no matter who's in power, the progress we've made is not erased.

We're not waiting for permission. We're not waiting for someone else to decide that investing in our communities is the "right" thing to do.

We are doing it ourselves.

Kat Garcia, Founder, Ground AI (Hispanic woman)

Fearless Fund's unwavering commitment to championing bold ideas and betting on people is exactly what drives a vibrant economy. The entire Fearless team is exceptional—they consistently go above and beyond, offering not just their expertise and network but also hands-on operational support. Their value add is real, and their impact is undeniable. I'm beyond proud to be working with such talented individuals that I can call more than investors but rather partners.

Chapter 14

Fearless Victory

> Because the Foundation's charitable grant program is expressive, the Alliance cannot force the Foundation to open the program to non-Black women under § 1981. The Alliance is not the first plaintiff to try using antidiscrimination laws to suppress opposing viewpoints on topics of public concern—here, whether charities may focus their funding on racial minorities who have long experienced discrimination. But the law is clear: § 1981 and other antidiscrimination statutes are not a license to "interfere with" a speaker's "desired message" or compel it "to include . . . other ideas with [its] own speech that [it] would prefer not to include." . . . The Foundation created the Fearless Strivers program to express a message of support for Black women entrepreneurs and raise awareness about inequities in access to capital. The Foundation's choice to exclude non-Black women from its grant and mentorship program is inherently "expressive."
>
> —Gibson Dunn, amicus brief filed in *American Alliance for Equal Rights v. Fearless Fund Management, LLC* in support of the Fearless Fund

SUMMER 2024

The time had come to consider our legal options. After losing our appeal in June 2024, we could either go en banc, presenting before all twelve judges in the Eleventh Circuit Court of Appeals, which would then issue a ruling, or we could appeal to the Supreme Court of the United States.

Our legal team filed an extension to go en banc. I was excited about that opportunity as our attorneys laid out the options to me. Well, let's say I was excited about going en banc until I considered the pool of judges we'd have to present before. By the end of the first Trump administration, he'd installed about 226 federal judges.[1] The Fearless Fund operates within a conservative circuit, meaning there were high odds the judges would rule against us. Since the circuit court ruling stated our program was "substantially likely to violate" section 1981 of the 1866 Civil Rights Act and "substantially unlikely to enjoy First Amendment protection," I realized I had to think strategically.

The prevailing climate suggested the Supreme Court would not receive our case favorably either. Appealing to the Supreme Court and losing could do more harm than good. Just as AAER's lawsuit against Harvard and UNC didn't just undermine affirmative action within those institutions alone, it undermined it in higher education nationally, if the Supreme Court were to rule against us it would have implications for everyone.

"The impact of this case could extend far beyond our fund," our counsel advised me. "It could set a dangerous precedent for other organizations working to support marginalized communities."

"Oh no, I can't see that day!" I exclaimed. "This could be dangerous. At least right now, what we have on our side is the fact what we do is still legal."

I didn't want to establish bad case law that would impact the entire Black community, causing the decision to become the law of the land. I realized my mission and responsibility were both to protect all the money we'd raised and were deploying to women *and* to protect the entire community.

For strategic reasons, we allowed time to pass as though we were going to appeal to the Supreme Court; however, our legal team ultimately chose not to continue the case. I thought strategic settlement was the best idea. Our lead counsel, co-counsels, and strategic counsels agreed. We returned to the Eleventh District Court to engage in settlement discussions with the plaintiffs. The settlement leaned in our favor and was narrow in scope. The Fearless Strivers Grant program had already distributed all but one $20,000 grant. The fund agreed to give up that one award. In exchange, Judge Thrash—the same judge who'd earlier ruled in our favor—granted a permanent dismissal of the big case accusing us of reverse discrimination.

This was a complete victory.

No dangerous case law had been established, the Fearless Fund would continue its mission, and we never stopped deploying grants at the foundation or investing through our venture fund, even as the court case played out. We protected both our money and that of the community.

Better yet, I held the ace of spades.

In August 2023, I'd struck a secret deal with a large financial institution to offer low-interest loans to the underresourced founders who power our economy. More than a year later, on September 11, 2024, the Fearless Fund announced its new $200 million debt fund to lend $5,000 to $250,000 loans to the underresourced women and men entrepreneurs who run small businesses and whom we'd always fought for. Our debt fund provides traditional business loans—regular debt, such as you'd have with a mortgage. This is a different approach from the larger venture capital investments the Fearless Fund had been making. Venture is important, but it's a whole different animal, because start-ups scale and grow at a very rapid and aggressive rate with plans to exit the business. Plus, so many of us find ourselves locked out. The debt fund allows Fearless to support many more businesses. I was incredibly excited to announce it—especially since I'd negotiated the deal in secret a year earlier. All that time and through all the stress, I had something up my sleeve that AAER didn't know about!

The way Judge Thrash structured the settlement, we could continue our mission and keep all our work going. The fact that he'd dismissed the case was reassuring. It meant the complaint couldn't be filed against us again—and we didn't need to alter our mission of supporting Black women entrepreneurs.

We didn't back down, we protected the work we'd already done, and we saved the Fearless Fund.

I'd like to tell you that's where the story ended, but things got even stranger.

While Judge Thrash structured the settlement both sides had agreed upon, the opposition throttled into high gear and began issuing press releases full of mis- and disinformation in a clear attempt to save face.

The temporary restraining order intended to stop our business fell flat on its face. The main case arguing discrimination was permanently dismissed. We never went to court on the discrimination case (only on the preliminary injunction), and with this settlement we will never have to. We gave up one grant, but that program was already winding down. If anyone thinks stopping one $20,000 grant while we still deploy millions is a win, that's not the math I learned in school. And if you won, why are you still suing other small organizations for the same thing? This is a win for us, not for you!

Not only did the Fearless Fund continue doing business, we expanded globally to include Africa. We are the first VC fund built by women of color for women of color—and we will continue our work as the first VC fund built by women of color for women of color!

As if AAER's strange behavior weren't enough, remember that incarcerated man who appeared out of nowhere? He filed a motion to somehow intervene in the case.[2] I don't know what his story is, but his motion, too, was dismissed. And I do know without a doubt that activists who believe in white supremacy will continue their attempts to turn civil rights law on its head and to reinstate barriers to the American Dream in front of Black and brown people, particularly women of color.

The Playbook

The Cure for Reparations

Whether in the context of affirmative action or post–George Floyd DEI programs, the topic of reparative commitments has been very tricky dating all the way back to Emancipation. On January 16, 1865, in Savannah—shortly after his infamous March to the Sea, which devastated both the Confederate army and infrastructure, and civilian and economic life in southern Georgia—Union general William Tecumseh Sherman issued Special Field Order No. 15. This edict allocated 400,000 acres of confiscated Confederate land to newly freed Black families in 40-acre plots, stretching along the southeastern coast, from South Carolina to Florida. Later, some of these families were also provided surplus army mules, giving rise to the phrase "forty acres and a mule." The land and mule were the first and only forms of repair offered to Black people for the physical and economic violence they suffered during the 246 years they experienced enslavement. But Sherman's promise was never fully realized. After President Abraham Lincoln's assassination four months later, Lincoln's successor, Andrew Johnson, overturned Sherman's order, returning the 400,000 acres of land to its former Confederate owners. This betrayal left newly freed African Americans vulnerable to even more physical and economic violence. It forced many Black people into sharecropping arrangements—another form of economic oppression—often for the very same men who had enslaved them. During Reconstruction—and overriding the veto of President Jackson—Congress passed the Civil Rights Act of 1866, the nation's first attempt to protect the rights of newly freed African Americans. The 1866 act identified all people born in the United States, including African Americans, as citizens and guaranteed Black people's right to engage in and enforce contracts. However, it did not establish any right of or means of restitution.

Human Rights Watch defines *reparations* as "steps to remedy and make amends for serious harm. . . . Broadly speaking, meaningful reparations efforts often include steps to achieve a range of different goals including restitution, compensation, rehabilitation, satisfaction, and guarantees of non-repetition."[3] Globally, Germany's approach to Holocaust reparations offers a model. The Luxembourg Agreement of 1952 established a formal reparations program between West Germany and Israel, recognizing the immense harm inflicted on Jewish communities during the Holocaust. Under this agreement, West Germany committed to paying approximately 3 billion Deutschmarks to the Israeli government (about $7 billion today) to support the resettlement of Holocaust survivors. An additional 450 million Deutschmarks were allocated for direct payments to individual survivors. The German government also enacted policies to return stolen property, establish pension programs, and fund healthcare and social services for survivors.

If a nation responsible for one of the most horrific genocides in history can acknowledge and take sustained action to rectify wrongs that took place over the course of twelve years,[4] why does America, built on centuries of slavery and racial exploitation, continue to sidestep its own responsibility? We have many benchmark examples of possible solutions. The United States has already practiced several forms of reparations,[5] where it has both acknowledged and provided financial compensation to groups of human beings who have suffered systemic harm. Though the recompense has in no way approached the level of injustice, the US government has paid Native American tribes billions in land settlements and economic restitution for various broken treaties and land seizures. . . . For example, after World War II the nation initiated a reparations program for tribes whose land had been seized by settlers. By the time the plan ended in 1978, more than $1.3 billion in restitution had been paid out ($641 billion in today's dollars). Sadly, this was the equivalent of only $1,000 per tribe member and the money was held in trust accounts rather than paid to individual Native Americans.[6] Still, there was some form of repair.

In 1988, when I was in elementary school, the US government passed the Civil Liberties Act, formally apologizing for the internment of Japanese Americans during World War II and providing $20,000 in reparative compensation to each survivor. The very next year Michigan congressman John Conyers[7] introduced HR 40, calling for the US federal government to establish a commission to study and develop a reparations proposal for African Americans. (He selected the number forty in honor of "forty acres and a mule."[8]) Congressman Conyers reintroduced the bill in every congressional session until he retired in 2018. After that, Representative Sheila Jackson Lee carried the effort forward. It wasn't until 2021, after the George Floyd protests, that the resolution progressed beyond committee hearings. Even then the Democrats didn't bring the bill to the floor, despite having more than two hundred co-sponsors.[9]

More recently, in 2023, Germany expanded its reparations, providing additional compensation for elderly Holocaust survivors and those excluded from earlier settlements. These measures reflect an ongoing commitment to repairing harm and ensuring justice is not just symbolic but materially transformative. Interestingly, the US government played a key role in the process, facilitating settlements from banks and corporations that profited from Nazi-era policies. These precedents prove that reparations are not an abstract or unattainable idea; they are a recognized and practiced form of justice.

In other words, the question is not whether reparations should happen for Black Americans, it is why they haven't happened yet. For despite the undeniable moral and economic case congressional representatives Conyers and Lee and other reparations experts have made, critics continuously attempt to unravel their arguments. One familiar claim is "the past is the past," as if history does not breathe within our present. Another is that reparations are too expensive, too complicated, too disruptive to the so-called order of things. Still other opponents insist that reparations are just not appropriate since no one alive shackled Black bodies in iron, stole the income they generated, or auctioned off children as though they were livestock. However, reparations are not just about the brutality of slavery itself, they're about continuous injustice, passed down from generation to generation. They're about the generational wealth stolen from African Americans, the systemic barriers that keep Black families from recovering, and the ongoing disparities that prove the harm never stopped despite field orders, President Eisenhower's Executive Order 9981 and other EOs, affirmative action policies, the Civil Rights Act, the Voting Rights Act, the Fair Housing Act, DEI, and more.

Disparities the Fearless Fund was addressing when it came under attack.

The irony is that in some instances even slave owners received reparations.

No, that is not a typo!

The *slave owners*—not the people who were harmed, but their immoral and viciously abusive enslavers. Authorized by the Slave Compensation Act of 1837 as part of the Slavery Abolition Act of 1833, the British government's compensation to enslavers throughout the British Empire—including the Virgin Islands in the Caribbean, the Cape of Good Hope in Southern Africa, and Mauritius in the Indian Ocean—stands as one of history's most glaring examples of economic injustice. Rather than financially compensating the formerly enslaved people for the forced labor and brutality they experienced for generations, the British government instead paid enslavers £20 million (equivalent to billions in today's dollars) for their "loss of property." Some payments were even converted into government annuities, allowing descendants of slave owners to benefit from wealth rooted in human bondage for nearly two centuries. Meanwhile, the formerly enslaved received no reparations, leaving them economically disenfranchised and forced into exploitative labor conditions throughout the British Empire.

This sum, which accounted for nearly 40 percent of the British Treasury's annual budget at the time, was so substantial that the debt incurred to finance it wasn't fully repaid until 2015. The fact that British taxpayers—including descendants of enslaved people—were still indirectly paying off this debt until the twenty-first century highlights just one way the legacy of slavery continues to shape modern economic disparities.

The precedent exists; what's missing is the political will to apply it equally. If there is a benchmark for the abuser, there must be a benchmark for the abused. A structured reparations program would not only serve as a form of justice but could also provide long-term economic benefits to our entire society and even the world.

A 2020 report from McKinsey & Company estimates that if the racial wealth gap were eliminated, US GDP would increase by 4 to 6 percent, adding approximately $1.5 trillion to the economy over the next decade. This huge economic expansion would stimulate consumer spending, increase homeownership, and improve business investment, as Black Americans would finally have equitable access to capital and opportunities. Reducing racial wealth disparities would also create a more stable economy. Fewer people would depend upon social welfare programs to stay afloat. More people would earn higher wages and own financial assets, which would increase tax revenues. Long-term, reparations would not just correct historical injustices but also lay the foundation for the economy to expand in sustainable ways. They would create pathways for generational wealth, stabilize communities, and create a more equitable financial system that benefits all Americans.

Critics argue the nation has already made reparations through concessions like affirmative action and social welfare, as if patches on a bullet wound could ever be called healing. Though they've been helpful, these programs do not address the accumulated loss or directly compensate for centuries of labor exploitation and systemic exclusion. And now, even these minimal efforts are under attack. The Supreme Court has overturned affirmative action, and the Trump administration, through Agenda 47 and Project 2025, is rolling back DEI initiatives as well as equal-opportunity policies. These moves are part of a broad strategy to eliminate the mechanisms that attempt to address racial disparities, making the fight for reparations even more urgent and necessary. And when we take it upon ourselves to close these gaps, we are met with resistance. The lawsuit against the Fearless Fund is yet another example of how any attempt to uplift Black communities economically is seen as a threat.

The promise of reparations must go beyond a symbolic attempt at restitution.

When we think about reparations for Black Americans, it's essential that we:

- Directly compensate descendants of enslaved Africans. Much like Germany's payments to Holocaust survivors, government-issued direct payments, tax credits, and trust funds that grow over time should be considered, offering Black people the opportunity to accumulate wealth over the long term rather than receive only one-time payouts that fail to address inequities that have built up over generations.

- Restore stolen land, correcting this nation's history of displacing Black families and communities through policies like redlining, urban renewal, and eminent domain. All across the nation—and in places as varied as Linnentown, Georgia, and the Fillmore District in San Francisco—Black people have had their property seized in the name of urban renewal, annihilating Black generational wealth. In 2019 former residents founded the Linnentown Project, to preserve the community's history and raise awareness of the long-term impact of urban renewal policies. The University of Georgia has partnered with them. But while these efforts acknowledge the past, they do little to rectify the material loss inflicted on displaced Black families.

- Compensate former landowners at the current market value of the property.

- Offer grants promoting Black homeownership and business development in historically Black neighborhoods.

- Address the impact of discriminatory housing policies by expanding access to affordable housing, eliminating barriers to homeownership for Black Americans, and offering down payment assistance to Black people who are purchasing their first home.

- Fund community land trusts—nonprofit organizations created to ensure land will continue to be affordable and controlled by local communities—in Black neighborhoods to prevent them from being displaced by gentrification.

- Provide free tuition at public universities for Black students, student loan forgiveness, and direct investments in HBCUs to help correct generations of intentionally underfunded education in Black communities as well as Black people's systemic exclusion from higher education.

- Expand Black communities' access to quality healthcare, mental health resources, and maternal care. This is a critical feature of a reparations initiative that meaningfully addresses the racial health disparities that have left Black Americans with higher mortality rates, including infant and maternal mortality; poorer health outcomes; and inadequate access to medical care.

- Establish federally funded grants, low-interest loans, and tax incentives for Black-owned businesses.

- End policies that promote discriminatory housing practices, dismantle predatory lending systems, and reform the criminal justice system to address its disproportionate impact on Black communities. These are all necessary to ensure that reparations do not become just another hollow promise.

- Identify sustainable funding sources. To overcome challenges in creating restitution, multiple viable mechanisms exist, including reallocating federal and state budgets, and diverting funds from programs that have historically disadvantaged Black communities (think: excessive policing budgets) and reallocating them toward reparative initiatives.

- Impose taxes on industries that historically benefited from slavery and segregation.

- Encourage corporations to contribute to reparations efforts through tax incentives or direct investments in Black economic development initiatives, which would foster greater accountability.

Achieving reparations will require a broad, multiracial, and multigenerational movement that unites Black activists, policymakers, grassroots organizations, legal experts, financial experts, investors, and allies. Just as the civil rights movement brought together diverse coalitions to push for legal and social change, the reparations movement must engage many sectors of society, ensuring that reparative justice is embedded into the nation's economic and political frameworks.

Telling the full story will play a critical role. The full extent of Black economic exclusion, from slavery to present-day disparities, must be documented, taught, and publicly acknowledged. However, today we are experiencing an aggressive attempt to erase this history from public consciousness. From book bans targeting works that expose America's racial injustices to politicians' attacks on DEI initiatives, a coordinated effort is underway to suppress the truth about systemic racism and its lasting consequences. These efforts to whitewash history are not just about controlling narratives, they are about controlling power. By attempting to erase the truth that Black people's economic freedom has been systematically subverted and wrestled away, policymakers and institutions seek to undermine the very foundation of the reparations movement.

We have already seen successful local efforts that prove reparations are possible when communities organize and push for change. In Evanston, Illinois, the city passed the nation's first municipal reparations program (State of Illinois, 2021), allocating $10 million in tax revenue from cannabis sales to fund housing grants for Black residents affected by historical redlining and housing discrimination. In California, the state's Reparations Task Force conducted extensive research and issued policy recommendations on how the state can address systemic harm through direct payments, policy reform, and community investment. These efforts serve as blueprints for broader national action.

Additionally, advocacy groups like the National African American Reparations Commission and the Movement for Black Lives have developed comprehensive reparations frameworks that address economic justice, land restoration, and policy change. Legal efforts have also gained traction, with lawsuits challenging institutions and corporations that profited from slavery and segregation. These victories remind us that reparations are not an unattainable goal but an issue that gains momentum when truth, advocacy, and collective action converge.

Building coalitions means amplifying these successes and pressuring policymakers to take reparations seriously. It means leveraging grassroots power, academic research, and media influence to push reparative justice forward. Reparations are not just about acknowledging history; they are about correcting systemic harm and ensuring Black communities have the resources and opportunities they have long been denied. The time for debate is over; it's time for action.

Chapter 15

The New DEI Playbook Is DE

For far too long, we've avoided the difficult conversations essential for real systemic change. The truth is, addressing our collective fears openly and honestly is not just important—it's necessary. As we talk about creating more equitable systems and redistributing resources to ensure everyone has a fair shot, we can't ignore the deep-seated fears that many have about losing control or power. These apprehensions are real, and they reflect strongly entrenched societal structures. But they cannot be addressed by skirting around the issue or pretending it doesn't exist. It's time to have the uncomfortable conversations and do so without creating hostility or defensiveness.

There is a tendency for people's opinions to polarize and for some of us to view those who resist change as the enemy—especially when it comes to DEI. But I'm not here to fight against those people. I'm not here to argue or create unnecessary conflict. What I am advocating for is the courage to face the hard truths together. Because if we don't, we will continue to perpetuate the same systems that have caused harm for generations. Conversations about economic freedom and economic equity shouldn't be seen as battlefields but as opportunities for growth and healing. It's essential to acknowledge the fears people have, whether it's trepidation about losing power, the fear of feeling inadequate in the face of change, or anxiety about the unknown. But at the same time, we must create space for those conversations to happen without turning them into arguments that shut people down.

Fear of losing economic control and status leads to resistance to policies, including DEI initiatives, that could help redistribute wealth and opportunities to create a more just world, where everyone experiences opportunity. These are not just isolated issues; they are deeply interconnected, and unless we confront them head-on, we will continue to reproduce the same inequities. My goal is to bring people who are against DEI into the conversation in a way that creates resolve. I believe that change happens when we can sit together, look at the issues openly, and work toward solutions that don't benefit just one group but everyone.

Adults need to start adulting.

Growth can only happen when we admit that we don't have all the answers, acknowledge that we have room to grow. At that point we create the possibility for real dialogue and lasting change.

I understand that it's easy to view DEI initiatives through the lens of "us vs. them." But this issue isn't about attacking people who don't want change; it's about helping everyone recognize that real progress benefits all of us. When marginalized communities gain more economic influence, when our educational systems are more equitable, when we start dismantling barriers to homeownership, it creates a stronger, more inclusive society for everyone. The more we can normalize having these conversations, the less threatening they become, and the more likely we are to find solutions that work for everyone.

Diversity is not about another box to check. Creating true diversity and inclusion means more than merely adding a few more people of color to a leadership team or improving diversity in the workplace overall. It involves dismantling centuries-old systems established to keep certain groups at the top and others at the bottom of our society. It's about confronting the underlying power dynamics built into corporate structures, educational systems, and societal norms.

When the numbers say one thing but the actions don't align, as often happens, clearly something is off. Companies might talk about their commitment to diversity, publish reports about how they've improved in certain areas, and even invest millions into diversity initiatives. But the composition of their leadership teams, and the number of people of color and women in key roles, such as board seats, often don't line up with their stated goals. The actions don't match the promises. From profits, to productivity, to innovation, to retention, to customer satisfaction, to market share—we know businesses thrive when they embrace diversity. But it takes real courage for companies to put their money where their mouth is and to face the uncomfortable truth that, for many businesses, the idea of diversity goes against the grain of everything they've been built on. The mission to oppress and suppress often seems so much stronger than the mission to make money, because real change would require dismantling the systems that have allowed the powerful to stay powerful.

I'm not just talking about hiring more Black or brown people; I'm talking about changing the way businesses operate. We need to create environments where people of color can thrive, where policies actively support inclusion, and where leadership teams reflect the communities they serve. We must continue to demand that businesses align their actions with their words. We have to hold companies accountable not just for their corporate diversity statements but for their results. It's time to stop pretending that businesses can't afford to prioritize diversity. They can, and they should. But more important, they must. Because in the end, the businesses that embrace diversity won't just be the ones that are more profitable—they'll be the ones that are more sustainable, more innovative, and more in tune with the world around them.

Systemic oppression is not just about failing to diversify—it's about actively working against equity. Policies, hiring practices, and organizational cultures are often designed to ensure that power and wealth remain concentrated in the hands of a select few. Systems that are supposed to support diverse talent often exclude, undermine, or actively suppress it. We know that funding diversity leads to higher financial returns, yet the resistance to implementing meaningful change continues. It makes you question whether the true mission is economic growth, or preserving control and avoiding the inevitable shifts that come with genuine inclusion.

A beautiful example of the power of having faith in one another can be found in the movie and book *The Best of Enemies.* In 1971, African American civil rights activist Ann Atwater met with Ku Klux Klan leader C. P. Ellis in attempt to resolve a dispute about segregated schooling in Durham, North Carolina. In the beginning the two hated and wanted nothing to do with each other; however, they were forced to meet at the local charette—a very intense, often multiday, collaborative design process in which a group of decision-makers and stakeholders gather to solve a problem. In this charette, participants met twelve hours a day for ten days.

Well, the charette sessions were filled with theatrics and drama—they didn't go well at first. But by the time they ended, Ann Atwater had won over Klan president C. P. Ellis, who then voted for the local school to desegregate, shocking everyone in attendance. Not only that, C. P. ripped up his KKK membership card in front of everyone, including his Klan colleagues. Enraged, the Klan threatened his gas station; Ann rallied the Black community to support him. Subsequently, C. P. and Ann traveled to various cities sharing their story, remaining so tight over the years that Ann gave the eulogy at his funeral in 2005.[1]

I wish we held more charettes today, because so often people form opinions or make generalizations without hearing their perceived adversary's personal story, which could cause them to experience empathy and close relationship gaps. Another reason I love this story is because racism and sexism are often influenced by our proximity to one another. Many people don't know the stories of people beyond those who look like them because they do not live or interact closely with them. *The Best of Enemies* reminds us that when people are placed in proximity with diverse people, racial/ethnic outcomes can be different.

Similar to what took place in the charette, we can all come together as a collective to design solutions to the world's greatest problems. We cover specific solutions more in depth throughout the book's "The Playbook" sections, but my point is that from a high level there is nothing to fear.

Though I'm an advocate of DEI, as I write this book it's clear conversations *about* DEI won't go much further. For too many, DEI feels like a mandate, and nobody likes to be told what to do. Others have been misinformed and wrongly believe that DEI means something less than fielding a team of the most talented people. Still others know that the combination of a diverse talent pool and equitable treatment of people increases competition and requires everyone to up their game or risk losing power and wealth. I support the idea of reparations as well because of the magnitude of the economic imbalance. But if people don't accept a common narrative about the past, they won't buy into a fix in the present.

Since there's no doubt businesses, societies, and economies benefit when the most talented people are at the table and in the game, it's important we design ways to resolve this impasse. We've spent too much time treating the problem through stopgap programs that take the edge off the pain but don't cure it. The time has come to dig to the root of the economic injustice issue so we can create true economic freedom for all humankind.

During most of my childhood, Coleman Young served as mayor of Detroit. Already in office for seven years when I was born, in 1981,

Mayor Young served thirteen years more. As the first Black mayor in the city's roughly 275-year history, Mayor Young embodied the story of the Motor City. When he was a child, Young's family escaped Ku Klux Klan violence in Alabama and migrated to the Motor City. He worked on an assembly line at the Ford Motor Company, becoming a union organizer, and was later a postal service employee, a steelworker, a US Army Air Forces Tuskegee Airman during World War II, and a Michigan state senator before becoming mayor.[2]

Coleman Young was Detroit through and through.

Mayor Young understood the importance of equity and representation in a way few leaders did back then or do now, even today. Remember, the difference between equality and equity is subtle but crucial. *Equality* means giving everyone the same thing. *Equity* means treating people justly according to their circumstances and providing them what they need to succeed. By *representation* I'm referring to the importance of including diverse people, voices, and perspectives, especially from people who normally have been left out of the economic equation.

Mayor Young promised Black Detroit residents a better future than they'd experienced in the past—knowing that in addition to being systematically discriminated against in workplaces, unions, and government, they'd been prohibited from bidding on city contracts because of their race.

Mayor Young didn't just talk about change for Black people—he made it happen.

I will always remember his economic mandate: he required that the demographics of the people who were awarded city contracts, business opportunities, and other forms of funding match the demographics of the people who were paying the city taxes. Over previous decades (if not centuries), nearly 100 percent of those opportunities had been awarded inequitably, almost exclusively to white people, though Black people had lived in the city since the early 1700s. This historic practice contributed to vast racial wealth gaps and economic inequality that unfairly advantaged the city's white residents over its Black ones. Once Coleman Young became mayor, everything changed. His economic mandate required *demographic equity*. Detroit was 88 percent Black at that time, so the city awarded 88 percent of the contracts to Black people. This helped ensure that the people making up the majority of the taxpaying population received their rightful slices of the economic pie. For the first time in the city's 275-year history, all the residents of Detroit had the same opportunity to benefit from the city's resources and contracts as anyone else.

I watched Detroit grow under Mayor Young's leadership as he put this simple but powerful principle into action. Black business owners, contractors, and entrepreneurs were no longer shut out of opportunities that previous administrations had carved out solely for others. Businesses that once had no access to the sizable city contracts that could make or break a company suddenly gained a seat at the table. Mayor Young created a level playing field where people who had been historically excluded could finally participate in Detroit's economic prosperity. This wasn't about favoritism; it was about fairness.

Mayor Young's policies transformed previously neglected parts of our city. As people who had long been cut out of the economic conversation gained opportunity, large previously neglected swaths of Detroit became prosperous. Mayor Young's approach was revolutionary. It wasn't only about fairness; it was also about justice. Finally Black people—the city's primary residents—could access the very resources their tax dollars funded. Those funds no longer flowed out of their wallet and into the suburbs where so many white people had relocated; instead, more of those dollars stayed in the communities that earned them. Young's approach wasn't about excluding anyone; nor was it about quotas or giving special treatment. It was about addressing a history of economic and social inequality that had excluded communities of color from participating in Detroit's economic life and development.

Even as a child, I understood the significance. I understood that fairness wasn't just a nice idea—something promised but rarely delivered. Fairness was real; justice was real. And when people who looked like me were given the same resources, opportunities, and platforms as everyone else, magic happened. The city flourished. It wasn't just about making sure the people at the top had a seat at the table—it was about making sure the entire community had the opportunity to thrive.

The mayor's policies strongly impacted the trajectory of my life. Since so many white people had fled the city, almost everybody I saw succeeding was Black. Our leaders looked like us; our judges looked like us; our schoolteachers looked like us; people working in government looked like us; our mentors looked like us. The economic transformation meant that Black people owned the grocery stores, clothing stores, gas stations, and restaurants we patronized. On a day-to-day basis, the images of success Black residents we were seeing looked like us. I realize that having the most successful people look like you is the everyday experience of most white Americans; however, it was rare then and is rare now for far too many Black Americans. Representation matters.

Despite all the examples of Black success, until well into my adulthood, both local and national media focused excessively on Detroit's struggles to navigate the city's diminishing tax base. There was always a narrative from one media outlet or another that painted Detroit in a negative light and focused upon the darker side of the story. Because by the time Coleman Young was elected, Detroit had long been struggling from decentralization, as superhighways were built leading to the growing suburbs, and deindustrialization, as corporate leaders shut down automobile, auto-parts, and other industrial manufacturing plants, relocating to Southern states, Mexico, and overseas to reduce labor costs so their shareholders would benefit. Detroit's racial unrest sped up the process.

Yes, it's true that after major corporations abandoned the city and massive numbers of people lost their jobs, many Detroit residents became unable to pay their mortgage and lost their home to foreclosure or abandoned it, and parts of the city experienced decay. Yes, some people resorted to selling drugs to provide for themselves as they lost their jobs. Yes, a crack epidemic developed as some people self-medicated their pain. Yes, the murder rate rose as a small number of people became desperate. It's true that Detroit struggled with the same types of human issues filmmaker Michael Moore showcased among mostly white residents in his documentary *Roger & Me,* after General Motors shut down its manufacturing plant in his hometown of Flint, Michigan. But you didn't see consistent prime-time news specials about the comparable struggles white people faced. In fact, today when white people struggle with similar heartbreaks and life challenges, people often use the compassionate phrase "diseases of despair" to discuss their addiction to opioids, deaths by suicide, and mass shootings.

Though Detroit experienced challenges typical of areas with an unstable or declining economic base, it was also a land of opportunity. There were many more stories to tell—stories of communities fighting for survival, yes, but also thriving; stories of Black people building empires. When members of our community came together to address the challenges the city faced, everyone was offered the chance to sit at the solutions table. The drug dealer sat next to the pastor, who sat next to the lawyer, who sat next to the business leader.

> **I learned that talent is everywhere and that people some overlook, despise, or even fear can thrive when given a positive environment and the opportunity to belong.**

Mayor Young's legacy wasn't just about creating policies; he also taught the Black citizens of Detroit that we deserve the same opportunities as anyone else. Though the media was quick to highlight Detroit's struggles, our leaders ensured our successes were noticed. I carry that with me every day. It's the reason I believe in the power of representation and equity, the reason I fight for fairness and justice in everything I do. It's also the reason I understand success isn't just about what you achieve for yourself; it's about making sure that others can achieve it too. Because when one of us rises, we all rise. And given the tools to succeed, there's no limit to what we can accomplish.

Though the example I used centered on race, I ask you to stay with me, especially if you're white. Demographic equity is not a racial concept. I used the example of race to make the theory easy to follow; for instance, I could have used gender. According to the central principle of demographic equity, any large organization should identify their constituency, whether the citizens you govern or the audience of your consumership. Their business practices should merely support those supporters, the people they serve, whoever they are. Over time, the population an organization serves might fluctuate. As demographics change, groups should revise their practices over time. In Atlanta, today the population is about 45 percent Black. If one day it becomes 45 percent Latino, then demographic equity says the city's best practices should reflect that shift.

The brilliance of Mayor Young's mandate was that it was very simple. It wasn't about labeling people or communities as "underserved" or "overserved." It was about common sense. His mandate was not a minority mandate; his administration's goal was simply to be of service to the people he served. If the majority of the city's population were white, then the largest percentage of city contracts would go to white people. The Young administration's structure and funding directives reflected the people they governed. Under this model no outside entity tells people how to run their organization. All you're doing is reflecting the people you serve.

As we approach the year 2043 and the shift to a majority-minority population, if demographic equity were applied it is likely that fewer funds would flow toward white people. This would not be unfair. If this approach feels like a problem, then we must immediately address the vast economic inequities experienced by Black people. What's good for the goose should be good for the gander. Everybody should be getting their fair share. If the current demographic trends hold, in time the vast majority of that contract money will flow toward Latinos.

For those who are fearful, this at least establishes a benchmark and process. It's far better than the fear of a racial takeover so many white people harbor or the idea that the atrocities white people have inflicted upon Black people and other people of color will soon come home to roost.

By creating frameworks that support diverse funding avenues, we begin dismantling barriers that have historically excluded marginalized groups. Establishing fair funding plans for governments, corporations, and venture capital funds is a dynamic process—similar to creating art, it's not a one-size-fits-all formula. There's no algorithm for fairness. There's no blueprint that applies equally across governments, corporations, or VC funds. We listen to the needs of each party involved and look for the connections, gaps, and opportunities others might miss. This takes time, patience, and the ability to see beyond the immediate. The goal is not merely to fund something, it's to ensure the funding is fair, equitable, and sustainable. We ought to look at the bigger picture, consider the long-term implications, and understand the ripple effect of every dollar spent across the company, region, and even planet.

I realize the road to creating a fair funding plan can be uncomfortable, especially when those involved come from vastly different backgrounds or have competing interests. The government has its bureaucracy, corporations have their bottom lines, and VC funds? Well, they're notoriously driven by high returns—or so they say. It's easy to see why these discussions can become heated or difficult. But this is where we lean into the discomfort. We can't expect to make any real progress if we're not willing to confront the tension that inevitably arises when we start discussing what is fair and who deserves what.

"The Negroes of Montgomery seem to have taken a lesson from Gandhi—and our own Thoreau, who influenced Gandhi. Their own task is greater than Gandhi's, however, for they have greater prejudice to overcome.

"One feels that history is being made in Montgomery these days, the most important in her career. It is hard to imagine a soul so dead, a heart so hard, a vision so blinded and provincial as not to be moved with admiration at the quiet dignity, discipline and dedication with which the Negroes have conducted their boycott....

Chapter 16

The New Leader Is You

When Rosa Parks refused to give up her seat on a segregated bus in Montgomery, Alabama, she sparked a revolution. In that one moment, she not only stood her ground, she also ignited a flame of change that spread across the nation and beyond. She became the face of a movement that fought for justice, equality, and human dignity.

Mrs. Parks didn't set out to be a revolutionary. She wasn't looking for fame or attention. She simply did what she felt was right, and in doing so changed the course of history. Her refusal to be treated as less than human led to the Montgomery Bus Boycott, the rise of Dr. Martin Luther King Jr. as a national leader, and the eventual dismantling of segregation laws all throughout the United States. It all started with one woman, sitting in one seat, in one moment of defiance. Opposite are some of her handwritten notes and reflections regarding the boycott.

Mrs. Parks's notes provide a powerful reminder that change doesn't always come from the top down. Sparking it doesn't require an army or a grand plan. Sometimes, all it takes is one individual, one act, one decision that has the potential to inspire others to take action. Rosa Parks demonstrated that one person can ignite a movement, and that is a lesson we can all apply in our own lives.

We live in a world that desperately needs change. From social justice issues to environmental concerns, to inequality and the fight for mental health awareness, there is so much work left to be done that it can feel overwhelming. The problems seem too large, too complex, too ingrained, for one person to make a difference. But this is where the story of Rosa Parks offers hope. It shows us we are often capable of more than we give ourselves credit for. It demonstrates how one person, with a belief in their own power and a commitment to doing what is right, can transform the world.

The new leader we need today is not a celebrity or a politician—it's you. You have the power in your own life, in your community, and beyond. We are the people we have been waiting for. There is a scripture in the Bible that states, "Creation is waiting for the children of God to be revealed." In other words, creation is waiting on you to take your rightful place. When you do, people see God's hand on your life; it's very evident.

It's so important that you take your place.

Whether you're standing up for what you believe in, lifting others up, or being the change you wish to see in the world, your actions matter. Just like Rosa Parks, you can spark a movement in your own life. The world is waiting for you to step into your power. You are capable of catalyzing the change we so desperately need. It starts with one act of courage, one decision to stand firm, and one belief that you can make a difference. Just like Rosa Parks, you have the ability to inspire others, to ignite a spark that could grow into something much larger.

Leading people isn't always about titles, power, or even specific responsibilities. It is more often about influence, connection, and the impact you have on others. It's when you encourage someone to grow, to overcome something personal, or to believe that there's more within them than they thought possible. You don't have to be at the front of the room. In fact, sometimes leadership is most powerful when you don't even realize it's happening. We all have the ability to lead, not through titles or power but through actions and the energy we put into the world. Even without speaking a word, we influence and inspire just by being present, just by showing up.

Though many of us are experiencing tremendous uncertainty and antidemocratic forces are on the rise, it's also true that systems that once held us back, that told us we had to follow a prescribed path to leadership, are crumbling away. And I believe that this shift is one of the most liberating things we've experienced in modern times. Leadership isn't something that has to be earned or bestowed upon you anymore.

We are all the new groundbreakers, regardless of our backgrounds, titles, or where we are in our journeys. We don't need to wait until someone else confers leadership upon us. We can own who we are, step into that power, and embrace the responsibility that comes with it. When you take ownership of your journey, it doesn't just impact you; it also affects the people you interact with, the spaces you occupy, and the ways in which you create positive change. Like when you light a candle in a dark room, your path isn't the only one the flame illuminates; it brightens everything and everyone in its vicinity.

Leadership is the same way.

The more we own our light, the more we inspire others to find their own.

When we give ourselves permission to lead, it encourages others to do the same. We can all light up the world around us with our unique gifts, perspectives, and talents. When we claim our power, we create space for others to claim theirs too. And that's how true change begins—with individuals owning their light and letting it shine for the benefit of all.

Each of us holds the potential to create lasting, positive change. When we harness our unique gifts and abilities, when we channel our energy toward something bigger than ourselves, we can be catalysts for transformation. Whether it's within our families, our communities, or the larger world, the power to make change is in our hands. And when we do this, the effect is often far greater than we expect.

As I was writing this book, the news broke that another major corporation, Target, had pulled back on its DEI initiatives. Target's move is yet another reminder that if we want real, lasting change, we can't afford to be passive. We must actively protect and advance opportunities for business owners, especially those from underrepresented communities. But action without strategy won't get us very far. If we want to make a meaningful, long-term impact, we must move together—boldly, intentionally, and with purpose. It's easy to feel overwhelmed by the challenges ahead, but we can't let that keep us from moving forward.

After the news about Target spread on social media, some encouraging developments took place: Target investors came together to file a class-action lawsuit, demanding accountability for the company's decision. This is an example of collective voices in action. On social media I posted a plan for the Black, brown, and female business owners on Target's shelves to jointly petition Target's board. Collectively these brands make Target a lot of money, and when they signed their distribution deals they did so under the premise that DEI was included in the company's value system. If they all signed a letter and had their attorney make demands, they could get some things done, but they need to move as a collective. Various communities Target had previously supported also came together to boycott the brand. The company's business has been significantly down ever since, leading to a change in leadership, though not yet a change in policies. Many of the Black and brown brands have established direct sales through their own sites or websites. In the meantime brands like Costco, which openly embraced diversity, have prospered as many people who previously shopped at Target moved their dollars to a retailer that appreciated them and better reflected their values.

When we come together, we are powerful. Our voices, our actions, they matter.

The Target shareholders' lawsuit shows that when people are united in their resolve, they can drive real change. It reminds us that we don't have to settle for companies that say one thing and do another—we have the power to hold them accountable. Consumer boycotts of Target for betraying its core values are creating consequences for the company that hit it where it hurts: its bottom line.

The Montgomery Bus Boycott victory wasn't born solely out of morality—it was also about economics. While the moral cause was clear, what drove the change was the economic impact of the boycott on the bus system. For over a year, Black Montgomery residents refused to ride the buses, effectively crippling the transit system's revenue stream. Financial power, when used wisely, can shift the tide of injustice. People who didn't get or didn't care about the moral issues understood Black people's power to cripple the bus system's bottom line.

Economics alone didn't win the day though—the powerful leadership of Rosa Parks, Martin Luther King Jr., and countless others was key. These courageous trailblazers stood up to a corrupt system and experienced the moral and economic ramifications of their actions. They understood that true change requires sacrifice, and they were willing to face those hardships.

Despite the DEI rollbacks, certain companies are standing strong in their values, demonstrating that running a business, doing the right thing, and building a more inclusive economy don't have to be at odds. In fact, they go hand in hand. We need to support these businesses, uplift them, and celebrate their efforts, because they show us what true commitment looks like. They remind us that it is possible to be both profitable and principled.

Social media, online communities, and digital platforms allow anyone with a message or a cause to be heard. The world is literally at our fingertips, and with it comes the opportunity to use our voices to bring about the change we believe in. But with that access comes responsibility. How we choose to wield that power matters. We need to be intentional with our influence, grounded in our values, and committed to making a difference for the better. Positive change requires more than loud voices or big gestures; it also involves quiet, consistent efforts we make every day. Whether it's standing up for justice, advocating for kindness, or simply doing the work to improve ourselves and the lives of those around us, we all have a role to play.

When we each take ownership of our power, we become part of something much bigger than ourselves. We become a collective force for good. The time to step up, to lead, and to make a difference is now. The world is waiting for us to assume our power and create the change we want to see.

I often think about a quote from New Zealand's prime minister Jacinda Ardern: "If we focus only on being seen to be the strongest, most powerful person in the room, then I think we lose what we're meant to be here for." When we focus only on being the loudest voice or biggest personality, we can easily lose sight of the fact that we are here to live our purpose, make a mark, and leave a legacy that reflects who we are, not who we think we should be. Regardless of the size of our impact, it's important we learn to view our role, our purpose, and our impact as uniquely ours, not someone else's. The only true measure of success is how fully you align with your own truth rather that fitting a mold someone else has created. It's about defining your own path, your own goals, and your own impact.

Your value isn't tied to external validation or comparison to others. Your mark on the world is yours to make, and it doesn't have to follow anyone else's timeline or criteria for success. You have the power to create a legacy, to be a leader in your own life, and to make an impact that is uniquely yours.

I encourage you to take a moment and reflect on your own leadership. Ask yourself: What is my unique offering to the world? What is the mark I want to leave? It might not look like anyone else's, but that's exactly what makes it powerful. When you embrace who you truly are and follow your own path, you'll discover a strength within you that can move mountains. And in the end, it's not about being the strongest person in the room—it's about being the most powerful, authentic version of yourself.

The reality is, you are the cure. You walking in your purpose and playing your part in society is healing to the world. "Leadership is about making others better as a result of your presence and making sure that impact lasts in your absence," former Facebook COO Sheryl Sandberg said, reassuring people that it's not about the grand gestures, the accolades, or even the title—it's about the lasting impact you make on others. It's about how you help people grow, how you inspire them, and how you guide them in ways that continue to reverberate even after you're gone. True leadership happens not just through what you do, but through who you become.

We all have the potential to be great leaders, and that greatness comes from our willingness to develop our human potential. It's not enough to just read books or take courses on leadership. The real work happens inside us. Becoming more self-aware, recognizing where we need to grow, and being willing to do the work to evolve into the people we are meant to be are all part of it.

Every time I start a new company, including the Fearless Fund, or take on a new project, it requires a new and elevated version of me. Personally, the process of becoming greater is not just about learning new strategies or acquiring more knowledge. It is about looking inward and recognizing that in order to step into all that I am, I need to grow in areas that aren't visible on the outside but reside deep within me. I can clearly see the person I desire to become, but I also know that I have to embody it.

The real work isn't about adding tasks to my to-do list, it is about growing my capacity to handle the demands of the new elevated place and to show up in ways that are authentic, compassionate, and sustainable. I understand that I need to focus on evolving my internal self before I can take on the external responsibilities. The court case required me to take many moments for self-awareness and reflection. There were areas within me that needed development—the ability to remain calm under pressure, the discipline to stay focused even when things got chaotic, and the compassion to empathize with others even when I felt overwhelmed. These weren't tasks or skills I could just learn in a workshop or a seminar. These were qualities that had to be nurtured through my commitment to growth.

The most effective leaders continuously work on themselves, expanding their capacity and cultivating the inner qualities that will allow them to serve others in meaningful ways.

Rosa Parks once said, "You must never be fearful about what you are doing when it is right."

There will be moments when the path is uncomfortable, unconventional, and maybe even unpopular. But the most powerful and lasting changes often come from stepping outside the box and doing what others might fear or question. There's something incredibly powerful about knowing that the decision you are making is rooted in conviction and purpose, and in doing the right thing.

I've come to learn, just as Rosa Parks did, that once your mind is made up, your actions align with your values, and you know what you're doing is right, fear starts to fade. It may not disappear entirely, but it becomes manageable, something you can push through. Knowing what must be done, and knowing why it must be done, creates the strength to face any obstacles that may come. Nervousness is natural; it's also something that can be managed, channeled, and used as fuel. Because being fearless isn't about the absence of fear, it's about moving forward despite it. You step out of your comfort zone into something bigger, something that will push you to grow and make an impact.

It took fearless authority to establish the Montgomery Bus Boycott. Icons like Dr. King didn't just speak out; they stepped into the trenches, aware of the personal and professional cost as they faced obstacles like threats, violence, and a system designed to break their spirit. Yet they stood firm, knowing that their courage could spark a revolution in how we view power and resistance.

If those brave souls could confront the challenges they did—facing down segregation, risking their lives, and pushing through the intense economic pressure—then there's no reason why we can't be fearless today. The stakes may look different, but the goals remain the same: standing up for justice, leveraging the power of unity, and confronting the uncomfortable truths about the systems that continue to oppress us. It's time we take on today's battles with that same fearless leadership.

Fearless leadership isn't just about you; it's about the people you are leading and the impact you make on the world around you. When you lead with courage, when you step into your power and take risks, you show others that they too can do the same. You become a beacon of possibility, a symbol of what can be accomplished when you decide to move forward despite the fear.

As you step out as a new leader, remember this: Fear will come, but it doesn't have to control you. When you are clear about your purpose and your vision, fear diminishes, faith increases, and you can navigate with ease something that drives you rather than holds you back. Your courage and boldness will inspire others. Disruption, when done for the right reasons, inspires progress, and progress is what we need to drive positive change in the world.

Epilogue

Imagining Equality

As a Black person who travels all throughout the African Diaspora helping people increase their level of economic freedom, I know from firsthand experience that humanity will benefit greatly when people begin approaching Black people in ways that acknowledge our genius, our talents, our labor, our land, our businesses, and our resources with dignity and fairness. In other words, when Black people are engaged without the exploitation and abuse that have characterized their treatment for hundreds of years by those of various racial and ethnic groups who have bought into white supremacy, the shift will benefit all of humanity. No matter where we live on the planet, Black people are some of the kindest and most resourceful individuals you could ever work with. Whether in the workplace, in communities, or within families, we bring a wealth of talent, creative perspectives, and dedication to whatever we do. Though we have a legacy of resilience, it's time for the world to finally recognize that our genius is not merely a product of survival—it's a product of thriving, of creating something out of nothing, of crafting solutions even in the most challenging environments.

The key to unlocking our brilliance and ensuring that Black people and other people of color can contribute fully and fairly to society is to approach us with respect. Instead of holding on to the systems that have historically oppressed, degraded, and left behind

Black people, imagine what could happen if those systems shifted. We have contributed stellar discoveries and innovations while experiencing oppression. Just imagine that same creativity unleashed in a much more supportive system. Our contributions have the potential to reshape industries, economies, and cultures.

I'd like you to join me in imagining what could be possible if economic equity and economic freedom were to exist.

Just imagine if, instead of facing systemic barriers, Black people were met with partnership, with support, and with investment in our communities, in our businesses, in our potential. The world would benefit, not just in small ways but on a grand scale. Black people would help to create solutions to global issues often ignored by those in power. Whether it's climate change, poverty and economic disparities, global health crises, or other issues, these challenges should be addressed by more than a select few. Global cooperation means including the voices, ideas, and contributions of Black people. Working together, we can create systems that benefit everyone.

Also imagine a world with true diversity of thought.

What might this look like in practice? It looks like fair wages for the labor of people of all races and sexes. It looks like investment in businesses owned by all races and sexes. It looks like a society where all voices are not only heard but elevated. It looks like everyone being able to walk into a room and have their worth acknowledged. It's about seeing all contributions as valuable and even essential.

What we've learned as a community, time and time again, is that handouts among any group create a superior-inferior complex, where the person who gives is seen as superior and the person who receives as inferior. When I refer to "handouts," I'm talking about charity and other contexts where things are gifted to people who feel unempowered. In Proverbs 22:7, the Bible teaches that the borrower is subordinate to the lender—using the language "servant to the lender" or even "slave to the lender" in the New King James and New International versions, respectively. I believe doing business is better than charity because each party comes to the table possessing something to offer, avoiding the inferior/superior dynamics. In this way, collaborative approaches create an opportunity to share in the resources, to work in partnership, and for everyone to be treated with fairness and humanity. Because when everyone has access to the same opportunities and everyone is treated with respect and dignity, and everyone receives all the resources they need to succeed, the world will experience for the first time what the human collective can accomplish—and we all will be better for it.

Imagine a world with economic equity and freedom for all.

If economic inequality is leading to fear, loss of productivity, and a lack of progress, then if everyone had economic freedom, they would feel unleashed to be their most brilliant self. The world's leadership would be more diverse by gender, race, ethnicity, and other dimensions of diversity. All human beings would be well nourished and have a roof over their head and a comfortable home. People could afford to care for their health optimally and obtain a quality education that would allow them to thrive. Social services would respond to people's needs, which they would have fewer of because more of their needs would already have been met. From schools to playgrounds to buses and subways, the public infrastructure would prioritize everyone, not just the rich.

Black and brown people, in particular, could show up as their full brilliant selves in all aspects of life, including at work, and contribute to their full human capacity. Both people who are oppressed and the people doing the oppressing would be free of the bondage of low-vibration thoughts such as anger and fear. We would all embody the high morals we are created to experience. People could work in the areas of their gifts and passions instead of career tracks they've outgrown or are not interested in, or gig work they engage in just to pay the bills. People would feel free of financial stress—whether from their mortgage or rent, or their car note, or the cost of tuition or healthcare bills—similar to the indigenous residents of the United Arab Emirates and other oil-rich nations, who receive oil profits in the form of a monthly check. When society is equitable, there's no reason for people to feel financially desperate. This would result in lower rates of crime. As a result people could walk down the street at night and not clutch their purse for fear of being pickpocketed or feel the need to look over their shoulder. There would be less need for protective weapons such as knives and guns. Kids could attend schools without having to participate in active shooter drills and play outside without their parents worrying that they will get shot or harmed and never return. We would have fewer mass shootings, if any. And high-priced luxury events—from the Super Bowl to the Olympics to the US Open—would be financially accessible to all.

But people of all races would not merely experience a better individual quality of life (as though that goal were not worthy enough). Those improvements would ripple through families, across communities, and lift local, regional, and national economies. The increased creativity, productivity, and innovation would pulse around the world.

Afterword

Why DEI Must Not Die

by Stacey Abrams

For centuries, moments of great progress in our nation have been met with a coordinated and aggressive resistance dedicated to wiping away hard-earned progress. The Revolutionary War—a conflict waged in part to secure rights for nonlandowning white men who were denied the same privileges as the wealthy—was the first salvo. In 1787, dissatisfied by the incompleteness of the Articles of Confederation in addressing the economic hardship faced by newly minted Americans saddled by debt and ignored by their leaders, Shay's Rebellion forced a reckoning. The result was the Philadelphia Convention that gave us the US Constitution. The document's promise of liberty presaged and was born of the first stirrings of DEI.

Following the Civil War, the Thirteenth, Fourteenth, and Fifteenth Amendments abolished slavery in the United States, guaranteed citizenship to all individuals born or naturalized in the United States, and prohibited denying the right to vote based on race, color, or previous servitude. This period, known as the Reconstruction era, is characterized by Black Americans getting a few steps closer to full participation in a country that had subjugated them for nearly 250 years. Despite the historic economic and political gains made during this time, Black Americans faced reprisal in the form of Jim Crow laws and violence in an attempt to disenfranchise and control them.

In response to the Jim Crow laws that enforced racial segregation, the civil rights movement began. This historic movement led to the passage of the Civil Rights Act and the Voting Rights Act, and the establishment of the Equal Employment Opportunity Commission, the US Department of Justice's Civil Rights Division, and more. Finally, it felt as if our nation was living up to its founding ideals by ensuring that every community had an opportunity to achieve their own American Dream.

The civil rights era that began with the end of slavery created a blueprint for other historic movements in our nation's history to demand diversity, ensure equity, and inspire inclusivity—DEI. Labor movement uprisings like the Haymarket Affair, the Pullman Strike, and the Battle of Blair Mountain compelled the creation of laws to protect workers and their unions. The American Indian, Chicano, and AAPI movements responded to institutionalized racism that throttled economic access, and the Stonewall riots sparked the modern movement for LGBTQ+ rights. The passage of the Americans with Disabilities Act (ADA) mandated accessibility and equal opportunity for disabled people. Title I expanded the guarantee of public education to the poor, to rural children, and to children of color. *Roe v. Wade* and the Family Medical Leave Act (FMLA) secured a woman's right to bodily autonomy and the ability to remain in the workforce. Again and again, our nation has proved that it is at its best when we ensure that all people, no matter who they are or where they come from, have the freedom and opportunity to thrive.

For centuries, Americans of all backgrounds have fought to ensure that the next generation would face fewer barriers to opportunity and live a life of dignity that they could be proud of and build a legacy upon. These moments of progress—from the enactment of labor laws that protect our workers to the expansion of women's rights—comprise the relentless proof of the value of DEI. Without it, our nation would not have witnessed the gains of underrepresented communities across our economy, in educational systems, and in our elections.

DEI is a means of corrective action and vision-setting. It is a collection of laws, practices, behaviors, and aspirations that have moved our country toward its highest ideals and atoned for its worst impulses. Yet, with progress comes a shift in power dynamics. Those who have hoarded power and privilege are always threatened by competition and change. Afraid that loosening their grip will lead to losing unchallenged access, requiring instead that they prove their right to participate rather than taking success for granted. Those who are opposed to DEI are determined to kill it because they understand its value and know that it works. But the death of these foundational American values that undergird our economy and democracy will lead our nation to peril. Diversity, equity, and inclusion are core American values that benefit all people in our nation. If those values die, so too does America.

Opponents of progress often use the same playbook when attempting to stifle societal change, and the attacks on DEI follow the standard formula. They start by mocking how we define our ambitions, hoping that in the midst of defending our right to be, we will lose the thread of why we are indeed right. Consider the actions of naysayers and policymakers that try to use DEI as a punch line rather than a value statement. They hope that we will forget they are advocating for uniformity, unfairness, and exclusion—the apotheosis of DEI. In their telling, the aspirational goals of broad access to the American Dream are epithets. Because, like bullies on a playground, they know that if you make fun of someone, their instinct is to be embarrassed—whether it is warranted or not. When the mockery and attacks persist, more join in on the attack, hoping that it will keep the bullies focused on their target and not on themselves. Over time, when the victim has become so beaten down by both the onslaught and the abandonment, the bully successfully changes what the victims believe about themselves. By co-opting our language, opponents of DEI make us question our values and whether they are worth defending.

The term *woke* is the perfect example. *Woke* emerged in the 1940s among African Americans, finding usage over the decades, and it was fully popularized by activists in the Black Lives Matter (BLM) movement. The term obviously and intentionally encourages people to be aware of and engaged in important social issues related to racial justice. It worked. Progressives began to adopt the term of art to signify their engagement, setting a North Star for what they expected of a new century. In response, conservatives began to use the word disparagingly, trying to poison the effectiveness of this viral signifier. Over the next few years, what began as a call for communities to be aware of inequalities in our nation has become a way to dismiss the importance of actually doing what's right for marginalized communities. The word has been demonized by cynical politicians and activists who want to paralyze conversations and undermine actions that seek to disrupt the status quo. Their efforts too have worked. These days, we are as likely to hear mainstream leaders recoil from its use or spend their time debating the language, while opponents move on to their next tactic of eroding the positive behaviors the word evoked. The entire apparatus of the federal government has weaponized woke and DEI to justify a heinous retrenchment on American progress, where disabled veterans lose jobs because they reflect the perquisites of DEI.

As the founder of the pro-DEI American Pride Rises Network, I have pointed out that demonizing our language is only the first step. Next come the tactics of litigation and legislation. Litigation accomplishes the goal of dismantling the very laws that have protected so many of us from the worst impulses of those who despise progress. For example, in 2013, the Supreme Court eviscerated the Voting Rights Act in *Shelby v. Holder* by allowing states with a history of discriminating against voters because of their race to implement changes to the voting process without federal approval, making it easier for states to engage in voter suppression. In 2022, *Dobbs v.*

Jackson Women's Health eliminated the right of women to control their own bodies, forcing them to rely on states to determine the limits of their bodily autonomy. Both of these decisions gutted federal protections and re-created exclusionary policies that directly impacted the ability of all Americans to fully participate in our democracy.

In 2023, Students for Fair Admissions (SFFA) expanded their attacks to include higher education by singling out race as an illegitimate consideration in college admission decisions. Yet, the Supreme Court left untouched the ability of the same colleges to consider gender, religion, or legacy status. Only race is forbidden. But these were the opening salvos in an all-out attack on every aspect of progress. The Fearless Fund became one of the central players in their assault on the laws—trying to assert that their goal of uplifting women of color was somehow antithetical to American values. They were wrong.

First they undermine our language, and then they come after our protections. Finally, their ultimate tactic is prohibiting any return to progress. Using the cloak of states' rights, enemies of equality want to fracture the law and then use state legislation to permanently block its resurrection. And in 2025, we witnessed a raft of executive orders and economic threats to any organization that dared to pursue the central pillar of democracy that is reflected in DEI. If federal law abandons the marginalized, and state laws are divided against the disadvantaged, every community under threat is left to fend for itself. In the decade-plus following the *Shelby* decision, weakening voting rights, states have passed laws that expand voter suppression, especially among voters of color. Since 2021, more than 110 restrictive voting laws have been adopted across the country, and the Supreme Court is currently considering fully gutting the 1965 Voting Rights Act in the *Callais* case. And since the *Dobbs* decision in 2022, more than twenty states have banned or limited access to abortion. The fallout from Students for Fair Admission includes a reduction in the number of Asian American students admitted to elite colleges and the erasure of programs for first-generation students who might well become the last without support.

The issues of education, the economy, and elections are essential to DEI because they directly impact the ability of all people to participate in the American Dream. Education is about what you know. The economy controls what you do. Elections determine who is in charge. Since the Students for Fair Admissions decision in 2023, 440 anti-DEI laws have been introduced in forty states, with twenty-eight being signed into law—cutting across elections, the economy, and education. If you can dismantle who gets a say at the ballot box, you can control the political decisions made. Cutting back on access to resources dramatically impedes a person's ability to participate in the economy. If you control access to education, you place permanent barriers to knowledge and upward mobility. When DEI dies, so too does a pluralistic democracy and its intent.

The fundamental values of diversity, equity, and inclusion are under attack in our nation as a powerful, well-coordinated, and well-resourced opposition seeks to dismantle the core values that make our nation truly great. Despite the disinformation spewed by right-wing activists and politicians, DEI is corrective, not exclusionary. The laws at issue have only ever given people fair access to opportunity so they can build their own American Dream. Opponents of DEI are attacking our democracy, and they have intentionally focused on our economy to hoard opportunity for a select few.

In 2023, start-ups founded by women received less than 3 percent of venture capital funding. For Black women, that number is less than half a percent. These astonishing figures create barriers that prevent Black-women-owned businesses from thriving in our economy. The Fearless Fund is dedicated to supporting underresourced and underrepresented entrepreneurs by leveling the playing field and giving them the capital they need to scale their businesses. For too many entrepreneurs of color, starting and maintaining a business is challenging because they have less access to capital, higher loan denial rates, and difficulty accessing business networks.

One of the Fearless Fund's programs, the Strivers Grant contest, awarded $20,000 to Black-women-owned businesses to boost the meager amount of VC funding that Black women receive. Though small, the program was vital to helping Black women entrepreneurs grow their businesses. The program also garnered attention from anti-DEI activists committed to distorting civil rights law through legal bullying tactics that targeted small organizations attempting to expand economic opportunity.

As I mentioned earlier, in 2023, the Supreme Court decided in *Students for Fair Admissions v. Harvard* that race could no longer be used as a factor in most college admissions. Anti-DEI activists and politicians viewed this decision as a death knell for DEI and it emboldened them to use the courts to air out their grievances. The architect of the *Students for Fair Admissions* decision was the same person behind the *Shelby* decision that gutted the Voting Rights Act: Edward Blum. For decades, Blum has been on a personal vendetta to restore barriers to the key pillars of the American Dream: voting rights, education, and the economy.

Following the *Students for Fair Admissions* decision, Blum set his sights on private businesses and sued the Fearless Fund through his organization the American Alliance for Equal Rights, falsely accusing the Strivers Grant contest of being discriminatory against non-Black founders. This lawsuit was just one facet of a multipronged war on DEI waged by right-wing activists like Blum, Christopher Rufo, and Robby Starbuck, who believed that the Supreme Court's decision in *Students for Fair Admissions* gave them the license to bully private companies committed to DEI. The Trump administration and a raft of governors and state legislatures are eager to finish the job by nullifying progress and cementing barriers for the foreseeable future.

The values of DEI are not just nice to have; they are vital to the success of businesses in our nation and our economy overall. DEI drives innovation and growth for businesses, delivering benefits that directly impact and improve business performance. Research has shown that diverse companies are more innovative, make better decisions, and outperform their less diverse competitors. Companies that value DEI often attract and retain the best employees by widening the pool of skilled candidates. In fact, many applicants consider a company's stance on DEI while applying for jobs and are willing to turn down job offers from companies that reject DEI. Maintaining DEI commitments can also positively impact a company's reputation. Companies that once touted the values of DEI but retreated due to external bullying could suffer reputational harm with customers, stakeholders, and current and potential employees.

Despite the well-researched benefits of DEI on our nation's economy, why are so many committed to ending it? Because it levels the playing field. The values of DEI have worked for centuries to improve the lives of marginalized communities in this nation—communities that were left out of the economy, educational opportunities, and the voting booth, like the Black women the Strivers Grant contest focused on.

In their quest to end DEI, Edward Blum and his cynical acolytes are turning civil rights law on its head to make their flawed case. Blum filed his lawsuit against the Fearless Fund using the Civil Rights Act of 1866. This law was passed following the US Civil War and was the first federal law to define citizenship and to declare that all citizens are equally protected by the law. More specifically, Blum cited Section 1981 of the law as the basis for his lawsuit. This section was originally meant to protect formerly enslaved people from racial discrimination in contractual relationships. However, Blum used the law to support his baseless legal bullying and attack economic progress in our nation.

While the Strivers Grant contest was scheduled to wind down and the Fearless Fund announced a new $200 million debt fund that would offer loans to underresourced founders who power our economy, anti-DEI activists ratcheted up their attempt to turn civil rights law upside down to reinstate barriers to the American Dream. Years into the battle, we cannot lose heart. Instead, we must continue to take action and fight back to protect opportunity for all.

The first step to fighting back is to not shrink from who we are and not allow anti-DEI activists and cowardly politicians to delegitimize what we know to be true and beneficial. We must proudly proclaim our support of DEI and how it ensures that all communities in this nation have a pathway to the American Dream. That means also standing firm in the language of diversity, equity, and inclusion and its acronym, *DEI.* The reality is that DEI opponents are not concerned about what we call it, they are opposed to the values each letter upholds. Abandoning the term will not save us—only embracing our truth will. We must not allow them to win the battle of ideas without putting up a real fight or explaining the flawed reasoning behind their beliefs.

The second step is to block the noise. Often, DEI opponents deride our values with so many negatives that we begin to question whether what they're saying about DEI is valid. At a moment where DEI's main detractors hold some of the most powerful positions in our nation and use the bully pulpit to distract us with falsehoods and absurdities, it's easy to question whether or not the values we're fighting for are worth upholding. The distractions are the point and a key part of the anti-DEI movement's strategy. They want us to argue about whether natural or man-made disasters are the result of DEI so they can dominate and control the conversation. We must resist giving them that satisfaction. This moment demands that we remain steadfast about the values we hold dear and defend them on our own terms, not the opposition's.

Finally, we must speak up. Anti-DEI politicians and activists have made bullying a key part of their overall strategy. They bully corporations, small businesses, higher education institutions, and other entities that don't pledge allegiance to their cynical values and false rhetoric. Though a small but concerning group of companies and organizations has caved to the bullying, many more are standing firm at this moment and we need them to share their stories. When we are unwilling to proclaim our values or tout our successes, we make it easy for critics to define our values for us.

We must be vocal about what we believe in and resolute in the fact that it's beneficial. We have proof of DEI's benefits to our country—from the start of our nation, when the Declaration of Independence declared an ambition of equality. Today's fights are solely to ensure that the pathways of opportunity are widened for more communities in our educational systems, economy, and our elections. If DEI wasn't working, the opposition wouldn't be dedicating so much of their time and so many of their resources to stop it.

Opponents are betting on our silence and capitulation at this moment. To maintain the freedoms we currently have in our nation, and fight for even greater possibilities, we must be uncompromising in our commitment to DEI. Anything less risks abandoning the fundamental American values that have anchored our nation for centuries and have moved us closer to our nation's founding ideals. This story is one of many—and they all have the same narrative core: For us to rise, DEI must remain our rallying cry and mission statement. Because it works.

Acknowledgments

I give glory, thanks, praise, and credit to my Lord and Savior, Jesus Christ, for blessing me with this amazing life.

Thank you to my husband, Benjamin, for your support throughout this book process. To my family, especially my mom and dad, I can't thank you enough for providing me with an upbringing that has catalyzed positive change globally. And what would I do without my sisters, who have been my biggest cheerleaders?

I am deeply grateful to my incredible book team, who helped bring my dream to life: Tamira Chapman, Porscha Burke, Meredith Miller, Eula Smith, Hilary Beard, D'George Hines, Shevon Jones, and the entire staff at Storehouse Voices, Crown, and Penguin Random House.

I want to express my deepest gratitude to those who actively supported us throughout the court case: the Fearless staff as well as our Fearless advisors, donors, board members, portfolio companies, and grant recipients.

I would also like to acknowledge the following individuals and organizations, listed in alphabetical order:

Alphonso David
Anthony O'Neal
Attorney General Letitia James
Ben Crump & Associates

Bishop T. D. Jakes and Serita Jakes
Bishop William Murphy III and Pastor Danielle Murphy
Black Economic Alliance Foundation (BEA)
Congressional Black Caucus
Congresswoman Jasmine Crockett
Danielle Conley
Deanna Hamilton
Dejuana Thompson
Delta Sigma Theta Sorority, Inc.
Dennis Ellis
Derrick Johnson and the NAACP
Dia Simms
Dora Whitley
Gibson, Dunn & Crutcher LLP
Gregg Myers
Jacqueline Waters
Jotaka Eaddy
Kasim Reed
Kim Blackwell
Lawyers Committee for Civil Rights
Marc Morial and the National Urban League
Meagan Holston-Alexander
Melanie Campbell
NAIC and Robert Greene
Nikaya Brown Jones
Pastor Jamal Bryant
Rachel Noerdlinger
Rakia Reynolds
Reverend Al Sharpton and NAN
Richelieu Dennis
Rodney and Shanterria Sampson
The Rodriguez Family
Ron Busby and US Black Chambers
Samantha Jacobson
Shavon Arline-Bradley and NCNW

Stacey Abrams
Tamika Hawkins Adu
Tamika Mallory
Tasha Cobbs Leonard
Touré Roberts and Sarah Jakes Roberts
Zak Wallace

Permissions

Grateful acknowledgment is made to the following for permission to reprint previously published material:

Ben Crump "Foreword" *xi*

Black Economic Alliance Foundation "Brief of amicus curiae" *11, 19, 31, 67*

Pinky Cole "Testimonial" *43*

Gibson Dunn "Amicus Brief" *45, 157–58, 179, 195, 207*

Lawyers' Committee for Civil Rights Under Law, the Leadership Conference on Civil and Human Rights, National Action Network, National Association for the Advancement of Colored People ("NAACP"), National Urban League, National Coalition of Black Civil Participation, and LatinoJustice PRLDEF "Brief of amicus curiae" *87–88, 111, 141*

Excerpt from "Message to the Grass Roots"; November 10, 1963 *96*

Excerpt from "Speech at Ford Auditorium"; February 14, 1965 *97*

PERMISSIONS

Malcolm X ™ used with Permission from the Family of Malcolm X.

Excerpt from "The Other America," March 14, 1968 *99*
The Heirs to the Estate of Martin Luther King Jr. c/o Writers House as agent for the proprietor New York, NY. Copyright © 1968 by Dr. Martin Luther King, Jr. Renewed © 1996 by Coretta Scott King.

Denise Woodard "Testimonial" *121*

National Venture Capital Association and the Venture Capital Foundation "Amicus Brief" *123*

Deepica Mutyala "Testimonial" *135*

States of New York, Colorado, Connecticut, Delaware, Hawai'i, Illinois, Maine, Maryland, Massachusetts, Minnesota, Nevada, New Jersey, Oregon, Pennsylvania, Rhode Island, Vermont, Washington, and Wisconsin, and the District of Columbia "Brief of Amici Curiae" *167–68*

Kat Garcia "Testimonial" *205*

Stacey Abrams "Why DEI Must Not Die" *251*

Appendix

The Fearless Freedom Economic Justice Act

The legislative model outlined herein is designed to be universally adaptable. It may be revised to reflect the legislative processes of each respective country, state, province, or municipality while upholding the core principle: that public funding, contracts, and services be proportionally allocated in alignment with the demographic composition of the population served.

Federal-Level Legislation

Though this model is intended for use by national governments specifically the U.S. federal government, to ensure that federal contracts, goods, and services are equitably distributed in alignment with national demographic composition. It serves as a foundational model for any national-level implementation seeking to rectify economic disparities rooted in colonial or systemic exclusion.

XXXTH CONGRESS

1ST SESSION

H.R. ____

To balance the award of federal contracts to reflect the demographic characteristics of the United States, and for other purposes.

IN THE HOUSE OF REPRESENTATIVES

DATE, YEAR

Mr./Ms. ______ introduced the following bill, which was referred to the Committee on _______.

A BILL

To balance the award of federal contracts to reflect the demographic characteristics of the United States, and for other purposes.

Be it enacted by the Senate and the House of Representatives of the United States of America in Congress assembled,

Sec. 1. Fair Funding

(a) Short Title.

This Act may be cited as the "Fearless Freedom Economic Justice Act."

(b) Policy.

It is the policy of the United States to balance the distribution of federal contracts for the purchase of goods and services, public works contracts, and contracts for projects among individuals and businesses to reflect the demographic characteristics of the United States.

(c) In General.

(1) Notwithstanding any other provision of law, and except as set forth in this section, the head of each awarding federal agency may establish targets for awards to individuals or businesses with a specified characteristic, on the basis of competitive bidding procedures, for contracts or portions of contracts for the construction, reconstruction or rehabilitation of public buildings, the construction and maintenance of highways, and the purchase of goods and services (including pension fund management contracts and other services contracts).

(2) For each specified characteristic, the target established by such agency for the award of such contracts or portions thereof shall be an amount that approximates the percentage of individuals with such specified characteristic in the general population of the United States.

(3) If a federal agency establishes a target under paragraphs (1) and (2) for any specified characteristic, it must establish a target for every specified characteristic in the general population.

(4) In calculating the percentage of contracts to be set aside under this section, the awarding agency or contractor shall exclude any contract that may not be set aside due to a conflict with a federal law or regulation.

(d) Definitions.

(1) Business. The term "business" means any contractor, subcontractor, manufacturer, service company or corporation engaged in interstate commerce in the United States.

(2) Individual. The term "individual" means any person who is a resident of the United States.

(3) Specified Characteristic. The term "specified characteristic" means an individual racial trait that is tracked by a federal agency for statistical purposes.

State-Level Legislation
(Applicable to U.S. States or Equivalent Regions Globally)

This version is structured for passage by U.S. state legislatures (e.g., General Assembly, State Senate) and can be adapted for use by provinces, territories, or regions in other nations with similar governance structures. It directs state governments to establish demographic equity benchmarks in awarding contracts and public projects. This version begins with language appropriate for a state legislative bill and may be revised to reflect state-specific legal conventions.

Sec. ____________. Fair Funding

(a) Short Title.

This Act may be cited as the "Fearless Freedom Economic Justice Act."

(b) Policy. It is the policy of this state to balance the distribution of state contracts for the purchase of goods and services, public works contracts, municipal public works contracts and contracts for quasi-public agency projects among individuals and businesses to reflect the demographic characteristics of the state.

(c) In General.

(1) Notwithstanding any provisions of the general statutes, and except as set forth in this section, the head of each awarding state agency may establish targets for awards to individuals or businesses with a specified characteristic, on the basis of competitive bidding procedures, for contracts or portions of contracts for the construction, reconstruction or rehabilitation of public buildings, the construction and maintenance of highways, and the purchase of goods and services (including state pension fund management contracts and other services contracts).

(2) For each specified characteristic, the target established by such agency for the award of such

contracts or portions thereof shall be an amount that approximates the percentage of individuals with such specified characteristic in the general population of the state.

(3) If a state agency establishes a target under paragraphs (1) and (2) for any specified characteristic, it must establish a target for every specified characteristic in the general population.

(4) Municipalities. Notwithstanding any provision of the general statutes, and except as provided in this section, on and after January 1, 2026, each municipality when awarding a municipal public works contract may establish targets for awards to individuals or businesses with a specified characteristic, based on statistics for such municipality, in the same manner as described in paragraphs (1) through (3).

(5) Quasi-public agencies. Notwithstanding any provision of the general statutes, and except as provided in this section, on and after January 1, 2026, each quasi-public agency when awarding a public works contract may establish targets for awards to individuals or businesses with a specified characteristic, based on statistics for the geographic area served by such quasi-public agency, in the same manner as described in paragraphs (1) through (3).

(6) In calculating the percentage of contracts to be set aside under this section, the awarding agency or contractor shall exclude any contract that may not be set aside due to a conflict with a federal law or regulation.

(d) Definitions.

(1) Business. The term "business" means any contractor, subcontractor, manufacturer, service company or corporation that maintains its principal place of business in the state.

(2) Individual. The term "individual" means any person who is a resident of the state.
(3) Specified Characteristic. The term "specified characteristic" means an individual racial trait that is tracked by a state agency for statistical purposes.

Local/Municipal Legislation
(City or County Governments)

This version is intended for use by municipal legislative bodies such as city councils or county commissions. It empowers local governments to align their public funding, procurement, and contracting with the demographic realities of their jurisdiction. This model is particularly replicable across cities globally and can be customized to local charters or codes. It begins with:

Be It Ordained by the City Council of the City of ______ ________________________________:

The Municipal Code of the City of ________________ ______________________ is hereby amended by adding the following new section:

SECTION _________________.

(a) Short Title.

This Act may be cited as the "Fearless Freedom Economic Justice Act."

(b) Policy.

It is the policy of this city to balance the distribution of city contracts for the purchase of goods and services, public works contracts, municipal public works contracts and contracts for quasi-public agency projects among individuals and businesses to reflect the demographic characteristics of the city.

(c) In General.

(1) Notwithstanding any provisions of the Municipal Code, and except as set forth in this section, the head of each awarding city agency or department may establish targets for awards to individuals or businesses with a specified characteristic, on the basis of competitive bidding procedures, for contracts or portions of contracts for the construction, reconstruction or rehabilitation of public buildings, the construction and maintenance of streets and highways, and the purchase

of goods and services (including city pension fund management contracts and other services contracts).

(2) For each specified characteristic, the target established by such agency for the award of such contracts or portions thereof shall be an amount that approximates the percentage of individuals with such specified characteristic in the general population of the city.

(3) If a city agency or department establishes a target under paragraphs (1) and (2) for any specified characteristic, it must establish a target for every specified characteristic in the general population.

(4) In calculating the percentage of contracts to be set aside under this section, the awarding agency, department or contractor shall exclude any contract that may not be set aside due to a conflict with a federal or state law or regulation.

(d) Definitions.

(1) Business. The term "business" means any contractor, subcontractor, manufacturer, service company or corporation that maintains its principal place of business in the city.

(2) Individual. The term "individual" means any person who is a resident of the city.

(3) Specified Characteristic. The term "specified characteristic" means an individual racial trait that is tracked by a city agency or department for statistical purposes.

Notes

Introduction

1. Federal Reserve Bank of St. Louis, "Share of Net Worth Held by the Top 1% (99th to 100th Wealth Percentiles) (WFRBST01134)," FRED (Federal Reserve Economic Data), accessed January 16, 2026, at https://fred.stlouisfed.org/series/WFRBST01134.
2. Ben Harrell, "The Average Savings Account Balance in the US," Bankrate, last modified January 8, 2025, accessed March 16, 2026, at https://www.bankrate.com/banking/savings/emergency-savings-report/.
3. Mary K. Jacob, "How the Ultra-Rich Are Souping Up Their High-Tech Bunkers for the End Times," *New York Post*, August 9, 2024.
4. Sammi Caramela, "Billionaires Are Building Luxury Bunkers to Escape Doomsday," *Vice*, May 31, 2024, accessed January 16, 2026, at https://www.vice.com/en/article/billionaires-are-building-luxury-bunkers-to-escape-doomsday/.
5. World Population Review, "How Many Black People Are in the World?," accessed January 16, 2026, at https://worldpopulationreview.com/metrics/how-many-black-people-are-in-the-world.
6. Vincent Geloso, "Economic Freedom in the Literature: What Is It Good (Bad) For?," Fraser Institute, accessed January 23, 2026, at https://www.fraserinstitute.org/studies/economic-freedom-literature-what-it-good-bad.
7. Dame Vivian Hunt et al., "Diversity Matters Even More: The Case for Holistic Impact," McKinsey & Company, December 5, 2023, accessed January 16, 2026, at https://www.mckinsey.com/featured-insights/diversity-and-inclusion/diversity-matters-even-more-the-case-for-holistic-impact.
8. Stanford Teaching Commons, "Growth Mindset and Enhanced Learning," Stanford University, accessed January 16, 2026, at https://teachingcommons.stanford.edu/teaching-guides/foundations-course-design/learning-activities/growth-mindset-and-enhanced-learning.
9. Carol S. Dweck, "What Having a 'Growth Mindset' Actually Means," *Harvard Business Review*, January 13, 2016.

10. GandhiServe Foundation, "What Are Mahatma Gandhi's Views on God, Truth, and Love?," Mahatma Gandhi Institute of Education for Peace and Sustainable Development, accessed January 16, 2026, at https://www.mkgandhi.org/faq/q5.php.

Chapter 1: Emergency

1. The Education Trust, "A Brief History of Affirmative Action—and the Assault on Race-Conscious Admissions," *Education Trust Blog*, July 11, 2023, accessed January 16, 2026, at https://edtrust.org/blog/a-brief-history-of-affirmative-action-and-the-assault-on-race-conscious-admissions/.
2. New York University School of Law, "Civil Rights Act of 1866 and Section 1981," Twenty-Fourth Annual Derrick Bell Lecture on Race in American Society, accessed January 16, 2026, at https://www.law.nyu.edu/sites/default/files/Civil%20Rights%20Act%20of%201866%20and%20Section%201981.pdf.

Chapter 2: The Elephant in the Room

1. Brittany Farr, "A Demographic Moral Panic: Fears of a Majority-Minority Future and the Depreciating Value of Whiteness," *University of Chicago Law Review*, October 13, 2023, accessed January 16, 2026, at https://lawreview.uchicago.edu/online-archive/demographic-moral-panic-fears-majority-minority-future-and-depreciating-value.
2. Federal Reserve Bank of St. Louis, "Unemployment Rate—White (LNS14000003)," FRED (Federal Reserve Economic Data), accessed January 16, 2026, at https://fred.stlouisfed.org/series/LNS14000003.
3. Dame Vivian Hunt et al., "Diversity Matters Even More: The Case for Holistic Impact," McKinsey & Company, December 5, 2023, accessed January 16, 2026, at https://www.mckinsey.com/featured-insights/diversity-and-inclusion/diversity-matters-even-more-the-case-for-holistic-impact.

Chapter 3: A Strategic Assault

1. Brennan Center for Justice, "*Shelby County v. Holder*," August 4, 2018, accessed January 16, 2026, at https://www.brennancenter.org/our-work/court-cases/shelby-county-v-holder.
2. LegalClarity, "What Does a Motion Mean in a Court Case?," January 23, 2026, accessed January 26, 2026, at https://legalclarity.org/what-does-a-motion-mean-in-a-court-case/.
3. American Alliance for Equal Rights v. Fearless Fund Management, LLC, Defendants' Opposition to Plaintiff's Motion for Preliminary Injunction No. 1:23-cv-3424-TWT (N.D. Ga., filed 2023), p. 5.
4. FlowingData, "A Million Dollars vs. a Billion Visualized with a Road Trip," FlowingData, July 15, 2020, accessed January 16, 2026, at https://flowingdata.com/2020/07/16/a-million-dollars-vs-a-billion-visualized-with-a-road-trip/.
5. Ed Zimmerman, "I stand with Fearless Fund (I didn't coordinate this statement with them & I speak here solely on my own personal behalf)," LinkedIn, August 6, 2023, accessed January 16, 2026, at https://www.linkedin.com/posts/edgrapenutzimmerman_i-stand-with-fearless-fund-i-didnt-coordinate-activity-7094366074627870722-Ki59/.

NOTES

Chapter 4: A Seat at the Table

1. American Alliance for Equal Rights v. Fearless Fund Management, LLC, No. 1:23-cv-3424 (N.D. Ga., filed 2023).
2. National Humanities Center, "Mutual Benefit Societies, African American Community During Slavery," in *African American Identity: Volume I, 1500–1865* (Toolbox Library, 2006).
3. Grand United Order of Odd Fellows, "Grand United Order of Odd Fellows in America," Social Welfare History Project, Virginia Commonwealth University Libraries, accessed January 16, 2026, at https://socialwelfare.library.vcu.edu/eras/grand-united-order-of-odd-fellows-in-america/.
4. Equal Justice Initiative, "Lynching in America: Supplement—Lynching by County," Equal Justice Initiative, 2015, accessed January 16, 2026, at https://eji.org/wp-content/uploads/2020/02/02-07-20-lynching-in-america-county-supplement.pdf.
5. LegalClarity, "*Grutter v. Bollinger*: The Supreme Court's Ruling Explained," accessed January 16, 2026, at https://legalclarity.org/grutter-v-bollinger-the-supreme-courts-ruling-explained/.
6. Post-Secondary National Policy Institute, "Historically Black Colleges and Universities (HBCUs): A Background Primer," New America blog, January 1, 2015, accessed January 23, 2026, at https://www.newamerica.org/post-secondary-national-policy-institute/our-blog/historically-black-colleges-and-universities-hbcus/.
7. DJ Khaled, "God Did," featuring Rick Ross, Lil Wayne, Jay-Z, John Legend, and Fridayy, track 2 on *God Did*, We the Best Music Group and Epic Records, 2022.
8. Corporate Finance Institute, "Cap Table: Guide and Template," February 22, 2018, accessed January 16, 2026, at https://corporatefinanceinstitute.com/resources/valuation/cap-table-guide-template/.
9. Sophia Kunthara, "Black Women Still Receive Just a Tiny Fraction of VC Funding Despite Five-Year High," *Crunchbase News*, July 16, 2021, accessed January 16, 2026, at https://news.crunchbase.com/diversity/something-ventured-black-women-founders/.
10. Diversity VC and Atomico, "The Equity Record 2022," DATE, 2022, accessed January 16, 2026, at https://diversity.vc/wp-content/uploads/2022/11/The-Equity-Record-2022.pdf.
11. Shefali Luthra, "How the Biden Administration Is Trying to Make the Federal Government More Diverse," *19th*, February 16, 2023, accessed January 16, 2026, at https://19thnews.org/2023/02/biden-administration-diversity-federal-government-report/.

Chapter 5: Raised for This

1. Charisse Jones, "Affirmative Action: Who Really Benefits? White Women," *USA Today*, June 29, 2023, accessed January 16, 2026, at https://www.usatoday.com/story/money/2023/06/29/affirmative-action-who-benefits-white-women/70371219007/.
2. Rochelle Riley, "William Brooks, Champion of Detroit's Black Press, Dies at 85," *Detroit Free Press*, October 3, 2018, accessed January 16, 2026, at https://www.freep.com/story/news/columnists/rochelle-riley/2018/10/03/william-brooks-dies-85/1504482002/.

NOTES

Chapter 6: The Movement

1. United States Army Garrison Rheinland-Pfalz, "National African-American / Black History Month Observance," pamphlet, accessed January 16, 2026, at https://home.army.mil/rheinland-pfalz/1315/5410/0588/Black_History_African_American_Month_pamphlet.pdf.
2. Economy League of Greater Philadelphia, "Detroit: Past and Future of a Shrinking City," Leading Indicators, accessed January 16, 2026, at https://www.economyleague.org/resources/detroit-past-and-future-shrinking-city.
3. Eminem, "Beautiful (Official Music Video)," YouTube video, July 12, 2020, accessed January 16, 2026, at https://www.youtube.com/watch?v=lgT1AidzRWM.
4. Ruth E. Mills et al., *The Civil Rights Movement and the African American Experience in 20th Century Detroit, Michigan: Survey Report, Part 1: Historic Context,* Quinn Evans Architects and Michigan State Historic Preservation Office, April 2021, 54, https://www.miplace.org/4a72ad/globalassets/documents/shpo/programs-and-services/civil-rights-project/shpo-detroit-civil-rights-survey_websize.pdf.
5. Macrotrends, "Dow Jones Industrial Average 100-Year Historical Chart," accessed January 16, 2026, at https://www.macrotrends.net/1319/dow-jones-100-year-historical-chart.
6. Darrick Hamilton and Trevon Logan, "Why Wealth Equality Remains Out of Reach for Black Americans," *Conversation*, February 12, 2019, accessed January 16, 2026, at https://theconversation.com/why-wealth-equality-remains-out-of-reach-for-black-americans-111483.
7. PBS, "Timeline: Malcolm X's Life," *American Experience*, accessed January 16, 2026, at https://www.pbs.org/wgbh/americanexperience/features/malcolmx-timeline-malcolm-xs-life/.
8. King Solomon Missionary Baptist Church, accessed March 11, 2026, at http://www.kingsolomonchurch.org.
9. Malcolm X, "Message to the Grassroots," speech, Detroit, Michigan, November 10, 1963, transcript at BlackPast.org, accessed January 16, 2026, at https://www.blackpast.org/african-american-history/1963-malcolm-x-message-grassroots/.
10. Malcolm X, "Message to the Grassroots," speech, Detroit, Michigan, November 10, 1963, transcript at BlackPast.org, accessed January 16, 2026, at https://www.blackpast.org/african-american-history/1963-malcolm-x-message-grassroots/.
11. Brooklyn Museum, "A Timeline of African Art and History," Brooklyn Museum, accessed January 16, 2026, at https://www.brooklynmuseum.org/resources/africa-timeline.
12. Malcolm X, "Speech at Ford Auditorium," Detroit, Michigan, February 14, 1965, transcript at BlackPast.org, accessed January 16, 2026, at https://www.blackpast.org/african-american-history/1965-malcolm-x-speech-ford-auditorium/.
13. "Poor People's Campaign," Martin Luther King, Jr. Research and Education Institute, Stanford University, accessed January 16, 2026, at https://kinginstitute.stanford.edu/poor-peoples-campaign.
14. Martin Luther King Jr., "The Other America," speech at Grosse Pointe High School, Grosse Pointe, MI, March 14, 1968, Grosse Pointe Historical Society, accessed January 23, 2026, at https://www.gphistorical.org/mlk/mlkspeech/.

15. Lorraine Boissoneault, "Martin Luther King Jr.'s Assassination Sparked Uprisings in Cities Across America," *Smithsonian Magazine*, April 4, 2018, accessed January 16, 2026, at https://www.smithsonianmag.com/history/martin-luther-king-jrs-assassination-sparked-uprisings-cities-across-america-180968665/.
16. Zach Schrempp, "James Forman (1928–2005)," BlackPast.org, February 28, 2007, accessed January 16, 2026, at https://www.blackpast.org/african-american-history/foreman-james-1928-2005/.

Chapter 7: Knowledge Is Power

1. Ballotpedia, "Federal Judges Nominated by Donald Trump," accessed January 16, 2026, at https://ballotpedia.org/Federal_judges_nominated_by_Donald_Trump.
2. Ruth E. Mills et al., *The Civil Rights Movement and the African American Experience in 20th Century Detroit, Michigan: Survey Report, Part 1: Historic Context,* Quinn Evans Architects and Michigan State Historic Preservation Office, April 2021, 64, https://www.miplace.org/4a72ad/globalassets/documents/shpo/programs-and-services/civil-rights-project/shpo-detroit-civil-rights-survey_websize.pdf.
3. "Abernathy, Ralph David," Martin Luther King, Jr. Research and Education Institute, Stanford University, accessed January 16, 2026, at https://kinginstitute.stanford.edu/abernathy-ralph-david.
4. Detroit Historical Society, "Underground Railroad," *Encyclopedia of Detroit*, accessed January 16, 2026, at https://www.detroithistorical.org/learn/online-research/encyclopedia-of-detroit/underground-railroad.

Chapter 8: Backlash

1. NORC at the University of Chicago, EPOP Survey Project, Association for Enterprise Opportunity, "Women Business Owners Fact Sheet," accessed March 16, 2026, at https://epop.norc.org/content/dam/epop/media/in-the-news/pdf/2025-women-business-ownership-fact-sheet.pdf.
2. Maggie Elehwany, "NRHA Breaks Down the Rural Impact of the Latest COVID-19 Stimulus Package," National Rural Health Association blog, March 2020, accessed January 16, 2026, at https://www.ruralhealth.us/blogs/2020/03/nrha-breaks-down-the-rural-impact-of-the-latest-covid-19-stimulus-package.
3. Dame Vivian Hunt et al., *Diversity Matters Even More: The Case for Holistic Impact*, McKinsey & Company, December 5, 2023, accessed January 16, 2026, at https://www.mckinsey.com/featured-insights/diversity-and-inclusion/diversity-matters-even-more-the-case-for-holistic-impact.

Chapter 9: The African Queen

1. "Queen Amina of Zazzau: A West African Warrior Queen," Black History Heroes, July 2013, accessed January 16, 2026, at https://www.blackhistoryheroes.com/2013/07/queen-amina-of-zaira-west-african.html.
2. Jessica Snethen, "Queen Nzinga (1583–1663)," BlackPast.org, June 16, 2009, accessed January 16, 2026, at https://blackpast.org/global-african-history/queen-nzinga-1583-1663/.

Chapter 10: What's a War Without Soldiers?

1. Akkani Dorcas, "10 African Countries Still Paying Colonial Tax," Vanguard, accessed March 16, 2026, at https://www.vanguardngr.com/2024/12/10-african-countries-still-paying-colonial-tax/#google_vignette.

Chapter 11: Back in Court

1. Rebecca Beitsch, "Why Ron DeSantis Is Fighting with Disney," *Hill*, March 31, 2023, accessed January 16, 2026, at https://thehill.com/business/3935602-why-ron-desantis-is-fighting-with-disney/.
2. Editorial Board, "DeSantis vs. Disney Is a Fight Florida Can't Afford," *Miami Herald*, September 13, 2023, accessed January 16, 2026, at https://www.miamiherald.com/opinion/editorials/article279102084.html.
3. *American Alliance for Equal Rights v. Fearless Fund Management, LLC*, No. 23-13138 (11th Cir. oral argument, Jan. 31, 2024), audio recording, CourtListener, accessed January 16, 2026, at https://www.courtlistener.com/audio/90459/american-alliance-for-equal-rights-v-fearless-fund-management-llc/.
4. Khorri Atkinson Bellamy, "Black Americans Are Being Targeted by Disinformation Ahead of the 2024 Election, Experts Say," NBC News, July 25, 2024, accessed January 16, 2026, at https://www.nbcnews.com/news/nbcblk/black-americans-disinformation-election-social-media-rcna157096.
5. Southern Poverty Law Center, *The Year in Hate and Extremism 2024*, 2024, accessed January 16, 2026, at https://www.splcenter.org/resources/reports/year-hate-extremism-2024/.
6. Leadership Conference Education Fund, *Cause for Concern: The State of Hate 2024*, May 2024, accessed January 16, 2026, at https://civilrights.org/edfund/wp-content/uploads/sites/2/2024/05/CauseforConcernStateofHate-2024.pdf.

Chapter 12: Crowned for This

1. Niquel Terry Ellis, "Federal Appeals Court Blocks Fearless Fund from Awarding Grants to Black Women Entrepreneurs," CNN via Yahoo News, June 3, 2024, accessed January 16, 2026, at https://www.yahoo.com/news/federal-appeals-court-blocks-fearless-210239427.html.
2. Chandler Moore and Cody Carnes, "Firm Foundation (He Won't)," performed by Chandler Moore and Cody Carnes, Sparrow Records, December 10, 2021.
3. "Our Visit to the Slave Castles in Ghana," Black Travelers International, May 13, 2022, accessed January 16, 2026, at https://www.blacktravelersint.com/our-visit-to-the-slave-castles-in-ghana.
4. Ghana Tourism Authority, "Elmina Castle," VisitGhana, accessed January 16, 2026, at https://visitghana.com/elmina-castle-2/.
5. Simpson Thacher & Bartlett LLP, "Supreme Court's Affirmative Action Ruling: Implications for Corporate DEI Initiatives," client memorandum, June 6, 2024, accessed January 16, 2026, at https://www.stblaw.com/docs/default-source/memos/firmmemo_06_06_24.

Chapter 13: Sound the Alarm

1. Gerren Keith Gaynor, "Watch: White House Reacts to Calls from Fearless Fund, Orgs to Protect DEI," *Grio*, June 20, 2024, accessed January 16, 2026, at

https://thegrio.com/2024/06/20/watch-white-house-reacts-to-calls-from-fearless-fund-orgs-to-protect-dei/.

Chapter 14: Fearless Victory

1. John Gramlich, "How Trump Compares with Other Recent Presidents in Appointing Federal Judges," Pew Research Center, January 13, 2021, accessed January 16, 2026, at https://www.pewresearch.org/short-reads/2021/01/13/how-trump-compares-with-other-recent-presidents-in-appointing-federal-judges/.
2. *American Alliance for Equal Rights v. Fearless Fund Management, LLC*, No. 1:23-cv-03621 (N.D. Ga. filed Aug. 2, 2023), docket, CourtListener, accessed January 16, 2026, at https://www.courtlistener.com/docket/67658002/american-alliance-for-equal-rights-v-fearless-fund-management-llc/.
3. Human Rights Watch, "Why Reparations? A Q&A," June 19, 2025, accessed January 16, 2026, at https://www.hrw.org/news/2025/06/19/why-reparations-qa.
4. St. Louis Kaplan Feldman Holocaust Museum, "Holocaust Timeline," accessed January 16, 2026, at https://stlholocaustmuseum.org/learn/timeline/.
5. Ta-Nehisi Coates, "The Case for Reparations," *Atlantic*, June 2014.
6. Stephen Menendian et al., "Reparations: The Legal Case for Repair," *Fordham International Law Journal* (online), February 15, 2025, accessed January 16, 2026, at https://www.fordhamilj.org/iljonline/k73pddfmra65ecd-fxc5k-bdazp-npp5j-l8be9-kbndm-tlwlf-2pnhz-hpjc3-2bxkm.
7. Ruth E. Mills et al., *The Civil Rights Movement and the African American Experience in 20th Century Detroit, Michigan: Survey Report, Part 1: Historic Context,* Quinn Evans Architects and Michigan State Historic Preservation Office, April 2021, 64, https://www.miplace.org/4a72ad/globalassets/documents/shpo/programs-and-services/civil-rights-project/shpo-detroit-civil-rights-survey_websize.pdf.
8. John Conyers Jr., "Why We Need HR 40," *Journal of Pan African Studies* 9, no. 5 (2016): 142–51.
9. American Civil Liberties Union, "HR40 & Reparations,", published in 2021, accessed March 11, 2026, at https://www.aclu.org/sites/default/files/field_document/hr_40_toolkit_final_0.pdf.

Chapter 15: The New DEI Playbook Is DE

1. North Carolina Department of Natural and Cultural Resources, "Activist Ann Atwater," blog, January 28, 2020, accessed January 16, 2026, at https://www.dncr.nc.gov/blog/2020/01/28/activist-ann-atwater.
2. Branden Hunter, "Coleman A. Young: A History of the People's Mayor," *Michigan Chronicle*, May 24, 2018, accessed January 16, 2026, at https://michiganchronicle.com/coleman-a-young-a-history-of-the-peoples-mayor/.

About the Author

Arian Simone is an Ivorian queen, venture capitalist, entrepreneur, philanthropist, and author whose life reflects fearless leadership and impact. As founder and CEO of the Fearless Fund, the first venture capital fund built by women of color for women of color, she has secured backing from institutions like JPMorgan Chase and Bank of America to invest in diverse founders. Today, as Queen Wa of Dawa Grand Bereby in Côte d'Ivoire, she partners with the Ivorian government to empower underresourced communities and advance sustainable development.

About Storehouse Voices

Founded in 2024, Storehouse Voices celebrates stories from under-published voices across the globe. Our imprint elevates fiction and nonfiction that interrogates and reimagines our past and present and conceives of new futures. We are dedicated to amplifying culturally rich narratives and developing an environment that bolsters creators and engages the community as integral members of our publishing family.

Learn more about us and join our online community at

storehousevoices.com.